D1072207

SHERMAN MINTON

Indiana's Supreme Court Justice

Justice Sherman Minton outside his home in New Albany. (Louisville *Courier-Journal*)

SHERMAN MINTON

Indiana's Supreme Court Justice

WILLIAM FRANKLIN RADCLIFF

Guild Press of Indiana
Indianapolis, Indiana

Library of Congress
Catalog Card Number
96-75160

ISBN 1-878208-81-0

Manufactured in the United States of America

Designed by Sheila Samson
Type: Goudy Old Style

To Matilda Betts Radcliff
who believed
when there was little justification for her belief.

Contents

FOREWORD

Several recent biographies have given us fresh, detailed insight into the personality and character of Harry S. Truman, not the least of which is that written by Dr. Robert Ferrell, Professor Emeritus of History at Indiana University. When one looks at Truman alongside Sherman Minton, there are so many remarkable similarities it is no wonder that they became fast friends and remained so as long as either of them lived.

Both men were born in the upper middle South during the very end period of the Reconstruction following the American Civil War. They were profoundly influenced by the aftermath of the war and had family members who had served in either the Union or Confederate Army. Both served overseas in World War I and were active in veterans' affairs and politics soon thereafter. Both were associated with powerful political organizations, Truman with the Pendergast machine in Missouri and Minton with the McNutt organization in Indiana, and both men served in state or local government in some capacity at the insistence of these organizations. Minton and Truman were both elected to the United States Senate in 1934 and were sworn in on the same day in January 1935—they were, in fact, seatmates. Stalwart supporters of Franklin D. Roosevelt's New Deal, they stayed with him to the bitter end in the court packing fight of 1937.

Defeated for re-election to the Senate in 1940, Minton served briefly as a White House aide until his appointment by FDR to the United States Court of Appeals in Chicago, serving Indiana, Illinois, and Wisconsin. From there he was elevated to the Supreme Court of the United States by his friend President Truman in 1949.

Minton's academic credentials were superior to most, if not all, of his judicial colleagues, and he had used these academic achievements to claw his way out of deep rural poverty. A brilliant, formally educated man, he graduated from Indiana University and then earned a master's degree in law from Yale, where he studied constitutional law under William Howard Taft. He also attended the Sorbonne in Paris.

It is an interesting phenomenon that, as a legislator, this folksy Hoosier politician argued for the largest possible authority in both the federal executive and legislature, but as a federal judge on the Court of Appeals and the Supreme Court took a definitely restrained approach in contrast to what is now crudely called judicial activism. He was the last Truman court appointee, the first half of his service during the tenure of Frederick M. Vinson as chief justice, and after 1953 with Earl Warren.

Minton generally tended to be with the Frankfurter-Jackson part of the Court which often resisted the more judicial aggressiveness of Black, Douglas, and later Warren. But it was without hesitation that he supported Chief Justice Warren in support of his opinion in *Brown v. Board of Education*, and cast one of the four votes for certiorari under the rule of four to bring the *Brown* cases to the Supreme Court.

He loved politics, but he also understood his role as a lifetime federal judge and knew how to keep the judicial and political functions separate. His active public life from 1933 to 1956 cuts across more than two momentous decades in the history of this nation and the world, from the Great Depression to the Cold War.

Hugo Black burned many of his private and official papers before his death. Sherman Minton also left very little of a paper trail, a likely deliberate act on his part. Bill Radcliff has fully and carefully parsed the political and judicial records, which are closely interrelated. How a passionate partisan like Minton performed his judicial tasks at the two highest levels of federal judiciary is a story which itself justifies the author's effort. The Minton view of the federal judicial function very much deserves close attention, and William Radcliff has given it that attention.

—*The Honorable Allen Sharp*
Chief Judge, U.S. District Court
Northern District of Indiana

FOREWORD

The rotunda of the Indiana State Capitol Building in Indianapolis contains the busts of several prominent Americans. Some, like George Washington, are of men and women familiar to all Hoosiers. On a south-facing corner of the rotunda a bronze bust of Justice Sherman Minton looks across the expanse of marble toward his beloved home of Floyd County on the Ohio River. Though his name graces a federal building in Indianapolis, a bridge between New Albany and Louisville, and the Moot Courtroom at the Indiana University School of Law in Bloomington, the man who carried that name and had the distinction of being the only Hoosier ever to sit on the United States Supreme Court is relatively unknown to most of our citizens.

Bill Radcliff's biography is a major step toward introducing Sherman Minton to new generations, and his review of Justice Minton's career helps to put his accomplishments as a political leader, United States senator, and jurist into perspective.

"Shay" Minton was a Hoosier, born and bred, coming into the world in 1890 in a log cabin near New Albany. He attended New Albany High School, worked his way through Indiana University by waiting tables and firing furnaces, and went to Yale University School of Law on a five-hundred-dollar scholarship. He practiced law in New Albany, and ran for public office and lost. He served as Indiana's first public counselor before the first Utility Regulatory Commission, and then gained election to the United States Senate in 1934.

It was in the Senate where he spent the six most enjoyable years of his life, standing by the side of President Franklin D. Roosevelt and fighting for the New Deal. "We were in a revolution, and I was close to the throne," he wrote near the end of his life, reflecting on his term in the Senate.

Radcliff notes that Minton was a "bare-fisted fighter" during his career, both in Indianapolis and in Washington. During his "Little New Deal" days in Indianapolis following the elections of President Roosevelt and Indiana Governor Paul V. McNutt, Minton took on Indiana's powerful public utilities and forced rate reductions in the first days of utility regulation. He helped put together Indiana's first public welfare program, as well as programs that saved Hoosier schools from bankruptcy, and helped rescue Hoosier families from the darkest days of the Great Depression.

Minton was elected to the U.S. Senate the same year as Harry S. Truman of Missouri. The two of them became Roosevelt's staunchest allies in bringing many aspects of the New Deal into law. Radcliff's description of Minton's role in leading Roosevelt's ill-fated "packing" of the U.S. Supreme Court is especially interesting and illuminating, particularly since we are currently going through another time when the Congress and the President are at odds with each other as our country faces major adjustments in the distribution of power.

Minton's pugnaciousness gained him national notice and the friendship of FDR, who took him onto the White House staff following Minton's narrow loss in his 1940 Senate re-election attempt. A year later, Roosevelt nominated Minton for a seat on the U.S. Circuit Court of Appeals, Seventh Circuit, in Chicago, where he applied strict constructionist views and displayed a reluctance to substitute for the will of legislative bodies in making law.

His good friend President Truman nominated him for the U.S. Supreme Court in 1949. At that time, Minton's aggressiveness in leading the charge for Roosevelt's court packing plan came back to haunt him, but he refused to appear before the Senate Judiciary Committee considering his nomination to answer questions about it, saying his record spoke for itself. In this day and age, when every nominee for the Court seems to face a highly charged battle—including long hours answering questions before this panel—it seems surprising that the Judiciary passed the nomination on to the floor where it was ratified.

Radcliff does his most valuable service in treating Minton's record on both courts in some detail, revealing him as a hardworking, thoughtful judge who did his job well and played an important, supporting role in the Court's decision to end segregation in America. Minton's vote was one of the four needed to grant certiorari to the cases that led to the momentous *Brown v. Board of Education* decision striking down segregation. Without his vote, these cases might have been delayed even longer. But that wasn't his first stand for racial justice. He had worked as a senator for passage of antilynching legislation sought by the NAACP, and, to his critics who said the legislation was an invasion of states' rights, replied: "I am interested in states' rights, but I am more interested in human rights."

After his retirement from the Court in 1956, Minton's correspondence with his friend Truman increased, and it is this correspondence that many will find to be the most enjoyable aspect of this book. Mr. Truman and Shay Minton share observations on President Eisenhower, Joseph Kennedy, John Kennedy, Adlai Stevenson, and other giants of their times that are entertaining, enlightening, and often very funny. It is the type of correspondence that is vanishing in today's increasingly digital world. Unfortunately, it will be much more difficult for future historians to flesh out the personas of today's leaders as Radcliff has done in this book.

Inhabiting these pages are the men who made Indiana and this country into what it is today. Hoosier political giants walk again for this and future generations: McNutt, McHale, McKinney, Manion, Van Nuys, Capehart, Jenner, Denton, Pantzer, and, of course, Sherman "Shay" Minton, enshrined in bronze and now brought back to life, fighting again for the rights of the common man, a battle not yet won.

—*Governor Evan Bayh*
July 1996

PREFACE AND ACKNOWLEDGMENTS

Sherman Minton has been of particular interest to me most of my life.

Born in the southern Indiana community of Georgetown, in Floyd County, Minton attended a one-room elementary school and graduated from New Albany High School. Similarly, I was born and reared on a farm about five miles north of Fredericksburg in Washington County, Indiana, attended a one-room country school, and graduated from Hardinsburg High School, also in Washington County. As the crow flies, Georgetown and Fredericksburg are about twenty miles apart.

Our family on the farm couldn't afford a daily newspaper such as the *Courier-Journal*, published in Louisville. But we did subscribe to *The Salem Democrat*, a weekly publication from Salem, the Washington County seat. There were articles in this newspaper almost weekly about Sherman Minton while he was in the Senate.

But the focus on Minton in our neighborhood extended beyond the newspaper. One of my high school teachers, May Lester (now Mrs. L. D. Patterson of Oxford, Indiana) had a brother who received an appointment to West Point in 1935 from Senator Minton. Stories about Cadet Joseph S. Lester appeared frequently in *The Salem Democrat*.

One of my partners in our Muncie, Indiana, law firm was Marshall E. Hanley, now deceased. He had been a law clerk for Minton when he was on the Court of Appeals for the Seventh Circuit in Chicago, and Hanley entertained me with many stories about his former employer. In fact, when Hanley ran on the Democratic ticket for the 1958 nomination for United States senator from Indiana, then-retired Justice Minton was one of his staunchest supporters. Ultimately, though, Vance Hartke from Evansville won the nomination.

With all of these connections in my background, and with a sincere continuing interest in this remarkable man, I decided that when I retired from active practice of law (on December 31, 1987) I would write a book on the life and times of Sherman Minton.

In the course of my research, to find out what had already been written on this senator and Supreme Court justice, I was unable to locate a biography. I found several law review articles and two doctoral dissertations on his service as an associate justice of the Supreme Court; I also found two doctoral dissertations on his term as a senator. But no book had been written on his life.

This absence of a biography of Sherman Minton is puzzling. He had a distinguished career in the Senate form 1935 to 1941; he became majority whip of the Senate during that time, which was rare for a freshman senator. He was close to President Franklin Delano Roosevelt and his inner circle of New Dealers. Minton had served with distinction as a judge of the United States Circuit Court of Appeals for the Seventh Circuit in Chicago from 1941 to 1949. Finally, Minton had the distinction of being the only justice of the Supreme Court from the state of Indiana*, serving in that capacity from 1949 to 1956.

Thus, Minton was a key figure in the high tide of the success of the Democratic Party in Indiana in the 1930s. An early and ardent backer of Paul V. McNutt for governor of Indiana in 1932, he was named by Governor McNutt as Public Counsellor for the Public Service Commission of Indiana in 1933. He resigned this position in 1934 to seek, and win, the nomination of his party for United States Senator.

Minton's prominence in serving his country should have justified a biography long ago. The approach I have taken is to detail his public and judicial career, and whenever possible, to show the personal background and family life which made him the man he was.

I owe a tremendous debt of gratitude to the many persons without whose assistance this biography would not have been possible. Minton destroyed his Senate papers when he left that institution, and he burned his notes and papers when he retired from the Supreme Court. He did not write any "in-

---

* Justice Willis Van Devanter was born in Marion, Indiana, in 1859. He was reared and practiced law there before he moved to Wyoming at the age of twenty-five. He had been a resident of that state for twenty-six years when President Taft named him to the Supreme Court in 1910, and he remained active behind the scenes in Republican politics in Wyoming for many years after he joined the Court. Accordingly, most authorities, if not all, consider Justice Van Devanter an appointee from Wyoming, and the appointment is recorded as such.

side" accounts of events in which he participated, nor did he keep a diary. Therefore, it has been necessary to gather information by bits and pieces from a multitude of sources. Minton's daughter, Mary-Anne (Mrs. John H.) Callanan, has quite a collection of materials in her possession, which she generously and kindly shared with me. Son Sherman A. Minton, M.D., also generously shared many photographs of his father, the family, and other significant individuals in Minton's life. Thanks also are due to son John Evan Minton for his time and insight.

Much of my background research would not have been possible without several doctoral theses and dissertations, from which I have drawn extensively:

David H. Corcoran, formerly of New Albany, wrote "Sherman Minton: New Deal Senator" in 1977 at the University of Kentucky. This work traces Minton's early life through his Senate term. I have drawn heavily from this material.

Purdue University instructor Gordon R. Owen's "The Public Speaking of Sherman Minton" was written at Purdue in 1962. It contains biographical information and a rhetorical analysis of Minton, with emphasis on his career in the Senate.

"Mr. Justice Minton and the Supreme Court, 1946–1956" was David Neal Atkinson's thesis submitted to the Department of Political Science in the Graduate College of the University of Iowa in June 1969.

Elizabeth Anne Hull authored "Sherman Minton and the Cold War Court," November 1976, submitted to the Graduate Faculty of Political and Social Science of the New School for Social Research.

Information about Minton's life and law practice in New Albany was provided by John A. Cody, Jr., senior partner in the law firm of Cody and Cody, the successor firm to Stotsenburg, Weathers and Minton. Preston L. Prevatt, a partner in the law firm of Stutts and Bowen in Miami, Florida, generously and kindly furnished me with information about Minton's stint with that law firm in the twenties.

The staff at the Indiana Room, New Albany-Floyd County Public Library, the Indiana State Library, the Harry S. Truman Library, and the Dwight D. Eisenhower Library have been most patient, courteous, and helpful.

Much appreciation goes to Dr. George Geib of Butler University for his thorough reading of the manuscript. His comments and input were invaluable.

Sincere thanks must go to the secretarial staff at the law firm of DeFur, Voran, Hanley, Radcliff and Reed for their help in this endeavor. Particular thanks must go to Naomi Brown and Tonya Garland, who, with infinite patience and a vivid imagination, typed the first draft of the manuscript from my almost illegible handwriting on several legal pads. They also typed and retyped the several subsequent revisions.

Finally, hearty and heartfelt thanks are due to Pamela Gayle (Mrs. Steven D.) Murphy, who prepared the final manuscript, including bibliography and footnotes, and put it all together.

William Franklin Radcliff
Muncie, Indiana
January 1996

CHAPTER ONE

MR. JUSTICE MINTON
A Dream Realized

PRECISELY AT 10:30 A.M., ON WEDNESDAY, OCTOBER 12, 1949, PRESIDENT HARRY S. Truman walked briskly from his study at the White House onto the portico overlooking the Rose Garden. Following the President was Sherman Minton, leaning on a cane to help support the right leg which he had fractured earlier in August in a fall at his home in New Albany, Indiana.

It was a hot day in Washington—as hot as midsummer. Roses were blooming in the Rose Garden and the hedge was green. The garden was swarming with Hoosiers, hundreds of invited guests who had earlier stood in line to have their invitations checked by guards. These guests had come to Washington aboard three special railroad cars to see Minton, their friend and neighbor, receive the highest honor ever bestowed upon a citizen of Indiana. Though in actuality it was a ceremony to swear in a justice of the Supreme Court of the United States, it was really a sort of vindication of a state too often dismissed as inconsequential in the halls of power. Still, the whole affair had the down-home air of a Hoosier picnic.[1]

Mixed with the Hoosiers were dignitaries from all branches of government. The associate justices stood on the porch outside the President's study. Justices Hugo Black, Harold Burton, Tom Clark, Robert Jackson, and Stanley Reed mingled with the guests. Among the thirty distinguished senators who graced the event were Homer Capehart (Indiana), Tom Connally (Texas), William Jenner (Indiana), Scott W. Lucas (Illinois), and Claude Pepper (Florida). Speaker of the House Sam Rayburn was there too, along with Congressman and Mrs. John W. McCormack, and Congressman Adam Clayton Powell. Secretary of Defense Louis A. Johnson attended, as did Stephen T. Early, Undersecretary of Defense, and Undersecretary of the Interior Oscar and Mrs. Chapman.[2]

1

President Truman, nattily attired in a light tan summer suit and a checkered bow tie, paused before the microphone mounted on the portico and glanced at a roll of parchment he held in his hand as he spoke. "I am about to perform the most pleasant duty of my political career," he said. "That is to hand Mr. Justice Minton his certificate of office as a member of the greatest court in the world." Then, with a big grin on his face, the President handed the document to the towering Hoosier and said, "Here y'are, Shay." The new associate justice of the Supreme Court of the United States grinned back. "Thank you, Mr. President," he said, and accepted his commission.

Minton, wearing a blue summer suit with a striped four-in-hand tie, then introduced Mrs. Minton, who was demurely dressed in a dark blue suit adorned with a small orchid.

Chief Justice Fred Moore Vinson, the only member of the Court in his black robe, then asked Minton if he were ready to take the oath. "I am," was the reply.

With a solemn face, he repeated the oath of office after the chief justice:

I, Sherman Minton, do solemnly swear that I will administer justice without respect to persons and do equal right to the poor and to the rich, and that I will faithfully and impartially discharge and perform all the duties incumbent upon me as a judge according to the best of my abilities and understanding according to the Constitution and laws of the United States;

And that I will support and defend the Constitution of the United States against all enemies, foreign and domestic, and that I will hold true and faithful allegiance to the same;

That I take this obligation freely without any mental reservation of purpose and that I will well and faithfully discharge the duties of the office upon which I am about to enter, so help me God. [Federal law requires a justice to take an oath that is administered to all government officials and the judicial oath.]

Observers nodded, secure in the certainty that Minton actually would do as he said—sincerely "support and defend" the Constitution of the United States.

After the ceremony was over and the last picture had been taken, Minton retired to the Cabinet Room of the White House and stood for an hour shaking hands with the visitors. Mrs. Minton went off with Mrs. Truman, who also had attended the ceremony.

Kurt F. Pantzer, an attorney from Indianapolis and chairman of a special committee of the Indiana State Bar Association, presented Minton with a desk set—electric clock, calendar, and pens—bearing the state seal of Indiana. While making the presentation, Pantzer was flanked by Telford B. Orbison, also from New Albany and newly elected president of the Indiana State Bar Association, and John M. McFaddin, who had just retired. Mr. Pantzer praised the new justice for achieving "what no other native and resident of the state of Indiana has ever achieved—the placing of our bench and bar, as it has been in spirit, at the forefront of American law and American justice. Not only has every citizen of Indiana been honored by the distinction you have bestowed upon us, but our profession in Indiana is deeply conscious that it has grown in your shadow." The desk set given to Minton was engraved, "In token of our pride and affection, the bench and bar of Indiana, October 12, 1949. The candles you have lighted on the banks of the Wabash will gleam forever."

It was a Hoosier holiday in the White House. The visitors from back home chatted and lingered in the executive wing. One veteran reporter observed that it would be terrific government if everybody was as interested in public affairs as Hoosiers. When the long, hot ceremony was over, Minton—damp, tired, and happy—sat down in one of the big leather chairs in the Cabinet Room and loosened his collar. He would be fifty-nine in a few days and his leg hurt.

The crowd finally cleared from the White House and Justice and Mrs. Minton climbed into the sedan of their son-in-law, Dr. John H. Callanan, and were driven to the Supreme Court on the Capitol end of Pennsylvania Avenue.

That very day Minton donned his brand-new black robe and went right to work. When the "Hear ye, hear ye" signifying the opening of the court was heard and the robed justices filed to their seats on the high bench, none appeared more dignified or forceful than the justice from Indiana.[3] As Minton took the customary end seat—the one at the extreme left of the chief justice, the seat for the most junior member of the court—Chief Justice Vinson welcomed him, noting that "the President has nominated and, with the advice and consent of the Senate, has appointed Circuit Judge Sherman

Minton of Indiana to be associate justice of this Court in succession to Associate Justice Wiley Rutledge, deceased. He has presented his commission
and has taken the oaths prescribed by law. It is ordered that his commission
be recorded and that his oaths be filed."[4]

Among the guests who witnessed Mr. Minton take his oath of office on that
hot October morning were old friends to whom he owed much. One was
Paul Vories McNutt, governor of Indiana from 1933 to 1937. When the
Indiana Public Service Commission was created with authorization for a
public counsellor, Governor McNutt had appointed Minton to the office
on March 1, 1933. Minton had learned about politics and about Governor
McNutt through the American Legion. Members of the American Legion
of the State of Indiana, of which Minton was a leader, formed the nucleus of
the McNutt-for-Governor organization when McNutt and his advisers, led
by Frank M. McHale, decided in 1932 that McNutt would run for governor.
As the first public counsellor of the Indiana Public Service Commission,
Minton helped cut utility rates significantly. He thus pleased many Hoosiers, including McNutt, and set the stage to win himself a seat in the United
States Senate in 1934. Minton knew that he had won the nomination because of McNutt's support and that he had won the Senate race largely
through the personal popularity of the governor.

Another guest, Pleas E. Greenlee from Shelbyville, had been executive
secretary to McNutt from 1933 to 1936. Greenlee was the primary architect
of the campaign which gave Minton the senatorial nomination on the Democratic ticket in 1934. He defeated R. Earl Peters of Fort Wayne, chairman of
the Indiana Democratic party from 1926 to 1933.

As a senator in 1937, Minton had joined with Alabama Senator Hugo
Black, who was also present, in leading the fight in support of the court
packing legislation requested by President Roosevelt. Roosevelt rewarded
Black for his efforts by appointing him to the Supreme Court. Roosevelt
had considered Minton for the job, but Minton encouraged him to name
Black instead. Likewise, in 1945, Black encouraged President Truman to
appoint Minton to the Court, as successor to Owen J. Roberts, but Harold
H. Burton was named instead.

Thus, that October day was indeed a memorable one for the eighty-seventh American named to the highest court of the land. Sherman Minton must have been acutely aware that the office for which he had so often been mentioned was now his to occupy, along with all its awesome responsibilities.

Too, he must have considered the long journey from the poverty of his childhood in the hills of southern Indiana. From the blue overalls of a country boy to the black robes of a Supreme Court justice—it had indeed been a long and bumpy road.

CHAPTER TWO

THE EARLY YEARS

SHERMAN MINTON WAS BORN ON OCTOBER 20, 1890, IN THE HILL HAMLET OF Georgetown, Indiana, to John Evan and Emma Livers Minton. The third of four children, he had an older sister and brother, Ivy and Herbert, and a younger brother, Rosco.

Georgetown is located on State Highway 64 in southern Indiana, about eight miles west of the Floyd County seat of New Albany. The southern third of Indiana is hill country; the glaciers which flattened the northern two-thirds of the state, leaving rich layers of soil, did not reach the southern part. The soil is poor and the terrain is rough in that unglaciated triangle which extends south from Monroe County to the Ohio River, from Tell City to New Albany. It is an area of great natural beauty, but it boasts little prosperity.

Floyd County was formerly part of Clark and Harrison counties. Through the efforts of the Scribner family, later founders of New Albany, the county was organized on January 2, 1819, and named for Colonel John Floyd, a distinguished Virginian who was killed by the Indians on the Kentucky side of the Ohio River. Twelve years prior, in 1807, a man named George Waltz had entered a tract of land and laid out what would be the county's first settlement on the north side of a stream known as Whiskey Run (named Little Indian Creek later, around 1833). Waltz named the community Georgetown, gave two lots for blacksmith shops—the rural fabricators of the time—and watched the little village grow.

Sherman Minton's parents were of Indiana pioneer stock. His mother's family came from England, lived for a while in Maryland, and moved to southern Indiana in 1814. Anthony Livers, Minton's maternal great-grandfather, was one of the first settlers in newly formed New Albany,

7

just across the Ohio River from Louisville. The Minton side of the family came from Virginia by way of Kentucky and settled in southern Indiana after 1850. John Evan Minton, Sherman's father, was born in 1862 in Harrison County, the son of Jonathan S. Minton and Savannah Cline Minton Smith. John Evan never knew his own father, who died on May 11, 1862, while serving in the Civil War with Company E, Fifty-third Regiment Indiana Volunteers. He died of an illness while aboard a troop ship on the Ohio River near Evansville, Indiana.[1] In one of his campaign speeches while running for the Senate in 1934, Minton, in speaking of the ravages of war, admitted:

> My understanding and sympathy for the soldier goes back to the Civil War in which my Grandfather Minton fought to preserve the Union. He gave his life in that great conflict and left behind him a widow and a family of five children, of which my father was one. He was a war baby and never saw his father. He was reared in that struggling family of five children amidst poverty and desperate circumstances. The aftermath of war never permitted him the opportunities of a full education or of a life of comfortable surroundings. As a youth he set forth to help support his widowed mother and his brothers and sisters. The winning of each day's bread was an uphill struggle. My father slaved and toiled from dawn until dusk to provide for his family of four children. He won out against terrible odds, but we did not know the meaning of luxuries in my family. We thanked God each day that the aftermath of war had left us bread and soup and a will to live.[2]

Emma C. Livers was born in Harrison County, Indiana, the daughter of Lafayette and Martha Desper Livers. She married John Minton in 1883.

The four-room house in which Sherman was born originally was a log cabin. Frame siding was later added to the outside walls. His parents were poor and poorly educated. At the time of their marriage each had attended school five years. John found it extremely difficult to support his family, earning a bare subsistence at various times as a farmer and as a laborer on the Southern Railroad. Once, while working on the railroad, he suffered sunstroke. In an interview in connection with the celebration of his seventieth birthday, Sherman spoke about this calamity and attributed his own "liberalism" to his "experiences in life. I can remember when my father had a sunstroke. The railroad brought him home and dumped him at our house. That was all. He was out of work and it was our responsibility. This human wreckage of the railroad system was thrown on the doorstep of his family instead of their trying to alleviate it."[3]

After suffering the sunstroke, John was forced to take any job he could find to keep bread on the table. He worked at various times as a farmer, grocer, butcher, junk collector, and stock buyer.

Financial insecurity forced the family to move often. Early on they moved to a farm outside Georgetown which Minton later described as the "old hill farm."[4] The family then moved to a small brick building in the southwest part of Georgetown which had been built and used as the United Brethren church, and still later to a house next door to the Christian church, where young Sherman helped the sexton ring the bell to call the members for worship. The nickname "Shay" was coined by his younger brother Rosco, who pronounced "Sherman" as "Shayman," a term the family shortened to "Shay." The nickname stuck and he was known for the rest of his life as "Shay" by all close to him and on all occasions when formalities could be relaxed.

The boy was exposed early to politics. When Minton was five, his father took him to hear an address by William Jennings Bryan. Perched on the wide shoulders of the elder Minton, he listened attentively to the silver-tongued orator. Bryan remained Minton's idol for the rest of his life, for he was, as Minton said, the greatest orator he had known.

Shay's formal schooling was obtained in a one-room grade or "common" school in Georgetown, housing students in grades one through eight and taught by one teacher. Because the room was heated by a wood-burning potbellied stove, a boy could earn five cents a week by building a fire each morning and getting the school warm before the teacher and other students arrived. For this munificent sum the boy also was required to wash the blackboard at least once a week.

Equipment was sparse; a container of drinking water and two tin cups were in a corner in the back of the room. Drinking water was carried from the spring over the hill by a pair of boys selected from a list of volunteers. A trip to the spring during school hours was a most pleasant break for these energetic and confined lads. There were two outhouses—one for the boys and one for the girls—behind the school.

One of Shay's teachers was Harry K. Engleman, who later became a physician practicing in Georgetown and the surrounding countryside. The teacher of the one-room school in Georgetown in those days taught as many as fifty pupils in all eight grades for a salary of about thirty-six dollars per month. Engleman described young Shay as a bright but mischievous lad, always with muddy shoes, who had to be challenged with more difficult exercises to keep him busy. Years later Minton stopped in Dr. Engleman's office, announced himself and asked if he could enter the inner office to see the doctor. Dr. Engleman replied, "Come in, if your shoes are clean."[5]

Tragedy struck the Minton family in 1900. Sherman's thirty-six-year-old mother died of cancer of the uterus on April 12 of that year. An unsuccessful operation was performed on the kitchen table by the local doctor, but she succumbed to the intractable malignancy. Sherman was not yet ten years old when his mother died, and the horror of the operation and death stayed with him all his life.

John Minton advertised in a "lonely hearts" paper for a new wife and soon obtained results. On December 3, 1901, at the age of thirty-nine, the senior Minton and thirty-year-old Sarah Montague were married by John J. Richards, justice of the peace of Floyd County.[6] On the day that the new wife arrived at the depot in Georgetown from Kentucky, Shay and his friends greeted her, a self-appointed welcoming and inspection committee. Apparently she took up the wifing and mothering duties she'd "signed up for" without incident, but the adjustment could not have been easy.

There was time left over after school for Shay to work for money. His first job, at the age of eight, was washing buggies at ten cents a job for John Wolfe, owner of the hotel and livery stable in Georgetown. After work, Mrs. Wolfe, who knew the gargantuan appetite of young lads, would feed the hungry boy.[7]

Once a year his father purchased cattle in and around English, Indiana, to stock his butcher shop. Young Shay helped his father drive these cattle from English to Georgetown, a distance of about thirty miles.[8]

When he wasn't working he was generally getting into trouble with pranks. In school he had the reputation of throwing paper wads, apple cores, and turnips. He and a friend allegedly frequented the nearby watermelon patches and "borrowed" many of the best specimens from the farmers.

One of his classmates described young Minton as "smart—always picked a back seat and the second day the teacher always moved him to the front. I can still remember his gazing longingly at those rear seats."[9]

Once while in grammar school, Minton jumped from the second story of the building to escape from being "kept in" after school.[10]

Another time young Shay loosened a wheel on the family buggy. The wheel fell off when his brother Herbert was on a date, much to the mortification of that young swain.[11]

On one occasion young Shay's prank bordered on the dangerous. Mrs. Henry Mitchell lived next to the playground of the grammar school. Baseballs flew over the playground fence, landing in her backyard. Mrs. Mitchell grew tired of these baseballs cluttering her lawn and so kept each baseball that sailed over the fence, irritating the boys who owned the balls. One day Shay noticed Mrs. Mitchell cooking a big copper kettle of apple butter in her backyard. He threw a baseball made with an inner core of gunpowder over the fence. Mrs. Mitchell promptly picked up the baseball and angrily tossed it into the fire under the kettle. The explosion overturned the kettle, spewing apple butter in all directions.[12]

Whether Shay was the "meanest damned boy in Georgetown" or "just mischievous," Minton in later years lamented that "they've never known me around here [Georgetown] as a lawyer, senator or jurist. . . . Whenever a chick squawked in the henhouse at midnight, or a pane of glass was shattered and the rock went scooting across the floor, they thought of me, and they still do."[13]

Minton completed his grade school education in the common school in Georgetown in the spring of 1904. However, because there was no place else for him to go to school, Shay went through the eighth grade again, not because it was required, but because of some inner compulsion to learn as much as he could. He finished the eighth grade for the second time in the spring of 1905.

Brother Herbert left Georgetown sometime before 1905 and went to Fort Worth, Texas. After Shay's school let out in the spring of 1905, John Minton took the family to Fort Worth to join Herbert. There, Shay, who had been working in any job available to earn money since he was eight years old, obtained a job on the production line with Swift and Company trimming neck bones, cutting beef, and carrying boxes. The money he earned helped support the family.

Reminiscing about this job during an interview around his seventieth birthday, Minton recalled, "When I was fourteen, I worked ten hours a day, at fifteen cents an hour, for a packing house. I learned something about child labor, wages and overtime. I knew the need for social legislation. I knew about the wastage of human energy."[14]

Ambition, high character, and rugged determination soon began to assert themselves in this lad who now was almost sixteen years old. Perhaps that boy remembered the vow that he had made to his paternal grandmother. She had told him before she died that he had a good mind and had made him promise he would get an education. At any rate, in the fall of 1906 Shay used his meager savings to purchase a one-way coach rail ticket from Fort Worth to Indiana so that he could go to high school there. "It was too hot," he later recalled, "and the land too flat in Texas, so I came home to Georgetown. I alone returned to Indiana to go to school. The rest of my family remained in Texas. My father died in Texas. I didn't run away. I just listened to my own advice. I was imbued with the propaganda of the time that the Hoosier educational system just couldn't be beat. I convinced my parents I should go to school here."[15]

Back in southern Indiana, Minton again entered the work force rather than school—at least for a while. The event was described in a special broadcast on October 12, 1949, honoring him on his appointment to the Supreme Court by radio station WHAS in Louisville:

A kid in knee pants squatted under the floor of a penny arcade on Jefferson Street in Louisville. His job was to jerk the levers that worked a make-believe excursion boat. When he jerked, the boat above him wobbled from side to side. His cousin had invented the gadget that rocked the boat. He paid the kid fifteen dollars a week to work it. It was big money. He'd been at it two weeks when, in the middle of an excursion, homesickness hit him. He finished the ten minute tour, crawled out of his cubbyhole, and chucked his job. Justice Minton said that episode was the turning point in his career. He returned to Georgetown and school.[16]

Minton lived in Georgetown with his uncle Henry Clay Minton and in the fall of 1906 enrolled at Georgetown Township High School in

Edwardsville, about three and a half miles east of Georgetown. This high school was geared for attendance by farm boys and girls who were needed at home most of the year to help with the farm work. The high school, in fact, was merely a single room added to the grade school, with an academic year six months long, starting in October and ending in March. Young Shay walked the seven-mile round-trip between home and school every day.

However, the 1906–07 school year was the last one for the township high school. After it closed, Minton moved five miles farther east to New Albany, and in the fall of 1907 he became a member of the sophomore class at New Albany High School. He lived that year with his Grandmother Livers in her home on West Market Street. For the final two years of high school (1908–10) he lived at 716 Vincennes Street with the family of a classmate, Walter Sherman Heazlitt. Minton and the Heazlitt family remained friends for life.

These three years at New Albany High were important; it was there that he became a student, an athlete, and a speaker. Personality traits solidified—strength of character, high ambition, fierce competitiveness, and resoluteness that could not be weakened by any hardship or momentary failures which impeded his path. His goals in life surely were fashioned during this time. And most importantly, perhaps, he met and courted the young lady who would become his wife.

Minton first thought he wanted to be a civil engineer, but his low grades in mathematics altered his direction.[17] The young man's grade average in high school was 86 percent, with the highest grade in history, just under 90 percent. His favorite subjects were history and civics. Physics held some interest, botany none; yet he took and passed both courses because two science credits were necessary for graduation. He did very well in Latin, although at the time he "saw no sense in dead languages." English Literature he thought was "just silly" (the verses of Shelley were "just the kind of stuff a guy named Percy would write") but he did well in the course. The high school teacher who influenced him most was Albert L. Kohlmeier, who later continued his role as Shay's influential teacher as the head of the History Department at Indiana University.[18] Kohlmeier later recalled that "when Sherman entered high school, he had not had the opportunities that some of his classmates had. Minton's mind and character continued to develop, however, through-out his active career."[19]

This development of mind and character included a beginning fascina-tion with politics. When he was in high school in 1908 the textbook on government was a book by Woodrow Wilson, and in 1949 Minton recalled that he was just about the original Wilson man. He had a teacher who was a staunch Republican, and the day after Bryan was defeated for the third time, this teacher asked Minton "Well, who are you Democrats going to turn to now?" Without hesitation, Minton replied, "Woodrow Wilson." The teacher laughed, deprecating Wilson as "only a college professor."[20]

While attending New Albany High School, Minton helped organize and was the captain of his high school's first debate team. Kohlmeier was the sponsor and faculty adviser of the group. On April 15, 1910, Judge John Henry Weathers of New Albany presided at the debate between the team from Louisville Manual High School and the team from New Albany High School: Sherman Minton, Will Strack, and John Sweeney. New Albany defended the negative of the question, "Resolved, that the American Sys-tem of Legislation is Intrinsically Superior to that of Great Britain" and won by unanimous decision of the judges. Shay Minton, the second speaker, "displayed the best delivery of the evening."[21] Minton had read and ab-sorbed much of the political philosophy of his hero Woodrow Wilson in preparation for this debate: he emphasized that the President should be the real leader of the nation, emancipated from the control of Congress, and that political responsibility should rest with the President.

Kohlmeier always sought one member of his debate team to "do the spell-binding." For such tasks, he had "no difficulty in picking Minton" because "he had the height, a fine face, clear enunciation, a modulated voice, and terrific emotion." When Minton "spoke from conviction, his emotion and voice would ring the changes from sarcasm and ridicule to pathos."[22]

Perhaps it was this talent for debate and his keen interest in oratory, coupled with a dislike of mathematics (which continued throughout his life), that helped determine Minton's profession. However, he claimed that his vocational goal was determined earlier as a boy in Georgetown when he was fined three dollars for riding a bicycle on the sidewalk immediately after the town board had passed an ordinance to the contrary. Minton "was im-pressed by the proceedings." The justice of the peace "read out of a big book and everything was very formal. Right then I decided to study law. Maybe I thought it was an easy way to make three dollars."[23]

Athletic ability also surfaced while he was at New Albany High School, with the 1909 football yearbook reporting that "Shay was a green man at the beginning of the season but developed rapidly and should be a great tackle in the fall." When he graduated in 1910 the yearbook had these entries about him: Football—*Sherman Minton (Fullback): Energetic and daring, "Shay" is hard and determined offensive player. He is also a wonderfully accurate thrower of the forward pass.* Track—*Minton—Fast on the relay and good as a weight man.* Baseball—*Minton, Center Field—Best fielder and base runner ever in school.* Under his picture in the 1910 yearbook is the caption: *He has a work, a life purpose; he has found it and will follow it.* The class prophecy in the same yearbook predicted with amazing accuracy and uncanny foresight that "A band wagon with 'Vote for Minton for Senator' drove past." The "Character Book" page in the yearbook allowed that Minton would have as his goal "to convince a jury that black is white."

The boyish prankster had evolved into a strong-minded, high-achieving young man. Still, being an individualistic leader seemed as normal to him as getting up in the morning. On his first day at New Albany High School, he walked down the middle of the street toward the buildings leading some fifteen or twenty other students. He was wearing a large, wide, pink cravat around his neck. He walked boldly and confidently through the front door while the other students entered through the back door, the prescribed custom for freshmen. Within a week most of his classmates were wearing cravats—pink ones if they were available. He was soon the class leader, a role he occupied throughout high school. His followers seemed to want to know whether he was uptown or downtown during after-school activities. Shay obliged them: If he was downtown, he would turn the intersection sign for a doctor's office in that direction. If he was uptown, he would turn the sign in the opposite direction. This system seems to have pleased everybody but the doctor.[24]

He delighted in making the teeth of adults at New Albany High School rattle. His friend and classmate, Walter Heazlitt, recalled that both of them would ride an air chute to the school basement. On one occasion a teacher reached the chute just as Heazlitt and Minton disappeared into it and the teacher grabbed one of the boys. "He thought he had hold of me," Heazlitt recalled. "You never heard such a cussing in all your life. Little did he know he had a future Supreme Court justice by the seat of the pants."[25]

Another time, as a circus paraded through town, Heazlitt and Minton slipped aboard the monkey wagon. They sat atop the wagon picking imaginary fleas off of each other until Charles B. McLinn, the high school principal, spied them and ended the performance.

In the winter of his sophomore year, Minton dated a pretty senior, Ruth Rough, who was a wonderful singer. When Ruth won the high school vocal contest, Minton jumped from his chair, beside himself with joy and pride. Running out of the auditorium to the basement stairs, he shouted at the top of his lungs, "Hurrah for our side." The janitor in charge of the basement attempted to quiet him but to no avail. Finally a teacher arrived on the scene and suspended the unrestrained suitor from school.[26]

Later he was reinstated but not until he acknowledged in writing on February 20, 1908, that he had "disobeyed the rules and regulations of the High School, and failed to obey the orders of the janitor having charge of the basement in the High School building" and promised that "my spirit will be on the side of doing the right thing at the High School building in every way."

C. A. Prosser, superintendent of New Albany Public Schools, wrote sternly on his petition for readmission: "On the basis of the above promise please reinstate this pupil."[27] Minton also was required to make a public apology before the entire student body.[28]

Ruth was only a passing fancy. Undoubtedly, Minton's greatest reward in his high school career was meeting and courting Gertrude Frances Gurtz, the girl he would marry in 1917. When the young woman graduated from high school on January 20, 1911, the yearbook noted that "her peerless features approve her fit for none but a king." Through all her life she displayed a charm and grace which marked her as an ideal "lady" in the eyes of all who knew her.

The fifty-first annual commencement of the New Albany High School was held in the high school auditorium on Friday evening, May 27, 1910. Fifty-seven young men and women proudly received their diplomas that night, but none was more proud or conscious of having traveled a long, hard way to get there than Sherman Minton.

And the next step? Before he could attend college, he would have to reenter the work force to earn and save some money.

He again obtained employment with Swift and Company in Fort Worth, this time as a traveling salesman. For a year and a half Minton toiled, selling bologna, sides of beef, canned beef, and other products. Evidently he did it well; when he quit his job to attend college, Minton had to decline what one of the officials of the company called "a future for him at Swift."[29]

One of Minton's fringe benefits with Swift and Company was the opportunity to play in the outfield for the company's semipro baseball team. He had an arm so strong that he was spotted by Charles Comiskey, owner of the Chicago White Sox, who made him an offer to play professional baseball with the Galveston club of the Texas League. Minton turned the offer down to continue his education.[30]

Traveling as a meat salesman had another serendipitous effect on Minton. On one trip he found himself on the same train with his silver-tongued idol, William Jennings Bryan. Minton took the opportunity to talk with Bryan and to study his oratorical skills. In return, Bryan permitted Minton to hold his hat during his addresses from the rear platform of the train.[31]

On September 21, 1911, "Minton, Sherman, New Albany, 217 W. Main" enrolled at Indiana University in Bloomington. He gave as the name and address of his parent or guardian "Mr. John Minton, 1505 Lincoln, Ft. Worth, Texas."[32]

He was determined to become a lawyer; his total resources at this time were a hundred and fifty dollars. He kept himself in college by waiting tables and firing the furnace at his fraternity house, Phi Delta Theta, stacking planks in a lumber yard, selling washing machines which would not sell (Minton took meal tickets in part payment), refereeing football games, and doing any odd jobs that he could find.[33]

But he had little for himself beyond tuition. During summer school one year, he lived on ten dollars, sleeping in the Phi Delta Theta house, which was not serving meals. Through the week he lived on milk, eggs, berries, butter, and stale bread, which he bought two loaves for a nickel.[34] His salvation probably came from one of his friends, C. Severin Buschmann, who invited Shay to eat in his place on weekends. Buschmann paid four dollars and fifty cents a week to eat at a local boarding house, but he went home to Indianapolis on weekends, leaving a place at the table for Minton. "He'd load up on the boarding house food on the weekends and almost starve the rest of the week," Buschmann recalled.[35]

When Minton attended Indiana University, it was possible to combine the academic course with the law course and to graduate with a law degree in five years. The first two years consisted of undergraduate classes, with the last three years devoted to law.

Minton took this five-year course, but by hard work and attendance at two summer sessions he was able to complete the work in four years. His academic record for the two years of undergraduate work wasn't stellar: (1911–13) two A's, fifteen B's, and six C's. He received F's in Hygiene and Philosophy.[36]

Still, he seemed to feel the need for more schooling in his chosen career. In the fall of 1913, Minton entered the Indiana University Law School, and there found his niche. He took more than 106 hours of courses in law and received one B-minus (three hours), three B's (ten hours), one B-plus (five hours), and one A-minus (six hours). The rest of his grades were A's. He went to summer school in 1914, carried a heavy load of fifteen hours of law courses, and received a grade of A in twelve and a half of those hours with a grade of B-plus in the other two and a half hours. In 1915 he attended two sessions of summer school. During the first session, from June 29 to August 5, he received eleven and one-sixth hours of credit in his law courses with a straight-A average. For the second session, from August 6 to September 15, he received credit for seven and a half hours of law courses with a straight-A average,[37] a strong performance by any measurement.

Despite his heavy academic load and his work to support himself, Minton found time for athletics, debating and political office. Almost six feet tall and weighing 175 pounds, Minton played fullback and end on the varsity football team, center field on the varsity baseball team, and guard on the varsity basketball team.

In football he was a rugged tackler and a vicious blocker. His biggest thrills in football came from playing against All-Americans from other schools in the Big Ten. When the football team traveled to away games, Shay, who was then a complete teetotaler and nonsmoker, would go to his room early to study instead of joining his teammates in painting the town red. With chin jutting out in an aggressive manner and his dark eyes flashing, Minton spoke out when he thought something needed to be said. This fearless talk extended even to football Coach Childs, who was considered a tough coach. Minton wasn't one to let a problem fester. He insisted that grievances be aired and disagreements settled promptly. On one occasion such insistence cost him a cut hand, dismissal from football practice, and a bill from the university. During a heated argument which carried over from a class in the law school, fists began to fly and Minton looped an untimely left at his adversaries and hit a plate glass window.[38]

In baseball his strong arm rifled many a "strike" from the outfield, or by the combination of Minton to Sclemmer to Johnson (outfielder to short-stop to catcher), thus cutting down many an opposing runner at the plate.[39] In 1910 he stood at home plate in the old Eclipse Park, at Seventh and Kentucky in Louisville, then the home of the Louisville Colonels, and threw a baseball over the right center-field fence—a throw which many profes-sional baseball players in the American Association had attempted without success.[40] One of his teammates wrote about him:

Shay's enthusiasm and "talk-it-upness" during a game was something. He continuously shouted encouragement to our pitchers whether we were up or down; he was no slouch at razzing opposing pitchers and his terse com-ments on the bench did a great deal to stimulate the spirit to win.[41]

Minton later described his greatest thrill in sports at Indiana University. It came in the spring of 1915, during a baseball game at Ohio State, played on a Columbus field encircled by a cinder track. He wrote:

I came to bat. The pitcher threw one where I had been swinging for three years [high and outside]. Babe Ruth or Mickey Mantle never got the wood on the ball better than I did, and away it went over the center fielder's head.

As I rounded third base the center fielder chased the ball clear out of the playing field, and there it went down the cinder track, center fielder still chasing it. I walked in from third base. My teammates claimed that I kept the bat wrapped in tissue paper and would let no one else use it. That is apocryphal. If I had done that no one else could have batted, for we were practically a one-bat ball club.[42]

Minton was a member of the varsity debating team at IU during his freshman and sophomore years, vying successfully with Wendell Lewis Willkie, the 1940 Republican presidential candidate, and Indiana Governor Paul Vories McNutt, national commander of American Legion, high commissioner to the Philippines, and federal security administrator. When Shay entered the IU Law School he dropped his membership on the debating team due to lack of time. Throughout his collegiate career Minton continued the pattern of individualistic leadership which would later take him to the halls of power. On September 16, 1913, as a sophomore, Minton was elected as president of the Indiana Union, the all-campus organization for men, and served in this office in 1914 during his junior year.[43] He was a member of the board of directors, along with classmate Willkie, of the Jackson Club (young Democrats)[44] and held leadership positions in Phi Delta Theta.[45]

His sense of farce and the ridiculous also continued, and he loved to test the limits of the system. He instigated the famous (or infamous) Phi Delt snipe hunt and loved to tell about it in later years. On one occasion when Minton and some of his brothers determined to see an "all girl" show at the old Assembly Hall on campus, they built a scaffold to a second-story window to peep at the girls without paying. Some of the unlucky ones who were unable to reach the ringside seat at the top caused the scaffold to topple with a thunderous crash. Minton refused to go down with the scaffold. He alone hung high on the window ledge while his fraternity brothers scattered in all directions, leaving Shay as the only one left to answer for the crime.[46]

At commencement Minton graduated at the top of his class. In 1914 he had been awarded the annual Williams Jennings Bryan prize contest as the student showing the greatest proficiency in public speaking, with his subject "The Relationship of the Executive Department to the Legislative Department of the United States."[47]

Meanwhile, the romance with his high school sweetheart continued to flower. Although the young man sometimes was seen with another coed on campus, Gertrude seems to have had his heart, traveling frequently from New Albany to Bloomington to be his date for special events.[48]

Minton graduated from IU with an LL.B. degree on September 15, 1915. He won a set of law books for ranking first in his class and, had such degrees been conferred at that time, he would have graduated with "High Distinction." His top scholastic record entitled him to the office of law librarian as well as membership in Phi Delta Phi, the international honorary legal fraternity.

The outstanding law school record won Minton a five-hundred-dollar scholarship to the Yale University School of Law from the American Association of Law Schools.[49] In the fall of 1915 he headed east for the first time in his life for a year of graduate study at this prestigious school. Yale Law School in the academic year of 1915–16 had a distinguished faculty. Among the teaching scholars was William Howard Taft, former President of the United States and later chief justice who taught, among other subjects, constitutional law.

Other faculty members included Dean Swann, later a judge on the United States Court of Appeals for the Second Circuit; Henry Wade Robers, Senior United States Circuit Judge; Gordon Sherman, brother-in-law of Justice Mahlon Pitney, and two judges of the state courts of Connecticut.[50]

Minton took a course in jurisprudence, one in international and Roman law, and one in comparative European governments, as well as the usual courses offered by the Law School,[51] earning grades of A in ten courses and B in one. He earned his Master of Laws degree at Yale and graduated *cum laude*.

In later years when Shay was asked if he ever had dreams of being a member of the highest court in the land, he would smile and recall an incident that occurred in the constitutional law seminar of former President William Howard Taft. A Supreme Court decision under discussion was a holding that the government had the right to confiscate the nets of a fisherman who had been convicted of charges that he seined in a navigable stream. Taft and Minton became engaged in a heated discussion over the propriety of the ruling. Minton argued that the court was wrong because in his opinion, the fisherman had been wronged. "Naturally," Minton later explained, "I felt sorry for that poor devil who had lost his nets."[52] Taft argued that the ruling of the court was correct. Finally Taft, with the chuckle for which he was so famous, ended the argument with this prophetic counsel, "I'm afraid, Mr. Minton, that if you don't like the way this law has been interpreted, you will have to get on the Supreme Court and change it."[53]

Taft had another opportunity to examine Shay's legal abilities. The thesis on constitutional law which Minton wrote as the final examination in the seminar was declared by Taft to be "one of the best ever written at Yale."[54]

Minton's interest in oratory continued. He won Yale's Wayland Club prize for extemporaneous public speaking. A contestant drew a subject and devoted ten hours to preparation without knowing on which side of the question he was to argue. Shay drew the subject of "The Short Ballot" and won first prize.[55]

While at Yale Minton helped establish the Yale University Legal Aid Society, an extracurricular activity which must have been considered somewhat radical by the conservative elements of the school and the city of New Haven. However, Minton felt strongly that society in general and the nation constitutionally were obliged to offer legal rights to the poor.[56]

Even with the five-hundred-dollar scholarship, Minton had a hard time making ends meet. Poor and often hungry, he wrote to a friend that he had "grown an automatic appetite; it shut off after fifteen cents' worth."[57] But he was awarded his LL.M. degree from Yale in 1916. After his retirement from the Supreme Court, he commented in a letter to Justice Felix Frankfurter on his legal education at Yale and especially cited the legacy of William H. Taft. He despaired that Taft was one from the "bird dog school" who believed that a judge should "first find what the court has said and stick to it." For himself, Minton commented, "I think my training and practice were too much in that school. I did believe a great deal in stability, which was a fetish with Taft."[58]

The day of graduation from the Yale Law School in 1916 found Shay absent. The young lawyer was out earning money to open his law office. He took a job that summer as platform manager of a Chautauqua lecture troupe in the Midwest.

As manager of the Chautauqua troupe, Minton hired Alvin Nugent "Bo" McMillin, the "praying colonel," an All-American quarterback from Centre College of Kentucky who later became head football coach at Indiana University and a College Football Hall of Famer. The two had known one another since boyhood days in Fort Worth where Shay's brother Rosco and Bo were high school football teammates. McMillin had reason to "owe one" to his friend's brother; Minton had recently dragged McMillin from Silver Creek near New Albany when the visitor had fallen off a dam and into the swirling current. Another man from New Albany, Robert Best, leaped into a rowboat to rescue Bo but fell out of the boat and drowned. McMillin grabbed a tree limb and Minton was able to reach him and pull him to safety.[59] Minton was glad to have Bo as a tentmate for the summer, and after the experience was over the two men remained close friends even though they pursued very different careers.

In later years, Shay would tell at football banquets how the young Bo once wrote him a letter saying he was operating a "pressing club" to help pay expenses at Centre College and needed an electric "iorn" to help him with his work. Shay saw to it that Bo received his iron. Bo's rejoinder to the story was that all he knew about the "iorn" was that he received what he requested "and that's more than most people get from their senator when they want something." [60]

Minton had to wear many hats as manager of the Chautauqua circuit; he even had to sing in a quartet on occasion. Interestingly, the position brought Shay in contact again with William Jennings Bryan, who frequently spoke on the circuit. Bryan could still arouse audiences, and Minton spent many enraptured hours listening to his hero. At the end of the Chautauqua's summer season, the young lawyer had achieved his purpose. He had saved three hundred dollars. Minton returned to New Albany in the fall of 1916 to open his law office. He was admitted to practice by the Floyd Circuit Court, and became a member of the Bar Association of Indiana in the fall of 1916. Later, in an address given on July 26, 1955, in the courtroom of the Floyd Circuit Court, Minton recalled an incident of his early career:

> *Kirke* [D. Kirke Hedden] *had just been elected prosecutor. A colored woman shot and killed her husband. It was Kirke's first murder case and he asked me if I wouldn't like to help him for the experience. I needed nothing so much as experience and I accepted with alacrity. A good woman had killed a bad man. It was cold-blooded first degree murder as a matter of fact and law. But Judge Paris knew it was not, under the eyes of Men— the jury. While Kirke and I gave the state a bang-up good prosecution calling for the vengeance of the law, the jury knew better and acquitted and I think they would have given the defendant a medal if they had the power to do so.*[61]

Human considerations come above the law—always. Minton barely had begun his practice in New Albany when on April 6, 1917, the United States declared war on Germany and entered World War I. Minton enlisted in the

Reserve Corps, and reported on May 12, 1917, to the first citizens training camp at Fort Benjamin Harrison in Indianapolis. He was a candidate for a commission in the Officers Reserve Corps.[62]

A fellow candidate at the time, C. Severin Buschmann, (the friend who had provided boardinghouse food at Indiana University) recalled that although patriotic, "Shay was not enthusiastic about military life. He was a little unorthodox at times about saluting" and other military protocol.[63] It soon became common knowledge that two law professors in camp from the law school at Indiana University would be commissioned as majors. Minton knew these professors—he had, after all, graduated from the IU Law School—and he was not impressed with the abilities of these particular men. "Shay didn't care too much for them," Buschmann recalled, "and he let it be known he didn't want a commission if they were to be his fellow officers." The commander of his company, Eighth Company, Ninth Provisional Training Regiment, heard about Minton's critical remarks and decided that Minton should not be commissioned with his class.

When graduation day came and the candidates were to receive their commissions, General Glenn, the camp commander, appeared to face the graduate assembly of would-be officers. In the front row were those candidates who were to be commissioned majors, in the second row those who were to be captains, in the third row the candidates who were to be first lieutenants, and in the fourth row those who were to be commissioned second lieutenants. And, in the last row were those candidates who would not receive commissions. There stood Minton.

"General Glenn walked up to Minton and looked him over," Buschmann said. "Shay was a handsome, powerful-looking man—176 pounds, height of seventy and three-fourths inches, and a girth of chest of thirty-six inches at expiration and forty and a half inches at inspiration on his physical examination.[64] Glenn turned to the company commander and demanded: 'What are you doing with this ace in the discards?' "

Minton repeated the training cycle, but before he did he requested and was given a discharge to take care of a most important matter. The marriage of Gertrude Frances Gurtz to Sherman Minton took place on Saturday, August 11, 1917, at New Albany. The happy couple would be "At Home, 610 East Market Street, New Albany, Indiana," reported the announcement mailed out by the bride's aunt, Mrs. Frances LaFaivre.[65]

Gertrude was born on February 2, 1893, in the tiny village of Frenchtown in Harrison County. Her father, Frank Gurtz, was a farmer. Her great-grandfather had come to America from Germany in 1848 and, along with about fifty other families who had come from France, settled in Frenchtown. (The community had originally been called St. Bernard for the local church, but when a post office was established, the name was changed to Frenchtown in remembrance of its early settlers.) Gertrude reputedly owed her beauty and charm to a French grandmother.[66]

When Gertrude was four, her parents had sent her to New Albany to live during the school year because the schools there were better than those near her home in Harrison County. She lived there with her widowed great-aunt, Frances Faust LaFaivre. When the school year was over, Gertrude would return to Frenchtown for the summer. After her graduation in 1911, she attended college for a year at St. Mary-of-the-Woods in Terre Haute, Indiana, where she received high grades.[67] After completing the program, the young woman taught in a free kindergarten in New Albany and did social work in a preschool program in the local schools.[68]

Throughout her marriage, the rearing of three children, and her life as a politician's and Supreme Court justice's wife, Gertrude Gurtz Minton seems to have enjoyed nothing but respect from the people who knew her. The November 1949 issue of *Cross Keys*, the magazine of Tri Kappa (she was initiated into Nu Chapter on June 11, 1917), described her thus:

> *Is she tall? Not very. She is small, petite and very charming, and when she smiles her big brown eyes light up with a sparkle. She wears her hair, which is brown, either long or short, according to whim or fashion. She dresses simply and becomingly, and always gives the impression of daintiness, even when wearing house frocks with frilly little aprons, a thing which she does frequently, for she likes to cook. And, by the way, she is an excellent cook, too.*

On August 27, 1917, the new bridegroom re-enlisted in the Reserve Corps in order to attend officer's candidate school again and to repeat the training cycle at Fort Harrison. It was no idle commitment; the Allies were struggling desperately to gain the upper hand in Europe. This time he was assigned to the Fifteenth Infantry Company, United States Training Center. On November 26, 1917, he was discharged as an enlisted man to accept a commission as an officer in the Army. The next day, November 27, 1917, Shay was appointed a captain, Infantry Section, Officers Reserve Corps.

His first assignment was to the Eighty-fourth Division, then stationed at Camp Zachary Taylor in Kentucky and later in Chillicothe, Ohio, at Camp Sherman. Because of his demonstrated ability, Minton was assigned to the Advance Element of the Eighty-Fourth Division, which sailed for France in July 1918. Overseas he was detached from the Eighty-Fourth and assigned to the General Staff under General John Joseph Pershing. He scouted roads and other routes to ensure the safe movement of troops, ammunition and supplies to the front. In the intense battle sectors at the Soissons and Verdun fronts, when a battle was raging or a drive was in progress, days and nights would pass with little or no sleep or food and no relief from duty. When the Armistice was signed on November 11, 1918, Captain Minton was in charge of supporting operations for troops at Verdun, and after the Armistice, he was assigned to headquarters company of the Thirty-Third Division in the American Army of Occupation in Germany.

In the spring of 1919, Minton and Buschmann, both officers in the Army of Occupation, were sent to school at the Sorbonne in Paris, where Shay took special law courses in the Faculté de Droit, studying international law, Roman law, civil law and jurisprudence under internationally known French teachers. Minton lived in l'Hôtel Des Grands Hommes (Hotel of Great Men), a very small place with twenty rooms. Buschmann later recalled, "Shay and Gertrude were expecting their first child. Shay immediately assumed it would be a boy, and he also wanted to run for Congress. So he saved his money. He ate the least expensive meals, he lived very, very economically; he literally lived on very little." [69]

Years later, in 1963, Buschmann visited Paris and sent his friend a post-card from l'Hôtel Des Grands Hommes. "I talked to the young girl clerk," he wrote. "She said many great men, like Voltaire, had lived there. I told her there was one she didn't know about—U.S. Supreme Court Justice Sherman Minton." [70]

Minton was pleased to be in Versailles on June 28, 1919, when the treaty of peace between the Allies and Germany was signed. Then he returned from overseas and on July 31, 1919, underwent his physical examination prior to separation from service. In the report Minton certified that "at the present time I have no wound, injury, or disease, whether incurred in the military service of the United States or otherwise."[71] The next day, August 1, 1919, Infantry Captain Sherman Minton was honorably discharged at Camp Zachary Taylor, Kentucky.

CHAPTER THREE

EARLY PRACTICE, POLITICS, AND THE SENATE

MINTON RETURNED TO NEW ALBANY AND FOR THE FIRST TIME MET HIS INFANT son, Sherman Anthony Minton, born on February 24, 1919.

Then he rehung his shingle and reopened his office for the private practice of law as a sole practitioner. Clients were few in the beginning; it was obviously necessary for him to rebuild his practice after an absence of more than two years in the Army.

Complicating the situation was the fact that the political bug had bitten him. In 1920 Minton announced his candidacy for the Democratic nomination for Representative to Congress from the Third Indiana District. He finished second in the field of five candidates, and at the appropriate time listed his total expenditures for the campaign as $302.75.[1] After that, he declined to become actively involved in politics for a number of years; probably he was not used to defeats and did not like the feeling of failure. He later admitted that his knowledge of practical politics in 1920 was sadly deficient.[2]

With the political itch now scratched, Shay began in earnest to build his law practice. His oratorical skills coupled with his wide knowledge of law made him a formidable competitor and a respected adversary. He soon earned a reputation as a terrific trial lawyer, and his practice grew steadily. Always endowed with a hearty sense of humor, Minton also could laugh at himself. A favorite story he told about himself had to do with a pauper client charged with a serious crime. Shay, the court-appointed attorney, had a long interview with his jailed client on the afternoon before the trial date. After the interview, the client, according to Minton, brooded over the problem of whether to put his life in the hands of this young lawyer or to place his trust and confidence elsewhere. Apparently he voted with his feet; that night he broke jail and fled.[3]

In 1922 Minton joined a well-established New Albany law firm which took him as a partner in what eventually was called Stotsenburg, Weathers and Minton. The firm had originally been formed in 1849 as Stotsenburg and Brown. In about 1880 it became Stotsenburg and Stotsenburg and under that name engaged in the practice of law until 1902, when the firm became Stotsenburg and Weathers, with the addition of Judge John Henry Weathers.[4]

Founder Evan B. Stotsenburg was a noted lawyer who had been active in politics and had served as attorney general of Indiana from November 11, 1915, to January 1, 1917. Weathers, from Crawford County, had earned a reputation as an excellent lawyer before a jury and had served as a judge. Legend had it that just before he joined Stotsenburg and Weathers, Minton had been so successful in a damage suit against a client of theirs that, in self-defense, they asked him the next day to join them. Both he and the firm prospered under the association.[5]

Meanwhile, the Minton family continued to grow. Daughter Mary-Anne was born on July 4, 1923, in the house at 612 East Market, which the Mintons rented after World War I from Mrs. LaFaivre.

In early 1925, however, Minton accepted an offer from Shutts and Bowen, then the preeminent law firm of Miami, Florida. He moved the family to Miami to join the firm in May.[6]

What induced him to leave the lucrative practice of Stotsenburg, Weathers and Minton in New Albany—really his hometown since high school days—is uncertain. Perhaps he was restless as a smalltown lawyer and yearned for the excitement and stimulation of Miami, which in the early twenties was the center of the real estate boom in southern Florida. Perhaps Shutts and Bowen, who were both from southern Indiana, had summoned Minton to be the trial lawyer for the firm, an attractive inducement. At any rate, the opportunity seemed one that he could not afford to pass up.

The new town of Miami had lured Colonel Frank B. Shutts in the first decade of the century. He had been born in Aurora, Indiana, received his law degree in 1892 from DePauw University, and ran unsuccessfully for lieutenant governor of Indiana. Fate sent him away from his native state to Florida, where he was appointed as receiver for a bank in Miami which had failed in the panic of 1907. He spent a year or so in Miami in the reorganization of the bank and returned to Indiana for a brief period. In 1910, however, Shutts returned to Miami and opened a law office.

The other founder of the firm, Crate D. Bowen, was from Union City, Indiana, and had attended Butler University in Indianapolis. He practiced law in Indianapolis for several years, serving as assistant city attorney of Indianapolis from 1906 to 1910; then he went to Miami in 1912 at Shutts' request to become a partner.

Preston G. Prevatt, writing the history of Shutts and Bowen, noted that Minton was a "fine litigation lawyer, tall, heavy, a fighter, aggressive." Circuit Judge John J. Kehoe, Dade County, Florida, recalled him well. In an impromptu campaign speech when Minton ran for the Senate in 1934, Judge Kehoe described him as a most successful trial lawyer who could "charm the daylights out of anyone."

Colonel Shutts personally prepared an "agreed" rearrangement of the partnership interests of the firm on January 1, 1926; in it three additional associates, including Minton, were permitted to buy into the firm. Shutts and Bowen, with nine partners and nine associates, generated gross receipts of $335,478. Minton's interest was six percent; based on the net income of the firm for 1925, he was projected to earn $10,476 in 1926. Gross receipts in 1926 in fact increased to $409,967 and Shay earned $12,639.45 that year, a handsome sum in the twenties.

All of this prosperity for Miami and its environs came to a sudden halt. After a severe hurricane hit the area in 1926, the economy lagged, many businesses failed, and construction slowed. The legal profession naturally reflected the slowdown; the gross receipts for Shutts and Bowen in 1927 dropped to $290,615 of which, interestingly, Minton earned $15,048.13.

On January 1, 1928, Minton suddenly left the firm. He sold his interest, which now had increased to 6.536 percent, to the remaining partners of Shutts and Bowen for $12,365.12 (reduced to $5,892.25 after debts were offset). These remaining partners gave promissory notes to Minton in payment of his interest. As to why Minton left Shutts and Bowen, his children speculate that their mother did not like living in Florida. Also with the deflation in Miami's economy, the need for lawyers, who had gravitated to the area in numbers, was not as great as it had been. Possibly another deep-seated consideration was the attraction for the hills of southern Indiana, an attraction which Minton, always a Hoosier at heart, had experienced as a lad of sixteen in Fort Worth when he left his family to "go home."

Whatever the reasons, Minton and his family left Miami on January 1, 1928, and returned to Indiana. There was a new member of the family now: John Evan Minton was born in St. Edward's Hospital in New Albany, on November 16, 1925. Minton had sent his wife and two children back home for the baby's birth. Named for John Weathers and Evan Stotsenburg, Minton's law partners, the child coincidentally also had his paternal grandfather's name.

Minton rejoined the firm of Stotsenburg and Weathers and the name of the law firm again became Stotsenburg, Weathers and Minton.

He plunged into the practice of law consciously or unconsciously determined to enhance his reputation as a "terrific trial lawyer." Minton handled most of the trial work for the firm—which was a diversified practice representing banks, insurance companies and plaintiffs (individuals, partnerships and corporations who had been wronged and who sought redress and damages against the wrongdoer). The firm also represented criminals—a practice not unusual for law firms in small cities in those days. Minton, however, was already showing the skills which would eventually elevate him beyond the ranks of most smalltown lawyers. Most country lawyers in those years were afraid to go into a federal court to try a case, but Minton did not shrink from the challenge. Drawing on extensive knowledge of the law, sound training, and broad experience as a trial lawyer, he felt equally at ease with a case in a federal court as he did in a state court.[7] Meanwhile his interest in politics and politicians, dormant since his abortive try for Congress in 1920, reawakened. Minton had campaigned actively in southern Indiana for the Democratic party in the presidential campaigns of 1920, 1924, and 1928, and had acquired a good reputation on the hustings. As one fellow Hoosier well-acquainted with him remarked, Minton would never say no to a speaking engagement, juggling his other appointments and accepting rugged travel requirements.[8] So he was in some ways a real "natural."

In 1930 Minton again ran for Congress in the Democratic primary in the Third Indiana District, the same district he'd lost in 1920. Again he was defeated, this time by Eugene B. Crowe of Bedford. Although his home county of Floyd gave him a three-to-one margin in the largest primary vote in its history, the rest of the district did not treat Minton so kindly.

Son Sherman, who often accompanied his dad to the chicken dinners and speechifying, recalled the rigors of back roads campaigning in the early thirties: "Nearly every trip we had a flat tire. We didn't have a spare tire, so repair was a major project involving patching the tube, putting it back in the casing, and inflating it with a hand pump. Usually someone from a nearby farmhouse would come out and help."

Minton finally began to find political success, thanks in large part to his membership in the American Legion. This organization produced many political leaders in Indiana and elsewhere in the 1930s and thereafter. It seems to have served as a springboard into an arena closed to young, fresh aspirants. One writer explained that "the older politicians were loath to relinquish their grandstand seats and, consequently, there was no room for the younger war veterans, so they joined the American Legion and eventually went on to political places."[9]

In the records of the American Legion Post 28 at New Albany, the Bonnie Sloan Post (named for the first soldier from Floyd County to be killed in battle in World War I), Minton is not listed as one of the sixteen charter members. He had not yet been discharged from the Army when the charter was granted. The minutes of the organizational meeting of the post held on September 3, 1919, show that Minton, acting as temporary chairman, gave a talk on the purposes of the Legion, and was appointed publicity chairman. He served as post service officer for many years, giving advice and aid to those members in need. He also served one term as post commander, and later at the state level as judge advocate and as chairman of the state legislative committee. Additionally, he attended and held numerous positions at district and state conventions and spoke often on the floor at those windy affairs.[10]

The work at the Indiana Department of the American Legion attracted the attention of Paul V. McNutt and his powerful ally, Pleas E. Greenlee.[11] Both were to play vital roles in Minton's career.

Paul Vories McNutt, whose middle name was given to him by his father in tribute to a family friend, was born on July 19, 1891, in Franklin, Indiana. His father, John C. McNutt, was serving as prosecutor of Johnson and Shelby Counties when Paul was born. But the following year, on the expiration of his term, the father accepted an appointment as librarian of the Indiana Supreme Court Library. The family then moved to Indianapolis.

Although Paul McNutt was not a patrician in the sense that Franklin Delano Roosevelt had been, neither had he been reared in poverty as had

Minton. McNutt graduated from Indiana University in 1913 and from the Harvard Law School in 1916. After Harvard, he went to Martinsville and entered into a law partnership with his father. McNutt ran for prosecuting attorney of Morgan County in 1916 and lost by five votes. It was to be the only election he ever lost.

In the fall of 1917 McNutt became an assistant professor at the Indiana University School of Law. On November 27, 1917, he enlisted in the Army, was sent to Camp Travis, near San Antonio, Texas, and became a captain in the field artillery. At a dance on Christmas Eve in 1917, he met Kathleen Timolat of San Antonio, and they were married on April 20, 1918, in the Episcopal Church at Fort Sam Houston, Texas.[12]

In 1931 Paul McNutt, now dean of the Law School at Indiana University and former State Commander and National Commander of the American Legion, decided to run for governor on the Democratic ticket. A small but vigorous support group laden with members of the American Legion formed the nucleus of the McNutt-for-Governor organization. Frank M. McHale was the head of the committee and Pleas E. Greenlee, who had served two years as state adjutant of the Indiana Department of the American Legion, was secretary. Clarence E. "Pat" Manion, professor of law at the University of Notre Dame, Clarence Jackson, past state commander of the American Legion, and Sherman Minton were leaders in the organization. Minton later became head of the Veterans Committee of Indiana, which declared itself for McNutt for governor.

In 1932 Minton, heading the pro-McNutt activities in southern Indiana, toured the state from Hammond to Vincennes, delivering rousing speeches for the candidate.

Raymond S. Springer from Connersville, judge of the Circuit Court in Fayette County, opposed McNutt. The Republicans never had a chance against "tall, tan and terrific" McNutt who, aided by Roosevelt's landslide victory, overwhelmed his Republican opponent. He outdrew even the President. McNutt's plurality was 192,330 while Roosevelt's plurality in Indiana was only 189,447. The new governor's majority was 157,345.[13]

McNutt took the oath of office as the thirty-fourth governor of Indiana on January 9, 1933. Obviously the new governor was indebted to his friend and ardent supporter, Sherman Minton. The debt was paid off, at least in part, when McNutt appointed Minton to the position of public counsellor of the newly created Public Service Commission of Indiana. Newspapers at the time offered the view that McNutt was trying to build outstanding future leadership for the Democratic party; and Minton, in the public counsellor's spot, could grow by demonstrating his skill as an advocate and as an orator.

In 1933, the state legislature abolished the old regulatory commission that had general jurisdiction over the rates and services of railroads, both steam and electric, and railroad matters affecting public safety. In its stead was created the Public Service Commission, with general jurisdiction over all public utilities. On March 2, 1933, McNutt appointed Democrats Perry McCart from Paoli and Samuel L. Trabue, Rushville, and Republican Moie Cook, Logansport, as members of the new commission.[14]

The legislation responded to a specific need. Since they were monopolies, the public utilities in Indiana had not reduced their rates to correspond with the general decline in prices during the earliest years of the Depression. The act provided for the appointment of a public counsellor to rectify this wrong by representing the consuming public in matters concerning public utilities. But because the position was a new one, its duties and authority were not yet clear. Minton took an unusual approach to the rate problem: instead of attempting to prove that utility rates were too high, he asked the commission to require the public utilities to show cause why their rates should not be reduced. The commission complied.

Thereafter the public counsellor appeared before the PSC on behalf of consumers in cases involving rates, instituted proceedings against public utilities for reductions of their rates, and held numerous conferences with public utility officials for the purpose of securing rate reductions without formal hearings. Minton used this "short method" in obtaining results when he persuaded the Indianapolis Power and Light Company to voluntarily reduce its rates by $525,000.[15]

Minton's program obviously worked; the *Yearbook of the State of Indiana* for the year 1934 reported that, because of rate reductions prompted by the public counsellor, Indiana rate payers saved more than five million dollars.

The salary of the public counsellor and his department for 1934, the *Yearbook* reported, was $11,158.33, a large increase over the $3,559.98 figure for the preceding year. This increase presumably was a result of adding more assistants and a larger staff to the payrolls.

Although his service as public counsellor for the PSC (often acknowledged by McNutt) was excellent proof of Minton's stewardship, it was in a larger sense a display of the ardor of the man for social reform through legislative action. The people, in his view, deserved low rates from public utilities, and it was the job of the public counsellor to persuade business to do its civic duty. His responsibilities in the new administration went beyond the commission and reflected his social conscience. Franklin D. Roosevelt had, of course, come into power in 1932 and was headed in a liberal direction Minton believed he could support. In these stirring times nationally, Minton was given responsibility for writing much of the progressive legislation that characterized the so-called "Little New Deal" of Indiana from 1933 to 1934, such as the public welfare law and the state tax law, which saved the Indiana's public schools from bankruptcy during the rocky thirties.

The Reorganization Act of 1933, a keystone of the Little New Deal, made a more radical change in state government than any since the adoption of Indiana's second constitution in 1853. It reduced one hundred sixty-nine agencies to eight departments and put the governor beside the administrative officer as the head of each. All of these actions had the direct result of saving Indiana from bankruptcy. From a large deficit in 1933, when McNutt left office four years later the state had a surplus of more than ten million dollars.

Thus the Democrats believed that they could unseat the incumbent Republican Senator Arthur R. Robinson in the 1934 election. To meet this goal, R. Earl Peters of Fort Wayne, who had been chairman of the Democratic party in Indiana since 1926, resigned his post and on November 14, 1933, announced his candidacy for the Democratic nomination for the United States Senate.

McNutt would have none of it.

Peters' announcement ignited an angry contest with the governor's forces. These forces, whose leader was Pleas E. Greenlee, the governor's patronage secretary, refused to back the former chairman because Peters was not a trusted member of the McNutt group, and because the two had feuded over control of the two percent contributions to the Hoosier Democratic Club, which McNutt had won. They looked for another candidate to oppose Peters for the nomination and found him in Minton.

Minton and Greenlee were forming bonds which would last three decades. Greenlee was indeed Minton's type of man: self-made, pragmatic, party-loyal. Greenlee was a native of Shelbyville, and had been in newspaper work for many years. He had not completed grade school. He served in World War I with the Rainbow Division (the Forty-Second division of the United States National Army, so called because it was composed of National Guard units from various parts of the United States) and while overseas he was elected clerk of Shelby County. He took his oath of office while still in France, and his wife had to fulfill his duties as clerk until he returned home. After the war, he was state adjutant of the Indiana American Legion for two years. When McNutt became governor on January 9, 1933, Greenlee was appointed executive and patronage secretary to the governor. Most observers shared the opinion that Greenlee was the primary architect of Minton's victory over Peters in the 1934 Senate race.

Minton officially announced his candidacy for the Democratic nomination for Senate on February 22, 1934. He affirmed that he would continue his "fight through state and federal channels for relief and justice to public utility patrons of Indiana. The records of a faithful beginning have been written at home and by the national administration heralding the new deal in utility regulation."[16] Although Governor McNutt refused to officially commit to Minton, it was common knowledge that Minton had the active support of Greenlee and thus bore the stamp of the Indiana Statehouse.

On March 3 Minton wrote to Henry Miller, a classmate at Indiana University:

> Well, my hat is in the ring. Really it looks good. I have some of the strongest men of the State of Indiana in back of me. Earl Peters, former State Chairman, is also a candidate, and is spending a lot of time and money in organizing his forces, but McNutt, [Senator] Van Nuys and the Organization boys are against him.[17]

The Democratic state convention, at which the candidate for senator and other candidates were to be selected, was held on June 12 at the Cadle Tabernacle in Indianapolis. Although encouraged to seek the nomination by the politicians in the Hoosier capital, Minton was apprehensive about his chances. The night before the convention he had been unable to sleep, according to his roommates at the Athletic Club. Harry McClain of

Shelbyville recalled that as a diversion Minton had composed an ode to a mouse that had invaded their quarters. In the morning, according to McClain, "Shay went to the window, looked out over University Park at the sun coming up, and said, 'It's going to be a helluva good day for somebody, but not for me.' "[18]

He had reason to be apprehensive. Strenuous efforts had been made the night before by the forces of the convention to persuade McNutt to accept a compromise on the senatorial nomination. Senator Van Nuys and E. Kirk McKinney, chairman of the Marion County delegation with 269 delegates and Indiana manager of the Home Owners Loan Corporation, were closeted with McNutt in the Claypool Hotel from the night before until 4:00 A.M. the day of the convention. Van Nuys and McKinney were backing Reginald H. Sullivan, the mayor of Indianapolis, as a desirable compromise candidate capable of erasing factionalism. But the governor held his ground and insisted on Minton.[19]

The convention opened at 10:00 A.M., and Minton was promptly placed in nomination by his law partner Evan B. Stotsenburg, who, as past attorney general of Indiana, was influential with the older members of the party. Judge Clarence McNabb, Fort Wayne, placed the name of Peters before the convention. The names of six other hopefuls also were placed in nomination in the belief that there would be a deadlock between the forces of Peters and the forces of Greenlee and McNutt. If so, perhaps one of these hopefuls would receive the nomination as a compromise candidate.[20] Peters led Minton on the first ballot—620.5 to 598. On the next ballot Minton topped Peters—682.5 to 639.5—but each had made only a small gain. As supporters for the dark horses threw their votes to one camp or another, by the third ballot Minton had 827 votes to 586 for Peters. Peters' strength had begun to slip and Greenlee, the Minton floor manager, had pushed the vote for Minton higher on each successive ballot.[21]

Tension mounted on the fourth ballot, as Minton inched closer to the 1,076 votes necessary for victory. The forces of Minton now made their grand push, realizing that if their candidate failed to obtain the necessary majority on the fourth ballot, in all probability he would be stopped.

The delegates at the convention voted by county in alphabetical order. Many of the counties on the fourth ballot shifted a vote or two to Minton, thereby increasing his vote to more than 950. Then the faction in South

Bend, St. Joseph County, which had been bitterly opposed to McNutt in 1932, made a grand gesture for political unity. After giving its votes to Manion the first three ballots, it cast its entire ninety-six votes for Minton.[22]

After the organist in the Cadle Tabernacle had been stopped from belting out his lively "we're about to have a winner" march and order had been restored, Tippecanoe County, which had been casting most of its votes for Peters, gave most of its votes to Minton. The victory was his. Peters moved for the nomination of Minton by acclamation, seconded by all of the other candidates except one.[23]

Minton would oppose Senator Robinson in the fall. "From this day forward it is open season on Arthur Robinson and his birds of a feather," Minton proclaimed when he appeared on the platform to vociferous applause. He complimented his opponents for their "magnanimous spirit" and thanked his supporters. "Today you have nominated the next United States Senator," he declared to enthusiastic applause and huzzas.[24]

The press began to notice, and on June 14 *The Indianapolis Star* described Minton as "a big, distinguished looking man with a flair for snappy clothes."

A civic celebration was held in New Albany on June 19 to welcome Minton home from the state convention. Mayor Charles B. McLinn, a Republican leader and former high school principal, was the speaker:

Now, for the first time in our history, we in New Albany have a candidate for the high office of United States Senator. Seldom has our state been offered men of youth and of modest means for this high office. Sherman Minton is young, but he is wise beyond his years. As a boy he had qualities of leadership that matured and have been tempered with the years. . . . These hills do something to a man that makes him plant his feet firmly on the earth, stiffen his backbone, and turn his face to the stars.[25]

Shortly after his nomination for the Senate seat held by the anti-New Deal Robinson, Minton was invited to the White House. He took the train to Washington to meet President Roosevelt for the first time on June 30, 1934. The President welcomed the man he hoped would come to Washington to help back his policies.

On August 1 Minton resigned his post as public counsellor for the Public Service Commission to begin his Senate campaign.

Another meeting that brought joy and pride to Minton occurred on August 22 when John Minton, whom Shay had not seen for twelve years, made the long trek from Fort Worth, Texas, to Corydon, Indiana, to see his son. The occasion was a political discussion at the Harrison County Fairgrounds, a joint program featuring Shay and Arthur Robinson, his Republican opponent. "I traveled more than a thousand miles just to hear my boy speak," the elder Minton said, "and I plan to stay with him for the next ten days and accompany him around the state."[26]

The Democratic campaign opened officially on September 11. Burly, boot-jawed Minton rode into the Senate in the somber days of 1934 with a straight New Deal platform and a vote-getting battle cry: "You can't offer a hungry man the Constitution."[27]

Other slogans by Minton likewise aimed at the Republican hue and cry over the New Deal's usurpation of the Constitutional powers: "You can't walk up to a hungry man today and say, 'Here, have a Constitution,' " and "You can't hand to the farmer who has been ground into the soil a Constitution and tell him to dig himself out." He was later to regret the statements.

For their part, the Republicans soundly denounced McNutt, his political machine, his two percent club (each state employee was required to contribute two percent of his or her salary to the Hoosier Democratic Club for use as a war chest), and the reorganization act.[28] Minton managed to keep himself out of the worst of the political fire which fell on McNutt.

Despite some dissatisfaction over the governor's policies, the Democrats won a sweeping victory throughout the state in the general election which was held on November 6, 1934. Minton defeated Robinson by 58,698 votes. It was generally conceded that Minton had won largely through the personal popularity of McNutt. Certainly the newspaper publicity over his work as public counsellor of the Public Service Commission did not hurt him.

On November 7 the newly elected senator proclaimed in victory, "The New Deal lives and I am proud to be a part of it."[29]

On January 14, 1935, the new Senator Minton wrote to his friend, author-turned-diplomat Meredith Nicholson, who then was with the United States Legation in Asuncion, Paraguay:

My election in Indiana was not only a vindication for the New Deal, but for McNutt, who was the issue in the latter half of the campaign. The

*retirement of Senator Robinson was about the most pleasing thing that
happened in the judgment of people here in Washington, and I shall enjoy,
by reason of his unpopularity, a certain probationary welcome here."*[30]

On January 3, 1935, Minton dressed in long tails, winged collar, and
spats (probably for the first time in his life). He was about to take the oath
of office as senator. Indiana's other Democratic senator, Frederick Van Nuys,
escorted the new legislator to the rostrum and presented his credentials to
the Senate. Then John Nance Garner, Vice President of the United States,
administered the oath of office. The murmuring in the crowd was that Minton
was "as handsome as a movie star." Pleas E. Greenlee headed the Indiana
delegation which was seated in the Senate gallery to witness the ceremony.[31]

Thus Minton became the thirty-fourth United States senator from Indiana. Not since 1916 had Indiana been represented by two Democratic senators. Moreover, Minton was the first senator from southern Indiana to be
elected since 1905, when James A. Hemenway, a Republican from Boonville,
served for four years. Thirteen freshman senators, all Democrats, took their
oaths of office on January 3, increasing the Democratic margin in the Senate to forty-four. These freshmen, soon to make their mark on the legislative history of the nation, were Minton; Harry S. Truman from Missouri;
Lewis B. Schwellenbach from Washington; Carl A. Hatch from New Mexico;
Rush D. Holt from West Virginia; Francis T. Maloney from Connecticut;
George L. Radcliffe from Maryland; Theodore G. Bilbo from Mississippi;
Edward R. Burke from Nebraska; A. Harry Moore from New Jersey; A. Vic-
tor Donahey from Ohio; Joseph F. Guffy from Pennsylvania; and Peter G.
Gerry from Rhode Island.

So many new Democratic senators came to the Senate in 1935 that an
additional bench had to be installed in the back row on the Democratic side
of the aisle to seat the thirteen. These new senators became the
"back-seaters." Their most distinguished member, Harry Truman, reported,
"The thirteen of us were always close together, and we came to be known as
the 'Young Turks.' "[32]

Truman and Minton were "seatmates" on adjoining back row seats. With
Truman on his immediate left, Minton also turned to others nearby, discussing
the New Deal political agenda with Les Biffle, secretary of the Democratic
majority under Joseph T. Robinson of Arkansas. Often Minton and Truman

would be joined by Hatch and Schwellenbach in their discussions with Biffle.[33]

It was a time for adjustment at the personal level. Mrs. Minton and the two younger Minton children moved to Washington, D.C., renting a house for the family at 4917 Garfield Street, NW. The Mintons enrolled twelve-year-old Mary-Anne at the Immaculate Seminary, and John, age seven, attended St. Ann's school. However, son Sherman, sixteen years old, was a senior at New Albany High School and was determined to finish school there. He stayed with the LaFaivre sisters, Mrs. Minton's three spinster aunts.

According to her children, Mrs. Minton never adjusted very well to her husband's political career in Washington and never felt at home in the nation's capital. She spent winters there but returned to New Albany for the summers, and also returned to her native county at Easter for the spring flowers, and at other times when she could manage it.

The Minton home was a few blocks from Cathedral Avenue and a couple of blocks from the residence of a new friend and neighbor, F. Ryan Duffy from Wisconsin. Duffy would walk to the Minton home and then the two of them would walk to Cathedral Avenue where they would meet Alben W. Barkley from Kentucky. The three senators then would stroll toward the Capitol through Rock Creek Park while discussing the business of the day.[34]

Minton's staff was small—five assistants. James C. Penman became political secretary in charge of patronage as well as campaign and other political matters, while John F. Sembower answered the routine correspondence, and there was plenty of it. Minton was plagued in the early days of 1935 by letters from people who wanted to test the mettle of the new senator. He received an average of eight hundred letters of the total of seventy-five thousand that went to the Senate each day. Each letter, regardless of content, was answered at Minton's insistence as long as the name and address of the sender were legible. This task placed a heavy load on the secretaries. In addition to handling the personal correspondence, Sembower prepared the form letters which were needed for this heavy volume of mail and wrote the press releases. He also helped Minton with his speeches, did research, and drafted proposed legislation.[35]

Committee assignments of course were of primary importance to freshman congressmen. Minton was appointed to committees on Interstate Commerce, Military Affairs, Privileges and Elections, and Pensions.[36]

The legislative programs of the New Deal to which Minton had so ardently committed had begun to lose some of their popularity in Congress and the country by early 1935. In the Washington offices of the Liberty League and other conservative strongholds, particularly, it was being said that the New Deal had delivered nothing but a bunch of expensive, empty promises that jeopardized American freedom. Senator Minton, elected as an ardent advocate and staunch defender of the New Deal, determined to do something about such heresy. On March 18, 1935, he introduced into the *Congressional Record* a series of sixteen editorials and news items from fourteen different newspapers, all of which reported material progress toward economic recovery, suggesting that this movement out of the Great Depression stemmed largely, if not solely, from the policies and leadership of President Roosevelt and the New Deal.[37] Minton was the first Young Turk to go to the floor of the Senate to announce his support of the President. These editorials and news items were his first entries in the *Congressional Record* aside from routine appointments.

Minton may have consciously planned this seemingly spontaneous defense of the President. Many of the old friends and dependable allies of Roosevelt on Capitol Hill now were pusillanimous in their support of the President; and even when they gave it, by 1935 such support was often qualified or conditional. It was time for Roosevelt to seek new faces and other voices to represent him, and Minton seems to have been positioning himself to fill that important need. When Minton rallied to his support, FDR sensed that in this freshman senator from Indiana he had a dedicated admirer. A review of his first votes shows Minton to be "regular" on almost all major positions of the White House. In 1935 he strongly backed passage of the National Labor Relations Act. He vigorously supported passage of the Guffey Coal Conservation Act of 1935 even though he doubted its constitutionality. Later events proved him right because a divided Supreme Court struck it down the next year. Only two times in six years did Minton fail to vote with the administration—once when he supported proposals to lower the interest rates for farmers, and the other time when he voted in favor of a bonus for veterans of World War I.

In January of 1935 Minton received a call from the White House to ask if he would make a speech at the Waldorf-Astoria to the Duchess County Association of New York. This was one of Roosevelt's pet groups, and consisted almost entirely of wealthy men who had given generously to Roosevelt's campaign fund.[38]

Shay, of course, was flattered by the call. Rising to the occasion, Minton praised the group for their support of the commendable goals of the administration and praised Roosevelt as a leader. Who can doubt that Roosevelt received favorable reports on the speech from his friends in the association?[39] Events during this early period show Minton's first steps to becoming a recognized face in the Senate; he was soon asked by Vice President Garner to preside over the Senate for a brief period.

Tradition dictated that a freshman senator wait until he had been in the Senate one year or one session before he gave his first speech. Minton observed this tradition. His "maiden" speech would not be delivered until January 16, 1936.

However, two issues in which Minton was involved during that first year in the Senate attracted national attention. Delving into these issues provided him with much knowledge of the inner workings of the Senate and gave him added stature in the eyes of his colleagues.

The first one involved Huey Pierce Long, the dictatorial Democratic senator from Louisiana. The series of events began when Roosevelt requested permission from Congress to read a special message before a joint session, a message which also would be broadcast nationally by radio. Roosevelt wanted to explain the reasons behind his veto of the Patman bonus bill, which provided for payment of nearly two billion dollars to veterans of World War I in 1936 rather than in 1945. Administration leaders introduced resolutions in both houses on May 21, 1935, to hold the joint session on the following day, and Minton supported the one in the Senate. Minton's enthusiasm in support of this resolution was not shared by many senators, who grumbled over Roosevelt's unmitigated gall in asking that Congress be used as a rostrum for a political speech. But these objections did not extend to denying the President the right to speak to Congress, even when his chosen subject was a political matter. No senator wished to defy tradition.

No senator, that is, except Huey Long, who leapt into action. "The Kingfish" did not care if he offended Roosevelt as long as he could attack him. He obtained the floor of the Senate and tried to prevent consideration of the resolution by a filibuster until the session for the day was ended—precluding consideration and adoption of the resolution. Long spoke for hours on subjects as diverse as the Bill of Rights and organized baseball. He delighted the galleries with frequent jibes at his favorite target, Senator McKellar of Tennessee, who rose finally to assert that the senator from Louisiana had so little influence in the Senate that he could not get the Lord's Prayer adopted if he tried. But Long reserved much of his energy for a diatribe against Roosevelt: "He is coming here to celebrate. He is coming here to be known. He is coming here to be embellished. He is coming here to be fawned over." Finally, after sixteen hours on the floor of the Senate and far into the night, Long thought that his goal was in sight and believed that it was safe to go to the rest room to relieve himself without losing the floor. He suggested the absence of a quorum and headed for the men's room. Minton was on his feet as soon as Long closed the door behind him. Shay asked the chair for permission to make a point of order: Senator Long had surrendered the floor, he asserted. Vice President Garner sustained the point. When Long returned from his brief recess, the chair denied him the floor. Approval of the resolution to hear the President was passed on motion by a vote of forty-four to four. Tired but happy senators who supported the administration rushed to congratulate and thank Minton.[40]

With this filibuster, Long was only adding to a lengthy list of tawdry political efforts in the years 1934 and 1935. In 1935 he was a national figure; after President Roosevelt, he was probably the most widely discussed politician in the United States. Although he had supported Roosevelt in 1932, he was now angry with the New Deal and led the anti-New Deal sentiment in the Senate. "His income tax returns were being questioned, Farley was withholding federal patronage from him, and WPA projects in Louisiana had been suspended because of irregularities in local administration. The Kingfish's chief grievance, however, was that he wasn't President, and he felt he ought to be," according to historian William Manchester.[41] Long's book, My First Days in the White House, rumored to have been ghostwritten by a Hearst reporter, scornfully mused that he would appoint Roosevelt Secretary of the Navy when Long became President.[42]

As a self-appointed watchdog for Roosevelt, Minton continued to harass Huey Long on the Senate floor. On June 12, 1935, when Long was droning endlessly in another one of his filibusters with only a few senators on the floor, Minton interrupted. As the Congressional Record has it:

MINTON: *Mr. President . . .*

PRESIDING OFFICER: *Does the Senator from Louisiana yield to the Senator from Indiana?*

LONG: *I yield for a question.*

MINTON: *With great deference to the Senator, may I suggest that he not talk so loudly? A number of people around here are asleep.*

LONG: [He was never at a loss for words] *I am sorry I awakened the Senator from Indiana. [Laughter]. We would have been better off if he had not waked up. The best thing the Senator from Indiana can do is to go back into the cloakroom and go right back to sleep* [Laughter].[43]

On August 24 Long was again filibustering and had threatened to join the Republican party. Minton interrupted:

MINTON: *Mr. President . . .*

PRESIDENT PRO TEMPORE: *Does the Senator from Louisiana yield to the Senator from Indiana?*

LONG: *I yield for a question.*

MINTON: *The question takes this form:*

> *Oh, Huey! Oh Huey! come home to us now!*
> *The clock in the steeple's half past.*
> *You wander across that little green aisle,*
> *Pray, tell us how long will it last?*
> [Laughter.]

LONG: *I do not yield for that purpose.*

PRESIDENT PRO TEMPORE: *The Senator refuses to yield.*[44]

Two days later, on August 26, Long still was filibustering. Once more, Minton heckled him about whether he would be re-elected as a senator from Louisiana. Finally, Senator Long retorted, "There is not enough power under the canopy of heaven to beat me in an election to come back to this body, but men like the Senator from Indiana will be back over in Indiana with an RFD address when I am still here. I shall be here many years."[45]

Minton's badgering of Huey Long on the Senate floor did not go unnoticed at the White House. Long was a consummate politician and he probably was one of the few, if any, political enemies who frightened Roosevelt. Even before the publication of his book, *My First Days in the White House*, it was clear that Long was not satisfied with his ownership of Louisiana. He was prepared to move beyond the bayous. Asked if there would be a Long-for-President movement in 1936, his short answer was "Sure to be. And I think we will sweep the country."[46] A secret poll conducted by the Democratic National Committee in 1935 showed that Long might take four million votes away from Roosevelt if the Louisiana politician ran on a third-party ticket, carry eight or nine states, and throw the election in 1936 to the Republicans or into the House of Representatives. Roosevelt was not about to allow Long to do to him what Theodore Roosevelt had done to William Howard Taft in 1912.

But there would soon be no need for the White House to mount a spirited political opposition to Long.

On September 8, 1935, a young physician named Carl Austin Weiss hid behind a marble pillar in the rotunda of the statehouse in Baton Rouge, Louisiana, gun in hand, waiting for Long to emerge from the chamber where he was giving orders to the legislature. When the Kingfish walked across the capitol rotunda at 9:20 P.M., Weiss stepped from behind the pillar and shot him in the stomach. The assassin paid the price instantly. Long's bodyguards riddled Weiss' body with sixty-one bullets. But the Kingfish was fatally wounded. He died on Tuesday, September 10. Huey Pierce Long, Jr., age forty-two, had been assassinated by the son-in-law of District Judge B. H. Pavy. Under the Kingfish's direction, Pavy's judicial district had just been gerrymandered by the Louisiana legislature so as to make his re-election almost impossible. And Judge Pavy had been enraged after Long reportedly threatened to "tarbrush" two of his in-laws by suggesting that they had black ancestors in their family tree.[47] When Minton, while visiting at Indiana University, heard the news of the death of Senator Long, he said:

> *Huey Long had one of the most brilliant minds of any man I have known. He had boundless energy and a world of courage but he didn't have the ability to play ball. Long had to be head man. If he had had the ability to work with others, he would have been one of the great leaders of the nation.*[48]

Roosevelt was aware that the senator from Indiana had come to his defense, speaking out against Long when other leaders in the administration—both in and out of the Senate—remained silent. He was in Minton's debt.

Jim Farley, that astute politician and fortune teller of votes, told Harold Ickes in September of 1935 that if Huey Long had lived, he would have polled more that six million votes in the presidential election of 1936.[49]

The other issue which enhanced Minton's reputation and helped to make him a national figure in 1935 was the Holding Company Act, or the Wheeler-Rayburn bill. This legislation contained what is sometimes called the "death sentence" clause, providing that any holding company not able to prove its usefulness to its community within five years would be dissolved. The fight over the passage of this act provided a good example of how far big business would go to fight Roosevelt.

With his Public Service Commission experience in Indiana influencing him against the powerful "fat cats," Minton supported the bill as enthusiastically as he had supported other New Deal measures. The twelve-billion-dollar public utility industry opposed the act bitterly as did almost the entire press. Senator Minton took a major part in explaining, clarifying and arguing for the bill, which passed the Senate by a margin of one vote in June of 1935.[50]

After the bill was passed by the Senate, Congress was inundated by two hundred and fifty thousand telegrams and five million letters demanding rejection of the holding company death sentence. The House of Representatives, responsive to the deluge, eliminated the death sentence provision.[51] There was an uproar of opposition when the bill went to the House-Senate conference committee. The press screamed about widows and orphans "deprived of their all" because most trusts for widows and orphans held stock in holding companies.

Administration observers noticed a certain uniformity about the messages and press comments, and Senate leaders decided to investigate. A committee under the chairmanship of Senator Hugo Lafayette Black from Alabama was formed to do the task. Minton and Schwellenbach were named Democratic members on the committee of five senators. Senator Lynn J. Frazier, Republican of North Dakota, and Senator Ernest W. Gibson, Republican of Vermont, were the other members. The Black committee found a national pattern of large sums of money used by the public utilities for lobbying purposes but charged to operating expenses and passed on to consumers. Of the thousands of messages received by Congress from four of the more populous states, only three had been paid for by the senders. The rest had been paid for by public utilities.[52] Harry S. Truman from Missouri alone received thirty thousand of these fake messages from voters. He burned all of them and remained loyal to Roosevelt. For Minton the death sentence lobbying was a giant step forward in his career; it provided him an opportunity to work with Senator Black—a powerful senator—and gave him significant notice by the media. The Wheeler-Rayburn bill passed on the last day of the session. The final version included the "death sentence" clause to eliminate utility holding companies except those essential to the operation of an integrated public system. Black had high praise for Minton as a member of the committee. "He has a quick, alert mind which made him a very valuable member of the committee, both as to research and the examination of witnesses," Black said. "He showed himself to be a fluent speaker."[53]

In the 1935 session, Congress also passed the Emergency Relief Appropriation Act, a soil conservation act, the National Labor Relations Act, the Social Security Act, the Banking Act, the Public Utility Holding Company Act, the Farm Mortgage Moratorium Act, and the Guffey Coal Conservation Act.

In what must have been a welcome change from the political battles in Washington, Senator and Mrs. Minton journeyed to Manila in October 1935, to attend the inauguration of its first president, Manuel Luis Quezon y Molina. As guests of the new commonwealth government in the Philippine Islands, they were treated with ceremonial courtesy.

With the new year under way, Minton knew it was time for him to come before the Senate with his maiden speech. Events gave him a strong topic. The Supreme Court on January 6, 1936, declared the controversial Agricultural Adjustment Act unconstitutional. Minton decided to take the Supreme Court to task.

The revolutionary act had been passed in May of the preceding year. It empowered the Secretary of Agriculture to provide for reduction in the acreage or in the production for market of wheat, cotton, field corn, hogs, rice, tobacco, milk (and its products), and other commodities. Rental or benefit payments were to be paid to individual farmers from money obtained by a processing tax collected from the first processor of the commodity.

On July 14, 1933, the Secretary of Agriculture, with the approval of the President, had announced that rental and benefit payments should be made for cotton, and the case grew out of the taxing of Hoosac Mills Corporation, the first processor involved.

When taxes were demanded of Hoosac Mills for cotton it had purchased from growers, the company fought the claim. The case made it all the way to the Supreme Court, which ruled in favor of Hoosac Mills, calling the Agricultural Adjustment Act unconstitutional. Mr. Justice Roberts, writing for the six-to-three majority, held that agriculture was not a national activity, but instead was a state or local activity, that the act invaded the reserved rights of the states under the Constitution, and that the act was a statutory plan to regulate and control agricultural production—a matter beyond the powers delegated to the federal government by the Constitution.[54]

The Supreme Court's stand, then, was Minton's immediate target as he planned the maiden speech. But he, and the administration, had additional reason to be outraged at the court.

Earlier, on May 27, 1935, the Supreme Court had, in a unanimous opinion by Chief Justice Hughes, held the National Recovery Administration unconstitutional. It was not so much the rejection of the NRA which shocked proponents as it was the extraordinary vehemence of Hughes' opinion. The chief justice came close to calling Roosevelt an outlaw, and he warned both the President and Congress not to base broad federal statutes on their constitutional right to regulate interstate commerce.[55]

Senator Minton, along with others in the administration, feared the Court's decision regarding the Agricultural Adjustment Act and its implications. The Court held that Congress could not use its delegated powers to accomplish legislative ends which fall within the reserved powers of the states. Under that premise, the entire New Deal, including Social Security and the Wagner Act, might be in deep trouble. The Agricultural Adjustment Act was the very heart of Roosevelt's farm recovery program. When it was declared unconstitutional, other vital New Deal legislation could be doomed also.

Senator Minton carefully prepared to address the Senate and read the speech from a manuscript, the only time in the Senate that he spoke from a script. The wording was all his. One of his staff, John F. Sembower, reported that "Minton prepared all his own speeches . . . did all his own phrase-making;

I contributed factual data now and then."[56]

Minton made the speech on January 16, 1936, and began with statements that confirmed his nervousness about his maiden speech as well as his sincerity about the subject:

> Mr. President, it is with great deference that I rise to address this distinguished body at this time. I propose to discuss very briefly the recent decision of the Supreme Court in which it held the Agricultural Adjustment Act unconstitutional. Lawyers of far greater distinction than I, and statesmen of proven wisdom and ability who honor this body by their presence, are better able to discuss it than I.[57]

After declaring his respect as a lawyer for the Supreme Court, he asked his colleagues in the Senate to remember that in every case before the Court "some good lawyer finds that he is mistaken about what the Constitution provides, and very frequently some members of the Court are mistaken"[58] about what the Constitution provides. "What the Constitution provides rests in the minds and hearts of nine eminent and distinguished gentlemen of the Court who have the last guess."[59]

Minton reminded the Senate "that there is nothing sacrosanct about the opinions of the Court" because "their opinions can be changed." Then he exploded into the meat of the matter:

> I hold no brief for this most important opinion of the majority of the Court. I disagree with the majority emphatically. I think their opinion is the most strained, forced construction of the Constitution, and the most highly flavored political opinion to come from that Court since the Dred Scott decision.
>
> I accept the Court's decision in the same spirit in which Abraham Lincoln accepted the Dred Scott decision, when he said, first, in his debate with Douglas: "Somebody has to reverse that decision, since it is made, and we mean to reverse it, and we mean to do it peaceably." And, second, when he said in his first inaugural address: "At the same time the candid citizens must confess that if the policy of the Government upon vital questions affecting the whole people is to be irrevocably fixed by the decision of the Supreme Court, the instant they are made in ordinary litigation be-

tween parties in personal actions the people will have ceased to be their own rulers, having to that extent practically resigned their Government into the hands of that eminent tribunal."[60]

Minton included in his remarks an array of facts about the farm industry and farm prices which demonstrated the ill health of the economy and the effect of the Great Depression on farm prices, thus confirming the necessity for legislative action:

- Agriculture was the largest single industry in the nation.
- Forty-five percent of the population were directly dependent for their living upon the tillage of the soil or rendering some service to the tillers of the soil.
- Because of the Agricultural Act, prosperity returned to farmers from the ruin of 1933 with prices rising for corn from ten cents a bushel to thirty cents a bushel, for wheat from thirty cents a bushel to ninety cents a bushel, and for hogs from three cents a pound to twelve cents a pound.[61]

Then he moved to deal with the Court's refusal to decide on the validity of Congress' action under the general welfare clause of the constitution:

The tilling of the soil as an industry may be committed by the present form of the Government to the care of the states, but the welfare of the industry as a whole and its prosperity are a national concern. If the industry as a whole is not prosperous, it affects vitally the welfare of the entire Nation.[62]

The solution to the problem proposed by Minton was to amend the act to provide for the payment of the tax into the Treasury. Congress then would appropriate this money from the Treasury for the benefit of agriculture. It was his opinion that the Supreme Court must conclude that such an appropriation involved the general welfare.

In the conclusion of the speech, Minton made some belligerent statements which were to come back later to haunt him. During Minton's hearing before the Judiciary Committee on his nomination to be an associate justice of the Supreme Court in 1949, Senator Donnell of Missouri recalled the strong words Minton made in this speech in 1936:

> *Mr. President, I conclude, in agreement with the distinguished junior Senator from Alabama* [Mr. Bankhead], *that we may tax and then spend for the general welfare, and that saving agriculture would be spending for the general welfare, and therefore within the power granted to the Federal Government under the Constitution.*
>
> *Although the Court has gone out of its way to wreck a system that works, it has not gone so far, in my humble opinion, as to make our condition hopeless. I hope I am not wrong in my judgment of the scope of this important decision. If I am, and the Court has effectively paralyzed the arm of Congress to act to relieve the people who constitute the Government, then the people must act to reclaim their own Government.*
>
> *The blight of the cold, dead hand of the Court must not be permitted to contaminate the blood stream of the Nation and destroy the right of the people to live and prosper.*[63]

The speech had attracted national attention. It also was received with much favor at the White House. According to the *New Albany Tribune* this "speech by Minton admitted him into the 'hot dogs' circle led by Felix Frankfurter, a small cadre of liberal advisors at the White House." Frankfurter, later appointed to the Supreme Court by President Roosevelt, was a distinguished, nationally known law professor at Harvard University. When Roosevelt became President in 1933, Frankfurter, who had advised him during his term as governor of New York, advised him on New Deal legislation and other matters. Frankfurter undoubtedly praised Minton to the President. Events were to show that Minton's provocative attack on the justices of the Supreme Court gave him greater prestige with his colleagues and started his rise to power in the Senate.

Right: As a youth, Sherman "Shay" Minton wasn't quite the serious-minded fellow he seems during this dress-up affair with two unidentified female classmates.

Below: A fun-loving scoundrel on occasion, he got in his fair share of schoolboy scrapes. Many times his cohort was Walt Heazlitt, a boyhood friend who joined Minton at Indiana University. In this high-school-era photo are, *from left:* Minton, Mary Stotsenburg, an unidentified friend, Gertrude Gurtz (who would later become Minton's wife), and Heazlitt.

Left: The years at Indiana University were a busy, rewarding time for Minton. He worked hard at his studies, school activities and at athletics, but found his greatest reward in courting Gertrude.

Below: He lived at the Phi Delta Theta fraternity house along with Walt Heazlitt, who's pictured beside Minton in the background of the photo.

Travels 1,000 Miles to Hear Son's Speech At Corydon

Above left: Minton's father, John Evan Minton, in 1915, while Shay was attending IU, and nearly twenty years later *(right)*, when the elder Minton traveled from his home in Texas to join in his son's Senate campaign appearance at Corydon in 1934.

A collage of postcards the newly married Minton sent home to Gertrude while he served in France between July 1918 and July 1919. When he returned home, he saw his first son, Sherman Anthony, for the first time.

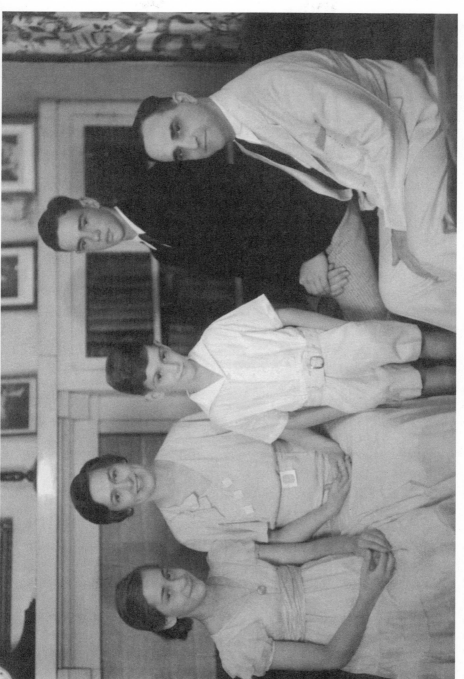

The whole family, about the time of Minton's successful run for the Senate. *From left:* Mary-Anne, Gertrude, John Evan, young Sherman, and Minton.

Senator Sherman Minton and his wife Gertrude share a light moment at a banquet in Washington with Indiana Governor Paul V. McNutt during McNutt's quest for the presidency.

CHAPTER FOUR

SUCCESS IN THE SENATE

—— ◄►═◄► ——

PRESIDENT ROOSEVELT WAS UP FOR RE-ELECTION IN 1936. TO ENSURE HIS success, the White House needed someone to battle the "economic royalists" strongly opposing the President. Foremost in the royalist category was the American Liberty League. This group of forces on the extreme right had been chartered in August 1934, initiated by conservative business leaders and newspaper publishers. Its members included Pierre S. DuPont, New York Governor Al Smith, and John W. Davis, attorney for industrialist J. P. Morgan. The executive director of the Liberty League was Jouett Shouse, former congressman from Kansas and assistant secretary of the Treasury under Woodrow Wilson.

But Democrats soon joined the ranks. John J. Raskob, a wealthy industrialist who had been a loyal Democrat and national chairman of the Democratic party for Al Smith, was one of them. Now Raskob defected from the party and joined the Liberty League, along with other distinguished Democrats such as Newton D. Baker and Dean Acheson, former Democratic presidential candidates Smith (in 1928) and Davis (in 1924), and Democratic governors Joseph B. Ely of Massachusetts, Albert Ritchie of Maryland, and Eugene B. Talmadge of Georgia. The party's public social policy was too radical for the Democratic defectors.

On January 25, 1936, Al Smith, wearing a high silk hat, addressed two thousand men in full dress and women wearing evening gowns and ermine stoles in the Mayflower Hotel in Washington, D.C. The Liberty League was launching its campaign against Roosevelt's re-election. *The New York Times* reported that the members of the Liberty League who attended represented "either through principals or attorneys, a large portion of the capitalistic wealth of the country." Smith, who now was fighting legislation which would prevent child labor, declared that "The New Deal smells of the stench of Communistic Russia." DuPont called Smith's speech "perfect."

Minton wrote on February 3 to James A. Woodburn of Indiana University: "I will never go wandering off after Al Smith or anybody like him." He labeled Smith a "rat" for abandoning the poor people of New York.[1]

Raskob was showing himself one of the more vocal members of the new royalist group, and on January 30 sent thousands of letters to inform citizens of the purposes and good works of the Liberty League. Minton received one of these letters and responded on February 3:

> I, too, come from humble surroundings, and, as one poor boy to another, let me tell you I am still with my gang, while you and your friend, Governor Smith, have run out on yours. I still have the poor man's point of view, while you have lost it now that you have become rich. I not only offer thanks for what I have, but I have some sympathy for those who haven't anything. Al Smith picked the right crowd to talk to about balancing the budget. How would that speech have sounded down under the Brooklyn Bridge, made to the boys and girls from the sidewalks of New York, especially if he had told them the rest of the story, that to have balanced the Budget would have taken from them their last crust of bread? "Balance the Budget!" When, sir, did you or your associates, the DuPonts, raise your voice about an unbalanced Budget in 1917 and 1918, when the Budget was unbalanced to buy your munitions of war to kill American boys? It was all right to have an unbalanced Budget then, but wrong to have one to feed starving Americans.
>
> You speak of socialism and communism. I believe in this administration, and I am no Socialist or Communist. I don't even know one. I hope you will pardon me for saying so, but I think I am as good a citizen as you. I love my country as much as you. I thought enough of it to offer my life in defense of it in May 1917, while you were engaged in unbalancing the Budget. . . .
>
> I resent your intimation that liberty-loving Americans can find no place to rally except under the banner of the American Liberty League.[2]

Minton was baring his fists in defense of the program he deeply believed in; more was to come. He gave a radio address Monday night, February 24. In it he discussed the recent decision of the Supreme Court upholding the constitutionality of the act of Congress which created the Tennessee Valley Authority. Among other things, Minton said:

> In short, the opinion holds that under the war powers and commerce clause of the Constitution Congress may build these great dams in the navigable streams of the country. That the water power thus created may be converted into electricity, instead of permitting it to go to waste, and when the electricity is generated it is the property of the United States. That any surplus energy thus generated may be sold by the Government and in order to enable the Government to market the surplus the Government may acquire the transmission facilities for the purpose of conveying the surplus to the market. . . .
>
> The critics of this administration have been charging the TVA to be socialistic and communistic and subversive of the purposes of our Government. The Liberty League, through its president, on last July 1, over the radio said: "If any experiment could be more radically socialistic or more wholly contrary to the whole basic conceptions of our Government than the TVA, I am at a loss to imagine it. . . ."
>
> So, in conclusion, let me assure you that if you have been reading Liberty League propaganda and have been looking in the closet and under the bed every night expecting to find a Socialist or Communist with a red flag in one hand and a cheese knife in the other to be lurking there, you may now rest your weary head upon your pillow in peace for the Supreme Court assures you that TVA is constitutional and American. You need no longer fear, nor believe in, the communistic and socialistic bugaboo of the Liberty League.[3]

His defense of the administration's policies brought him before the American Bar Association at Washington's Mayflower Hotel, on March 4, 1936, which was honoring Judge William L. Ransom. Minton's speech may have pointed the way toward Roosevelt's eventual court packing plan.

In the speech Minton proposed that Congress "can and should provide that when a litigant challenges an act of Congress on constitutional grounds in the United States Supreme Court, the act of Congress shall determine his right unless he is able to convince at least seven (out of nine) judges of the Supreme Court that the act conflicts with the constitution and therefore is invalid."[4]

At the beginning of his speech, Minton, knowing that the guest of honor and probably most of the lawyers in attendance disagreed with him on these views, acknowledged such disagreement but said he was confident that Judge Ransom would join him in the sentiment of Voltaire, "I may not agree with what you have to say, but I will fight for your right to say it."[5]

Minton concluded this speech:

> *Such regulation by Congress is logical and consistent with the mechanics of checks and balances and the philosophy upon which our form of government is constructed. I therefore deny that ours is a government by the majority, and that the Supreme Court is only carrying out the theory of the rule of the majority. I assert that ours is a government of checks and balances, and it is unwholesome and dangerous to place in the hands of five men, however eminent, able, and patriotic, the exercise of so great power in a sphere so remote from the source of all power—the people themselves.*[6]

The fight had just begun. In Congress, on March 4, 1936—the third anniversary of the New Deal—Senator Lester J. Dickinson, a Republican from Iowa, castigated the record of Roosevelt. "In the entire annals of our history, no period can be found which offers such a strange compound of muddled thinking, contradictory purposes, and callous political exploitation of a nation's distress."[7]

Such sentiments could not be allowed to stand. Minton immediately joined Majority Leader Senator Joseph T. Robinson in an attack on Dickinson.

Using facts supplied by Minton from a February 14 speech in Indiana, Robinson declared that "the country on the whole is prosperous. Cotton prices declined 61 percent under Hoover but had increased 92 percent under Roosevelt. Industrial production declined under Hoover but had increased under Roosevelt." Finally Dickinson relented. He fired a parting salvo, however, insisting these improvements had been purchased at the expense of taxpayers. Not so, retorted Minton. The money had been borrowed "from the very people who have profited by it."[8]

Obviously not all of Minton's time was consumed in defending Roosevelt.

The junior senator from Indiana also took an active role in opposing the trial of Halsted L. Ritter, judge of the United States District Court for the Southern District of Florida in April of 1936. Ritter had been impeached by the House of Representatives because of alleged financial misconduct on the bench. Thereafter he was removed from office by the Senate. Well aware of the vagaries of Florida politics, Minton believed that most of the seven articles of impeachment were invalid. He voted "not guilty" on the first six counts and "guilty" on the seventh. The rest of the Senate did not agree. The Senate's vote for Ritter's removal was fifty-six to twenty-eight.[9]

On May 19 and 20, Minton, as a member of the Senate Board of Visitors, inspected the United States Military Academy at West Point, New York, and met with the cadets from Indiana. Upon his return to Washington on May 20 he was informed he needed to hurry to the White House for a meeting. Roosevelt and Felix Frankfurter had called the meeting to elicit platform ideas from the "Hot Dog" Club senators. Other senators at the meeting which lasted from 3:30 P.M. to midnight, were Burton K. Wheeler (Montana), Lewis B. Schwellenbach (Washington), George W. Norris (Nebraska), Robert F. Wagner (New York), and Henrik Shipstead (Minnesota).

An important question hovered like a dark shadow over the meeting: Would the platform be important? Or would the New Deal's highly controversial strategies be the only issue in the upcoming contest? No one was certain. Uncertainty reigned in Minton's home state, too, as political opinions predicted that 1936 would be a volatile year in Indiana for both parties. Minton was keeping a watchful eye on political activities back home. He knew from history and his own experience that voters in Indiana could be unkind to Democrats, perhaps now more than ever.

McNutt had been the first Democrat to win the statehouse since Samuel M. Ralston (1912–16). Republicans had kept the governorship as their private prize since 1916, guiding the state with governors James P. Goodrich (1916), Warren T. McCray (1920), Ed Jackson (1924), and Harry G. Leslie (1928).

Although many conservative Republicans had voted for Roosevelt and McNutt in 1932 because of unemployment, bread lines, and general poverty caused by the Great Depression, Minton knew that these conservative voters were fickle. It was true that some of the programs of the New Deal—such as Social Security, insured bank deposits, loans to homeowners, payments to farmers, and rural electrification—were acceptable with these voters. But they questioned the wisdom or necessity of others, such as relief for the unemployed, pro-labor legislation, and tighter regulation of private enterprise.[10] Because McNutt was prohibited by the Indiana constitution from succeeding himself as governor, Indiana Republicans in 1936 were hopeful that they could regain the statehouse with the promise of a more conservative administration. Minton was determined that would not happen.

Minton, with his typical passionate and indomitable loyalty, supported his good friend Pleas E. Greenlee as the Democratic candidate for governor from the start. On February 14, he made a speech in Shelbyville, Greenlee's hometown. Minton made a general plea for support of successful Democrat programs, extolling the virtues of the Roosevelt and McNutt administrations and telling his audience that the administration in Washington considered the programs of McNutt as a model for economic recovery. Minton compared these programs and the record of McNutt with the "Old Deal" record of the Depression, using numerous statistics. He laid the New Deal on the line in exactly the way he wished it interpreted. "It is a fight on the one hand, between entrenched greed and special privileges, the forces of the Reactionary and Standpatter, and on the other, the Liberal and progressive forces of the country," he insisted.[11]

While Minton was championing Greenlee's candidacy, McNutt vacillated in his choice of a successor. He seemed indifferent to Greenlee. If he were honest with himself, Minton had to admit there were problems with the Shelbyville native's candidacy. Greenlee's lack of formal education would hurt him; his friend had not completed grade school. Still, Minton thought that Greenlee's uncommon amount of common sense would compensate for his educational deficiencies.

Greenlee's public image clearly needed improving, and Minton was willing to devote himself to that cause. As a member of the Military Affairs Committee of the Senate, on August 5, 1935, he introduced Senate Bill 3359 to authorize the presentation of Distinguished Service Crosses to Greenlee and George L. Robins for bravery during World War I. Greenlee and Robins apparently had carried wounded soldiers to a field hospital while under heavy shell fire on the Lorraine front on the night of March 9, 1918. It may have been too obvious a ploy; the committee failed to act.

Greenlee's competition soon emerged. E. Kirk McKinney, representing the conservative Democrat "old guard," had the endorsement of Senator Van Nuys. M. Clifford Townsend, lieutenant governor under McNutt, finally drew the backing of the McNutt machine.

Van Nuys, in an effort to slow the Townsend-McNutt effort, released a report submitted by Harry L. Hopkins of the Works Progress Administration. Hopkins' report alleged that the McNutt machine was bribing delegates to the Democratic State Convention to support Townsend for governor in exchange for jobs in relief work.

Before the convention, one forecast of delegate strength showed Greenlee with 687, Townsend with 684, and McKinney with 474. Then McNutt unleashed his machine. On June 16, 1936, when the first ballot was counted at the Democratic State Convention, the McNutt forces handily gave the nomination to Townsend.

Minton pragmatically switched horses at this point. He had seen the handwriting on the wall as the convention approached. Now, although he nominated Greenlee in a brief speech, it was apparent he was facing the realities of the situation and looking for a candidate who could win. He was, finally, not only resigned to Townsend's nomination but pleased at a pragmatic level when it was made unanimous. Party harmony was essential if his leader, Roosevelt, was to carry Indiana in the fall. The state convention elected Minton and Van Nuys as Indiana delegates to the Democratic National Convention in Philadelphia to be held later that year. Minton was now in a strong position to support the renomination of Roosevelt and the election of the national and state tickets of the Democratic party in November 1936.

More and more in that year Roosevelt considered Minton his faithful lieutenant for the New Deal in the Senate and made it a point to include the senator from Indiana in his circle of political associates. On June 14, Minton attended the dedication of the George Rogers Clark Memorial in Vincennes, Indiana, a project which had gone through many dreary phases and which finally culminated in a ceremony—attended by Roosevelt— to honor the Revolutionary War hero. Minton met again with FDR at the White House on September 4 and November 10.

During the summer and fall of 1936 Minton campaigned in Indiana for Democrats on the national and state tickets. He spoke to enthusiastic crowds in French Lick, Terre Haute, Noblesville, Angola, Frankfort, and Columbus. On November 2, the day before the election, the Democratic faithful paraded through New Albany and crowded into the Kerrigan Theatre, where they listened to Minton lambast the "scare" tactics of the Republicans. The message was that the New Deal would work—was already working. Minton recalled Hoover's unfulfilled prediction that "grass would grow in the streets if Roosevelt was elected," and with pride declared that "prosperity is not just around the corner but it is on a straight path." He was confident that the Democrats would win the next day.

Despite the strong history of conservatism in Indiana, Roosevelt carried the state by 250,000 votes. Not only did the President win in Indiana, he won almost every other state and buried Kansas Governor Alfred M. Landon 523 electoral votes to 8. Landon had won only Maine and Vermont. Townsend was elected governor of Indiana by 181,000 votes, and in Indiana eleven of the twelve candidates on the Democratic ticket for the House of Representatives won easily. Hoosiers—like most Americans—had accepted Roosevelt's new course for the ship of state.

When Minton called on Roosevelt on November 10 to congratulate him on his stunning victory, the meeting evoked rumors of a judgeship for Minton and a federal appointment for McNutt. Nothing of the sort happened. There were, however, clear signs that Minton would continue his rise to power in the Senate. Minton had supported the President on every issue in 1936 except the veterans' bonus bill, which passed over Roosevelt's veto. Further evidence of the emerging role of Minton as a leader in the Senate came when the he met with other congressional leaders in late December. Newspapers speculated that Minton might replace J. Hamilton Lewis as majority whip in the Senate as Lewis' age and infirmity were eroding his effectiveness.

When McNutt's term of office was about to expire at the end of the year, Minton spoke at a party honoring the governor and declared, "As we bid you good-bye at the statehouse, may we bid you Godspeed toward the White House."[12] McNutt was one man to whom Minton was loyal throughout his life, in spite of the fact that McNutt snubbed Minton in 1936 because Minton had supported Greenlee in the gubernatorial race rather than McNutt's choice, Townsend. To exact his revenge, McNutt kept Minton's name off the official program of the 1936 Democratic State Convention and ignored him at the Democratic National Convention in Philadelphia that year.

Promptly at noon on Tuesday, January 5, 1937, Vice President John Nance Garner banged his gavel to bring the Senate to order and to open the first session of the Seventy-fifth Congress. He faced a jubilant group of Democrats; after Roosevelt's landslide victory they controlled with an overwhelming majority of 75 to 17 in the Senate and 334 to 89 in the House.

The Democratic caucus re-elected Joseph T. Robinson of Arkansas as majority leader of the Senate and James Hamilton Lewis of Illinois as majority whip. Alabaman Hugo L. Black was elected as secretary. The majority leader was authorized by the Democratic caucus to appoint an assistant whip.

It was a necessary step. Not only was Senator Lewis, the majority whip, old and in poor health, he often voted against the administration on pending matters. Such insubordination by a party member—particularly one in a leadership role—was a source of embarrassment and annoyance to Senator Robinson. The majority leader firmly believed that a Democratic senator was duty-bound to vote for the presidential legislation even if the senator was opposed to a law on its merits. Lewis must be controlled—or bypassed.

Robinson acted without delay and on January 10 announced that Minton was his choice for assistant whip.[13] Minton now had the job of "assisting" Lewis to persuade and cajole Democratic senators to support Roosevelt and the party program on pending legislation.

Minton was forty-six years old and his appointment to a responsible job brought an infusion of sorely needed new blood to the Senate leadership, now primarily an old fogey's club. Lewis, his boss, was seventy-four; Robinson, majority leader, was sixty-four; Carter Glass, chairman of the Appropriations Committee, was seventy-nine; Pat Harrison, chairman of the Finance Committee, was fifty-six; and Royal S. Copeland, chairman of the Commerce Committee, was sixty-nine.

On January 18, soon after his appointment as assistant majority whip, Minton went to the White House to discuss the legislative package with Roosevelt. Later, Minton emerged to announce that the President soon would unveil a plan for judicial reform. Another strategy session would be held at the White House before the bill to reform the court was presented: the President, Attorney General Homer S. Cummings, Minton, and several congressmen would attend, Minton said.[14]

Roosevelt and Cummings unveiled their plan for court reform on Thursday, February 4, in the Cabinet Room at the White House before the Cabinet and Democratic congressional leaders. Secretary of the Interior Harold L. Ickes was delighted that he did not have to carry the fight in Congress. Ominously, many congressional leaders were silent. Representative Hatton Summers of Texas, chairman of the House Judiciary Committee, was utterly opposed to the plan from the moment he heard about it. He flatly announced to his colleagues on the way back to Capitol Hill, "Boys, here's where I cash in my chips."[15]

The comment, and significant opposition from absent leaders, presaged trouble for Roosevelt's plan. Still, the next day, February 5, FDR sent his Supreme Court plan to Congress.

The plan was not new. Attorney General Cummings had found in old Justice Department records a plan to invigorate the federal judiciary by appointing a new judge for every judge who had reached the age of seventy and had not retired. That document was dated 1913 and its author was then Attorney General James C. McReynolds. Now an associate justice of the Supreme Court, McReynolds was the most outspoken member of the court when it came to interference with the fundamental "laws" of laissez-faire economics. If the principle advocated by McReynolds were applied to the Hughes court in 1937, Cummings noted, Roosevelt could name six liberal justices to reverse the present court's trend to reactionary decisions with votes of six to three and five to four. When Cummings informed the President of the plan, Roosevelt was gleeful, exclaiming, "That's the one, Homer!"[16] He even is supposed to have called it "the answer to a maiden's prayer."[17] The famous (or infamous) court packing plan thus was born.

However, at this point Minton was diverted momentarily from the court battle. He needed to turn his attention to his home state, crippled by a natural disaster. In late December 1936, heavy rains began to fall throughout southern Indiana. More than nineteen inches of rainfall had been recorded in many areas by the end of January 1937 (three inches or less was normal for the month). "Rare meteorological conditions had created this calamitous inundation of almost biblical proportions," said a spokesman for the Army Corps of Engineers.[18] All previous flood records in the lower Ohio Valley were shattered; never had so much land been under flood waters for so long. Damage was enormous.

Ninety-five percent of Jeffersonville, Clarksville, and Utica were under water. The town of Leavenworth was destroyed. (It was later rebuilt on higher ground.) At Evansville, the Ohio River reached flood stage of thirty-five feet on January 10, crested at about fifty-three feet on January 31, and did not recede to flood-stage level until February 19.[19]

Minton returned home to seek relief for more than a million people left homeless and to obtain aid to offset the millions of dollars in damage caused by the flooding. Thousands of square miles were inundated. Surveying the Ohio River between Lawrenceburg and Evansville in early February, he said, "I little realized how things would look even from radio reports. All Washington was listening in, but the description of what was taking place did not present the picture at all," he said. "The whole stricken area reminds me of battlegrounds during the World War."[20]

Returning to Washington, Minton prodded, pushed, and dogged federal agencies and even asked the President for assistance in his efforts to obtain help for flood victims.

Assured of some form of assistance, he could turn his attention to the national scene again. The extremely radical plan to reorganize the Supreme Court was looming, and it was time to present it to the public. Under the plan, the President could appoint an additional federal judge for every sitting federal judge who had served ten years and had not resigned within six months after his seventieth birthday. Roosevelt claimed that "insufficient personnel" handicapped the efficiency of the federal judiciary and his solution would "accelerate" the legal process. In practical political terms Roosevelt could add six justices to the Supreme Court and increase their member to fifteen: Louis Brandeis was eighty, Willis Van Devanter was seventy-seven, James McReynolds was seventy-five, George Sutherland and Charles Hughes were seventy-four, and Pierce Butler was seventy.

The plan had stunned the Congressional Democratic leadership when it was unveiled because only the President and Cummings knew about the proposal. The attorney general, with the aid of a few trusted lieutenants, had drafted the bill and a presidential message to Congress to accompany it. Reaction at a national level was predictable. Just as the proposal stunned the Democratic leadership, it stunned the country.

The administration would have preferred that the bill be introduced in the House because of the 334 to 89 majority of Democrats there. House

members had to face the electorate every two years; they were more suscep-
tible to the pressure Roosevelt and his popular administration could bring
to bear on them. There was a major problem in the House, however. Hatton
Summers, chairman of the House Judiciary Committee, was unalterably opposed to the bill, and with the influence he had over the other members of
the Judiciary Committee, leaders feared that the bill might not be voted out
of committee and onto the floor of the House. So Roosevelt decided to
have the bill introduced in the Senate, and to wage the battle there.[21] Senator Ernest Lundeen of Minnesota introduced the court reform bill in the
Senate on Friday, February 5, 1937.

Minton entered the fray strongly, calling the President's court reform
plan "a sensible, statesmanlike approach to a most important problem. No
one can question the authority of Congress to act in line with the suggestions of the President. I favor enlarging the Supreme Court."[22]

Listeners knew all too well the background against which the highly
unusual proposal was being brought forth. It was obvious that the President
of the United States and the Supreme Court were at loggerheads and that
the opposition of the Court was going to jeopardize the practical function-
ing of the government. The list of grievances Roosevelt had against the
Court was by now long. On May 27, 1935, the Supreme Court had held the
National Recovery Administration unconstitutional. As has been discussed,
the Agricultural Adjustment Act was held unconstitutional on January 6,
1936, by a six-to-three decision. Thereafter in rapid succession, other major
legislation of the New Deal was declared unconstitutional by the Court—
much to the agony of the administration: the Securities and Exchange Act
by a vote of six to three, the Guffey Coal Conservation Act of 1935 by a
vote of five to four, and the Municipal Bankruptcy Act by a vote of five to
four. The grounds asserted by the Supreme Court to strike down the Municipal Bankruptcy Act, which permitted federal-state cooperation in the
readjustment of public debts provided the states took the initiative for such
cooperation, were so tenuous that many people thought the entire New
Deal, including Social Security and the Wagner Act, were doomed. Would
all federal participation in local problems be struck down by these conservative justices?[23]

Obviously there was a strong and decided judicial reaction to the very
process of governance at the executive level. Since the Supreme Court was

created by the Federal Judiciary Act on September 24, 1789, it had invalidated only sixty laws prior to 1935. In a little more than one year, starting on May 27, 1935, the Hughes Court had held unconstitutional eleven laws of the New Deal.[24]

The most alarming decision of all to the Democrats had come down on June 5, 1936, just before the Democratic National Convention. In *Morehead v. Tipaldo*,[25] the Supreme Court voted five to four to invalidate a New York state law which required minimum wages for women and children. Writing for the majority, Justice Butler held that "the right to make contracts about one's affairs is a part of the liberty protected by the due process clause. In making contracts of employment, generally speaking, the parties have equal rights to obtain from each other the best terms they can by private bargaining." So, the supporters of the New Deal asked whether, according to the court, a young girl in a sweatshop in New York had an equal right by private bargaining to convince a textile manufacturer that she should earn $2.39 a week. It was a ridiculous supposition, by its very nature irrational. The Court already had held unconstitutional a federal wages and hours act.[26] Now the Court held that neither the federal nor the state government could put a floor under wages or a ceiling over hours. It was a strong last straw.

Still, such a momentous change as that proposed by Roosevelt's court reform bill could not be submitted without difficulty. It produced a mighty uproar throughout the nation and a battle royal in the Senate. Seventeen different bills and fourteen joint resolutions on judicial reform were introduced. So many speeches were made and so much documentation was offered on the issue that two appendices were added to the *Congressional Record* to record the bitter debates.

Roosevelt asked Minton to make a major national address on NBC radio to support the court reform bill. The senator from Indiana delivered the speech on February 15, 1937, stoutly defending the administration's plan.[27]

The lines became sharply drawn as the debate on court reform heated up in the Senate. Several faithful Roosevelt followers parted company with him. Joseph C. O'Mahoney of Wyoming, Tom T. Connally of Texas, and Burton K. Wheeler of Montana all announced their opposition—as did the independent Senate liberals William E. Borah of Idaho and Hiram W. Johnson of California. Senator Edward R. Burke of Nebraska told a rally in Carnegie Hall that if the reform went forward, constitutional government faced "a rendezvous with death."[28] On the other side, Senator Kenneth D. McKellar of Tennessee defended the court reform plan by citing presidential precedents.[29]

Minton did everything in his power to make court reform a reality for Roosevelt. On March 2 he was able to stop debate on a pending matter and obtain the floor for Senator Marvel M. Logan of Kentucky, who spoke in favor of court reform, affirming that he saw "nothing unusual in authorizing the President to appoint an additional justice when one has passed the retirement age."

At this moment other senators, like Maryland's Millard E. Tydings and Walter F. George of Georgia, took issue with the charge that "old men" could not function effectively on the court.[30] Minton interrupted these senators to inform them that one justice, seventy-five-year-old McReynolds, had not written an opinion in five years.[31]

Roosevelt's original strategy had called for Senate majority leader Joe Robinson of Arkansas to lead the court packing fight with help from Barkley, Black, Schwellenbach, LaFollette, and Minton. However, now that the gloves were off, Minton emerged as the bill's most ardent supporter; a bare-fisted, aggressive competitor by nature, he wanted to be in the middle of this heated contest. In addition to praising the bill on its merits, Minton inserted into the *Congressional Record* favorable testimony on the proposed legislation from twelve eminent jurists from the lower courts.[32] Minton even cited Chief Justice Hughes, who in 1928 had lamented about judges who stayed too long on the bench.[33]

And, for the first time in its history, the Supreme Court itself emerged from lofty seclusion behind the pillared facade and entered the fray. When Roosevelt contended that the Court was over-aged, undermanned, and unable to handle the backlog of appeals, Hughes was furious. He called Senator Wheeler, the leader of the Democratic opposition in the Senate, and asked the senator to visit him at his home. When Wheeler arrived, the chief justice handed him a letter, addressed to Wheeler. "The baby is born," he said wryly.[34] Wheeler was to be the first witness for the opposition before the Judiciary Committee on Monday morning, March 22. He testified that after Attorney General Cummings had told the committee that the Supreme Court was unable to keep abreast of its docket, he had gone "to the only source in this country that could know exactly what the facts were."

Wheeler continued as silence fell on those in attendance in the Caucus Room, "And I have here now a letter by the chief justice of the Supreme Court, Mr. Charles Evans Hughes, dated March 21, 1937, written by him and approved and signed by Justice Brandeis and Justice Van Devanter. Let us see what these gentlemen say about it." He then read the letter:

> The Supreme Court is fully abreast of its work. When we rose on March 15th (for the present recess) we had heard argument in cases in which certiorari had been granted only four weeks before—February 15th— . . . there is no congestion of cases upon our calendar. This gratifying condition has been obtained for several years. We have been able for several terms to adjourn after disposing of all cases which are ready to be heard.

In his letter, Hughes had also added this critical comment:

> An increase in the number of Justices of the Supreme Court, apart from any question of policy, which I do not discuss, would not promote the efficiency of the Court. . . . There would be more judges to hear, more judges to confer, more judges to discuss, more judges to be convinced and to decide. The present number of Justices is thought to be large enough so far as the prompt, adequate and efficient conduct of the work of the Court is concerned. . . . [35]

Senator Wheeler later recalled that "you could have heard a pin drop in the caucus room" after he finished reading his letter.[36] The letter severely damaged the chance for passage. What hurt even more was the conservative justices' change of heart about liberal legislation of the New Deal. On Monday, March 29, the Supreme Court reversed itself on minimum wages for women and children and upheld the constitutionality of a minimum wage law in the State of Washington.[37]

On March 31, Minton delivered a speech in the Senate which was heavy with sarcasm and ridicule. Among other things, he said:

> Thus, after twenty years of unabated struggle, minimum wage legislation is for the first time sustained by the Supreme Court by a bare majority vote. Four members of the Court still insist upon putting an interpretation

*upon the words "due process" and "equal protection of the law," an inter-
pretation that is difficult for lawyers to understand and impossible for the
layman to grasp.*

*Only by the vacillating vote of a single justice was the constitutional
right of the state legislature reinstated after what seemed to be a hopeless
struggle—to paraphrase Justice Holmes—to educate the justice "in the obvious." A few weeks ago I pointed out the fact that three times previously
in the history of our country the Supreme Court had come in conflict with
the avowed policy of Congress, and three times the verdict of history was
against the Supreme Court; now for the fourth time the Supreme Court
has come in conflict with the avowed policy of Congress and of the states
and the verdict of history is against the Court.*

*I refer in the four instances to the Dred Scott decision, reversed by the
Civil War; the legal tender decision, reversed by the Supreme Court itself
within a period of a few months, and I may add that by its reversal Chief
Justice Hughes said in his book on the Supreme Court the Court itself then
and there inflicted upon the Court a mortal wound, which leads me to
observe that perhaps the decision of the day before yesterday may have
inflicted another. Then, there was the decision concerning the income tax
law which was held unconstitutional because one justice changed his mind
overnight. That decision of the Court was later reversed by constitutional
amendment. So, for an institution that has to support a halo, that is a
pretty bad record. . . .*[38]

Minton concluded his speech with an attack on the stability of the mind
of Justice Roberts, who had provided the swing vote in these cases. "I am
unwilling the policy of this country shall be committed to the instability of
Mr. Justice Roberts' mind." Two weeks after upholding the minimum wage
law in the State of Washington, the Supreme Court on Monday, April 12,
upheld the constitutionality of the National Labor Relations Act, more
commonly known as the Wagner Act, in a five to four decision.[39] Then on
May 24 the Supreme Court upheld the Social Security Act[40] and Roosevelt
and the entire administration gave a collective sigh of relief that this most
important piece of legislation had survived judicial challenge.

Still, the fight over the court bill continued in the Senate. Roosevelt
had from the beginning every reason to expect to win the fight—Congress

had uniformly bowed to his will during the first term. He seemed destined to win; after all, the Democratic majority was seventy-five to seventeen in the Senate. Then unforeseen events occurred which changed the face of the struggle entirely.

At least one of these wholly unpredicted events was the result of Republican strategy masterfully perfected by the politically wily Senator William E. Borah. The senator from Idaho realized that the Democrats were sharply divided on the court reform bill and decided to let the majority party fight it out among themselves on this controversial issue.

In 1937, Southern senators, all good Democrats, held all three key positions in the leadership roles of the Senate. First and foremost was Joseph T. Robinson of Arkansas, majority leader, who exercised more absolute authority over the body than even Lyndon B. Johnson later enjoyed. James F. Byrnes of South Carolina, and the shrewd and entertaining Pat Harrison of Mississippi, chairman of the Senate Finance Committee, were the partners of the majority leader. These senators, with all of their influence, should have been able to obtain passage of the court reform bill. Robinson alone had accumulated enough political IOUs from his fellow Democrats to have passed the court bill if he called them in.

As late as May 1937, thanks to the prodigious efforts of Senator Robinson, Roosevelt had enough votes in the Senate to put through a reasonable compromise of the court bill by reducing the number of new justices to be appointed from six to two or three. Many faithful Democrats in the Senate probably would have voted for a compromise despite their intense opposition to the court packing bill. Such a compromise would have been sufficient because Chief Justice Hughes and Justice Roberts had changed their positions and were voting for the administration. However, Roosevelt "had his Dutch up," as he was fond of saying. He would not think of compromise while he could count on those political IOUs in his pocket and in the pocket of Senator Robinson. He would hold to the original bill.[41]

One formidable problem with the original measure written by Cummings and submitted to Congress by Roosevelt was that it did not offer the justices over seventy a reasonable opportunity to retire. Both Van Devanter and Sutherland had indicated their desire to retire prior to 1937. However, justices of the Supreme Court then could retire from active service only by resignation. If a justice did resign, then Congress could reduce his compensation or retirement pay, as had happened to Justice Oliver Wendell Holmes when he retired.[42] No one wished to be cast adrift in his old age, so naturally the elderly justices clung to their positions despite ill health, senility, and other infirmities.

After the court fight began, opponents of the President's bill who wished to find a way to let the justices retire gracefully rushed a bill through Congress which enabled federal judges to retire without loss of income.

After the passage of this liberalized measure for retirement, Senator Wheeler of Montana, now bitterly anti-Roosevelt despite his earlier friendship with the White House, joined with Borah of Idaho to persuade Van Devanter to resign now, if he were going to retire. It was his patriotic duty, the argument went, and it would also help to defeat the court reform bill. Roosevelt could get a sop of appointing a justice of his choice—one who would vote in favor of New Deal legislation and thereby constitute a majority of the justices without the bill. On May 18 Van Devanter sent his letter of resignation to the White House and left for his farm in Maryland.

The resignation of Van Devanter had been timed to coincide with the vote of the Senate Judiciary Committee on the court reform bill on May 18. Wheeler made sure that each member of the Judiciary Committee knew that Van Devanter had submitted his resignation as the committee convened. Hence there was not any need for the bill because Roosevelt could appoint his new justice. After hearing eighty-five witnesses and 1.5 million words of testimony, the committee on that day voted ten to eight that the bill "not pass," and adopted a report calling the plan "a measure which should be so emphatically rejected that its parallel will never again be presented to the free representatives of the free people of America." Six Democrats on the committee had deserted their party and voted with the majority. Senator Minton inveighed against his colleagues on the committee for their action in voting against the bill.

The bill wasn't dead, but its course continued through difficult waters. The Senate must muster the will and support to see it through to law, and the Senate was becoming an increasingly hard place for Roosevelt to guarantee results.

Justice Van Devanter's resignation and the resulting vacancy on the court placed Roosevelt in a dilemma. The lifelong ambition of Senate Majority Leader Joe Robinson, who had served the President diligently and with absolute fidelity for four years, was to sit on the Supreme Court. Roosevelt had hinted that he could expect one of the places of the new justices after the court reform bill was enacted. Robinson, thus enticed, had labored nobly in the vineyard with single-minded purpose, carrying on the battle for the court reform bill, day after day and week after week, giving the bill twelve hours or more of his work each day throughout the long months that it had been before the Senate.

When the news of Van Devanter's resignation broke, the entire Senate flocked around Robinson's desk, congratulating him on his coming promotion and calling him "Mr. Justice." But Roosevelt was preparing to renege on his implicit promise. The President's New Deal advisors and strategists considered Robinson too conservative and too old to fill the single vacancy on the Supreme Court when the whole purpose of the court reform bill was to bring in younger and more liberal judges. Consequently, Roosevelt treated Robinson as if he were a poor relative too embarrassing to be acknowledged in public—no seat for him. The Senate was enraged. The whole climate in the Senate deteriorated for two long weeks and finally Roosevelt had to confront the hard facts: Robinson had to be the new justice.

Roosevelt invited him to the White House in early June, offered him the appointment, and authorized him to compromise the court reform bill on the best basis possible. Although Robinson left the White House with a light heart and a zeal to accomplish this thorny assignment, it was not to be. The fight over the bill already had taken too much out of him.

On June 11, 1937, Vice President Garner, president of the Senate and a vital part of the administration strategy, left Washington in disgust for his home in Texas because he did not want to work for a bill he despised. His departure left Robinson to carry the entire fight for court reform in the Senate. He used all of his personal prestige to plead not only for the plan but for his own future appointment; his colleagues realized he was begging them to help him to fulfill his cherished ambition to become a justice.

Joe Robinson was a big, heavyset, red-faced man with small eyes, jutting jaw, and an awesome temper which required constant control. Now sixty-five years old and exhausted from weeks of battle over court reform, he was in grave personal danger from stress and physical strain.

The compromise version of the court reform bill was introduced in the Senate on Friday, July 2. It allowed the President to appoint a new justice for each member of the Court over seventy-five, not seventy. Also, it permitted the President to make only one such appointment each year. Robinson led the fight for the bill's passage.

Minton backed the final attack on July 8, condemning "Justice Roberts for inconsistency, Justice Van Devanter for writing a minimal two opinions per year, and Justice Sutherland for not 'hurting himself with work.' "[43]

The next Tuesday, July 13, Robinson was sitting on the portico of the Senate when he asked a page to bring Minton to him. Minton was concerned when he saw Robinson, whose cheeks normally were rosy. "Joe was ashen," he later recalled. "I asked him if he wanted me to call a doctor but he said 'Hell no.' " Robinson told Minton that "it is only my indigestion and I am going home to rest a bit." With this statement, he placed Minton in charge of the Roosevelt forces during his absence and went home.

Home for Robinson was a five-room apartment on the fourth floor of the Methodist Building located just across Maryland Avenue from the Supreme Court building. It was the same building in which Justice and Mrs. Minton would later live. Robinson was alone in the apartment because Mrs. Robinson had gone to Little Rock for a week. At 8:15 the next morning, a maid who came to fix breakfast for him found Robinson sprawled out on the floor of his bedroom, dead of a heart attack. Near his right hand lay an open copy of the *Congressional Record*. "I guess I was about the last person to see Joe alive," Minton remembered with sadness.[44]

The Senate adjourned out of respect for Majority Leader Robinson; services were held for him in the Senate Chamber on Friday, July 16. Minton was among those senators appointed to attend the funeral at the First Methodist Church in Little Rock. A special funeral train left Washington for Little Rock on Saturday, carrying thirty-eight senators, Postmaster General James Farley, and Vice President Garner.

Garner remained unalterably opposed to the measure, and the funeral train provided a venue for lobbying against it with the very people he wished to convince. He plotted the defeat of the court reform bill on the trip back from Little Rock, holding court on the train with bourbon and branch water and talking to almost all of the thirty-eight senators. When Garner reported to Roosevelt upon his return on July 20, the President, who always wanted to know were he stood politically, asked: "How did you find the court situation, Jack?"

"Do you want it with the bark on or off, Cap'n?" Garner asked. "The rough way," answered the President. "All right. You are beat. You haven't the votes," was the defiant response.[45] Garner was right, of course. His insurrection, of course, meant that he would never run again with Roosevelt.

On July 20 Senator Barkley from Kentucky was elected as majority leader by the Democratic caucus to replace Senator Robinson, his margin of victory a single vote (thirty-eight to thirty-seven) over Pat Harrison from Mississippi. Roosevelt favored Barkley over Harrison because he was still doggedly determined to win on the court bill, and Harrison's election would be disastrous not only to the court reform bill but to his entire program.

FDR worked personally for Harrison's defeat. First the President applied pressure on the other senator from Mississippi, Theodore Bilbo, who disliked Harrison. Then he moved to Senator William H. Dietrich of Illinois, who was up for re-election and needed the support of Chicago political boss Ed Kelly. Roosevelt talked to Boss Kelly, and to help Kelly persuade Dietrich to do the right thing promised Dietrich two federal judgeships. Both Kelly and Dietrich could make good use of two such political plums. So Kelly called Dietrich and Dietrich's vote went to Roosevelt and Barkley.[46]

At Roosevelt's prompting, Minton and Schwellenbach also worked hard for Barkley's election. Minton was rewarded by Barkley and reappointed to his position as assistant whip of the Senate. But Roosevelt's cause was doomed anyway. The end of the court packing fight in the Senate came on Thursday, July 22. Senator Marvel M. Logan of Kentucky moved to recommit the bill to the Judiciary Committee, where it would be rewritten to exclude any reference to the Supreme Court but would deal only with retirement by lower federal judges. The motion carried by a vote of seventy to twenty with five abstentions. Facing reality again, Minton voted "aye," as a raucous laugh was heard in the Senate. Minton knew that the votes for passage were not there. Still, one newspaper in Indiana criticized Minton's abandonment of principle, asserting he instead chose to ride "the band wagon."[47]

The court packing bill had been defeated by two powerful blows: first, the engineered resignation of Justice Van Devanter, the staunch member of the "old guard" justices; second, the death of Senator Robinson. Joe Robinson had kept the plan alive in the Senate by the sheer force of his remarkable personality. And although Robinson had enough IOUs in his pocket to pass the bill, all IOUs die when the holder does.

Still, Minton was not quite ready to admit that court reform was dead. Judicial reform was sorely needed, he believed. On July 27 Minton proposed an amendment to the bill which would have required a two-thirds majority of the justices of the Supreme Court to hold an act of Congress unconstitutional. Minton was persuaded by his friends in the Senate to drop this proposal and the bitter fight over court reform finally ended.

Minton's courageous fight for court reform pleased Roosevelt, who seriously considered him to fill the Supreme Court vacancy created by Van Devanter's resignation. Secretary of the Interior Harold L. Ickes called Minton "one of the outstanding men on the floor of the Senate in the debate."[48]

But the strong stand exacted a price. Newspapers flayed him, friends turned against him. And on July 16, 1937, a large envelope containing a shotgun shell with a note wrapped around it was delivered to him. "Senator Minton. Don't mistake. I am educated. If you support Roosevelt's court bill we will get you—you dirty rubber stamp," read the note.[49] It closed with an obscenity which violated postal laws.

Routine Senate business had been going on, of course, during the fight to reform the court.

The *Congressional Record* for 1937 discloses that Minton found time to introduce approximately fifty amendments, petitions, bills, and resolutions beyond his gargantuan efforts to support Roosevelt's pet legislation.

Many of the pieces of legislation reveal his well matured political views. Undoubtedly spurred by the unpleasant memories of poverty from childhood after his father's injury on the Southern Railroad, Minton supported workman's compensation laws and fair labor standards. He believed that an energetic class of workers was crucial for economic growth and free enterprise as well as liberty. He once said that the only time some laborers had embraced communism was "when people were starving to death" during Hoover's term.[50]

Minton remained loyal to the basic rights of workers. Still, the labor unrest in 1937 which culminated in sit-down strikes bothered him. "Within my limitations as a lawyer, I know of no law that justifies the sit-down strike," he said.[51] In spite of that concern he favored an amendment to the bituminous coal law which would secure the right of collective bargaining for automobile workers and opposed Senators Borah and O'Mahoney who wanted the rights of corporations defined precisely to prevent infringement by unions or regulatory agencies. He also chastised Senator Bailey, who suggested that strikers wanted power rather than better working conditions.[52]

The death of Senator Robinson had relieved Roosevelt of his promise to put him on the Supreme Court, but the problem of selecting the successor to Van Devanter still existed.

Earlier, because of his outstanding service to the Democratic majority as assistant majority whip in securing the passage of measures such as flood control and relief, fair labor standards, public housing, antitrust laws and amendments to labor laws, it was rumored as early as February 1937, that Minton himself had an inside chance for an appointment to the Supreme Court. These rumors increased in proportion to his prominence as the fight over court reform raged. Minton denied such rumors in June. "I don't know who originated those rumors back home, but I am behind Joe Robinson," he said. However, deeply conscious that Indiana had never had a member of the Court, he added, "Indiana is entitled to representation on the Court."[53]

Roosevelt was given a list of fifty names as possible replacements for Van Devanter. On August 4 he told Ickes that he felt the choice "ought to come from the Wisconsin-Illinois-Indiana circuit which had not had a man on the Supreme Court bench for many years." Within the week Attorney General Homer S. Cummings sent the President a series of *curricula vitae* on eleven prospects, including seven state judges, the Dean of the University of Wisconsin Law School, Solicitor General Reed, and Senators Black from Alabama and Minton from Indiana.[54]

Roosevelt eliminated the Dean of the University of Wisconsin Law School and the state judges either because he doubted their liberalism or because he feared they might not be confirmed by the Senate. Despite the backing by Cummings, Solicitor General Reed was dismissed as "a good man but without much force or color."[55]

Senators Minton and Black were left. The Senate almost certainly would be compelled to accept either one of them as an act of collegial courtesy. Roosevelt recalled that while Robinson was living, the Senate would not have accepted anyone else because all senators knew of his ambition to serve on the Supreme Court and Roosevelt's implied promise to him. The

President would receive a wry satisfaction in knowing that the right-wing conservatives in the Senate would have to vote to approve a liberal reformer like Black or Minton.

Ickes expressed his preference for Minton when he met with Roosevelt on August 4. Ickes believed Minton had shown himself one of the New Deal's outstanding men during the Senate debate over the court bill. Minton was invited to the White House to confer with the President on the evening of August 11. The meeting was oddly equivocal. Roosevelt seemed to offer the appointment to Minton on the one hand, while on the other hand begging him to remain in the Senate where his services as assistant whip were needed. "Shay, I know of your ambition to be on the Court, but I need you in the Senate right now. There will be other vacancies in the future and you'll get one," Roosevelt told him.[56]

Roosevelt had carefully weighed the matter and his reasoning was strong. Minton was well-placed where he was: young and a leader in the Democratic Party in Indiana. Black was much too liberal for Alabama and facing a hard fight for re-election in 1938. In fact, Black had indicated that he might retire at the end of his current term rather than face re-election, thus being lost to the party. Roosevelt decided that adding a vigorous Southern progressive to the present court would be the soundest course of action for him to follow.[57]

On the evening of August 11, after Minton left the White House, Roosevelt met with Black. After the usual period of teasing that was so characteristic of his way of operating, the President showed Black a blank nomination form for the Supreme Court and asked Black if he might complete it by filling in his name.[58] Black agreed and Roosevelt completed the nomination by scrawling with his pen: "I nominate Hugo L. Black of Alabama to be an Associate Justice of the Supreme Court." The President later told Farley that he chose Black because he had served the New Deal longer and more zealously than Minton had. Farley recalled that Roosevelt concluded his recital with the gleeful statement, "And they'll have to take him, too!" Farley assumed that this reference was to the anti-court Democrats who would be under pressure of senatorial courtesy to approve Black.[59]

Roosevelt sent the nomination to the Senate on August 12, and Minton became Democratic floor leader with the job of obtaining Black's confirmation.[60] Minton's place was now secure.

Over the following weekend Minton was Roosevelt's guest on the presidential yacht for a trip down Chesapeake Bay. The voyage stirred speculation about the political future of the young senator from Indiana. Roosevelt, after all, only cruised with loyal liberals of his own ilk, and important ones at that. Governor Murphy of Michigan and Senator LaFollette, the progressive from Wisconsin, had been recent guests on the brass and mahogany *Sequoia*.[61]

During the debate over Black's confirmation, some niggling troubles did occur. Minton handled them skillfully. New York's Democratic Senator Royal S. Copeland, who was running for mayor of New York City and in need of the black vote there, raised the issue of Black's former membership in the Ku Klux Klan. In the context it was not seen as a serious issue, and Minton saw the nomination through as swiftly as he could. On August 17 the Senate confirmed the nomination by a vote of sixty-three to sixteen with sixteen abstentions. All thirty-two senators up for re-election in 1938 voted in favor of confirmation in the hope of gaining favor in the White House and perhaps getting some help from Roosevelt in the forthcoming election. The official commission was issued to Justice Black the next day.[62]

But the Ku Klux Klan issue would not go away. In September the *Pittsburgh Post-Gazette* first ran the story about Justice Black's Klan affiliations and then sold the story to the North American Newspaper Alliance. The statements in the press alleged that Black had donned white robes to take the oath of the Ku Klux Klan in Birmingham, Alabama, in 1923—three years before he defeated Oscar W. Underwood, an anti-Klan senator. The story said that Black resigned from the Klan in 1925 when he began his campaign for the Senate but that he had rejoined—actually had been reinstated as a life member in 1926.[63]

When this story broke, many senators who voted in favor of confirmation were embarrassed and stated that they would not have voted that way if they had known about Black's purported links with the Klan. Minton must bear some of the blame for the Senate's failure to more thoroughly investigate Black's fitness for this high office; he was pushing hard and fast for the political appointee without much reasoned evaluation of his credentials.[64]

Black was in London when the scandal surfaced. He kept silent until his return. On October 1 he made a radio speech to a national audience from the home of a friend. He admitted that he had joined the Klan but said that he later resigned. He also said that the unsolicited card which was given to him shortly after his nomination to the Senate was not a membership of any kind in the Ku Klux Klan because he never used it and did not even keep it. Black refused to denounce the Klan despite urging from his colleagues because, according to him, that would be letting down friends in Alabama who had helped him through the years.[65]

Minton found time in 1937 to help his own friends. He worked hard to have Roosevelt appoint old friend Paul McNutt as High Commissioner to the Philippines. Roosevelt made the Minton-sponsored appointment on February 17, 1937, and Minton took the lead in the Senate to gain McNutt's early confirmation. The Senate finalized the appointment on February 23. McNutt, who was just finishing his term as Indiana governor, was a much admired and esteemed Democrat who won Senate confirmation easily.[66]

Another cause taken up by Minton that year was that of his eternal ally Pleas E. Greenlee. When Wayne Coy resigned as director of the Works Progress Administration in Indiana to go with McNutt to the Philippines, Minton recommended Greenlee for the WPA job, provided that Governor Townsend approved. It was not an easy job. Not only did Townsend disapprove of an appointment for his political foe for governor, but he also discharged several friends of Greenlee at the Statehouse. Minton persevered—as was his habit—and persuaded Roosevelt to appoint Greenlee to the Federal Coal Commission (the agency which regulated the operators and miners on behalf of the public). "Those who may do a good turn for Minton are happy in the assurance that his obligations to them will be repaid. It makes little difference that taxpayers' money is being used to pay the obligations," decried the *New Albany Tribune* on June 19.[67]

Minton in that same time period gave a political boost to his friend and comrade, former governor McNutt, hoping to push him toward the White House. Minton told the press:

Roosevelt will not run for a third term and McNutt will be nominated. He's a natural. He gave Indiana the best administration it ever had. He put more legislation on the books of Indiana for labor and the farmer than

anybody ever did in the history of the state and he demonstrated his execu-
tive ability. He has acquaintances all over the United States. There isn't a
crossroad that doesn't have someone that knows him. He's a great cam-
paigner, too. There isn't a better one in the country. His views are sub-
stantially the views of the New Deal. [68]

The year 1938 opened brightly for the Mintons. The family was flourish-
ing in the complicated social environment of Washington by keeping a low
profile. The children, of course, were getting older. Sherman, almost nineteen, was a junior at Indiana University. Mary-Anne, soon to be fifteen, was
in school in Washington, D.C., as was John, who would be thirteen that
year. Mrs. Minton was managing the home as well as taking care of her
social duties, which that year included an invitation to the White House for
a visit with Mrs. Roosevelt. The life of the eighteen-hour-a-day senatorial
wife was yet in the future; most of the time Mrs. Minton was left alone to be
the good wife and mother that she was.

CHAPTER FIVE

FINAL YEARS IN THE SENATE
AND A JOB AT THE WHITE HOUSE

RUMORS IN WASHINGTON IN 1938 HINTED THAT HIGHER OFFICES WERE IN STORE for Senator Sherman Minton. The resignation of Associate Justice George Sutherland from the Supreme Court created a vacancy for which Minton was mentioned. There was even a "Minton for President" movement.

The continued ascendancy of Minton's political fortunes contrasted with the declining economic situation in the nation. The Great Depression continued to plague Roosevelt and his New Deal. Stocks were in a skid that was actually steeper than it had been in the first months after the crash of 1929. National Resources Committee statistics showed that 81 percent of the families in the United States lived on an annual income of less that two thousand dollars. By the spring of 1938 five million people who had found jobs since 1933 were out of work again, for a total unemployment of 8.5 million. Nearly 14 percent of the population was on relief. On the legislative calendar for 1938 were measures to deal with this gloomy picture.

Minton's Senate colleagues believed he should be in the forefront to deal with the problems facing the nation, and re-elected him as assistant majority whip. He was now experienced in the ways of the Senate and he was on the floor to defend the administration against all attacks. His unfailing support of the President produced heated debates and sometimes personal confrontations with many of his colleagues. The senator from Indiana remained unfazed. Minton was ebullient, outspoken, and an intense advocate of the New Deal—period. He was, as Justice Frankfurter once said, an "almost pathological Democrat."[1] His loyalty to Roosevelt and his dedication to the party line never wavered while he was in the Senate, in large part because his own school-of-hard-knocks convictions coincided with the

President's. He worked hard for the New Deal because he sincerely believed in it. Unfortunately, one must concede that Minton's ardor sometimes blinded him to its failures.

In the early part of 1938, Paul McNutt, now serving as high commissioner to the Philippines, left Manila to return to the United States and report to President Roosevelt on conditions in the Philippines and the Far East.

While McNutt was in Washington, Minton and Frank McHale, the new Democratic National Committeeman from Indiana and former campaign manager for McNutt, gave a huge party to unofficially launch the McNutt-for-President movement. Minton readily admitted that the purpose of the affair was to give everyone an opportunity to meet "Indiana's presidential candidate in 1940."[2] It was probably also an opportunity for Minton to make the statement in front of the other Democrats from Indiana that McNutt had "arrived."

The huge to-do was held at the Mayflower Hotel on February 23. Some three thousand people were invited to rub elbows with their fellows in the seat of power while enjoying the elegant decor of the Mayflower's Chinese Room. The guest list included all the Democratic members of the Senate and the House, Cabinet officials, major department heads, diplomats, high-ranking Army and Navy officers, newspaper correspondents, Indiana Governor M. Clifford Townsend, and other officials from Minton's home state.[3]

The menu featured gelatin of capon with salad Santa Maria, caviar, *croûte au chaud*, *buffet délice Diana*, hot meat snaps, four kinds of canapés, three kinds of mousse, and two massive eight-layer cakes, each eighteen inches in diameter, with one bearing the seal of the United States and the other the seal of Indiana done in delicate frosting.[4]

According to the gushing reports, the tables were decorated with tall red-white-and-blue candles in silver candelabra and great baskets filled with creamy-tan giant gladioli, rare black-purple Japanese iris, deep red roses, pussy willow, fern and smilax. There were five symbolic displays depicting the Washington Monument, Mount Vernon, a lighthouse, a yacht, and a pagoda.[5]

In describing the grandiose event, one writer said: "A hasty search of the records yesterday disclosed no precedent of any sort for the present reception. There have been many different and many tremendous parties in

Washington, but none like this, where a presidential bandwagon, newly painted, with at least four thousand seats on it and any number of handholds for last-minute jumpers, has gone on view more than two years before the nominating convention."[6]

Hoosiers always seem to have to be proving themselves, and perhaps this event fell into that category. They were determined that nobody was going to view these sponsors and their candidate as hicks. Still, the elegance of the event may have seemed a bit overdone when so many were still out of work. Furthermore, the White House was not represented at the reception; Roosevelt was keenly aware of McNutt's ambition to be President and he was not about to provide McNutt with good publicity. In fact there was a chilling response from the official family. President Roosevelt's Cabinet members also were noticeably absent from the affair, most of them declining the invitation with lame excuses. For example, James Farley was fishing in Florida; Frances Perkins had to attend a conference on the employment of older persons; Henry Morganthau, Jr., was detained on his farm in New York; Henry A. Wallace had a speaking engagement in California; and Cordell Hull was visiting old friends in Tennessee. Vice President John Nance Garner declined his invitation because he had a policy of attending only four social functions a year. The McNutt party was not one of the four.[7]

Estimates of the cost of the affair ranged from five thousand dollars to six thousand dollars (a tidy amount in 1938). When asked if the "Two Percent Club" in Indiana paid for the party, Frank McHale replied, "No, that would be a dumb thing to do. No, there would be a lot of criticism if that sort of story came out. This party is being paid for by a group of Paul's friends."[8]

It was still necessary to defend Roosevelt against the hungry wolves who snarled about everything he did. On April 28, 1938, the American Newspaper Publishers Association at a meeting in New York adopted a resolution which warned the public against the misuse of radio for propaganda purposes. This resolution obviously was aimed at Roosevelt's "fireside chats" and the national radio addresses given by other administration officials.

Minton was livid when he read the resolution. He decided to "aid newspapers in cleaning up their own house before they start cleaning up the radio," and forthwith entered the Senate Chamber, secured the floor, and voiced his angry objections. He introduced a bill which came to be known as the Press Gag. It provided that "any person or firm, corporation or association that publishes in the District of Columbia or publishes or causes to be transported in interstate commerce or through the mails any newspaper, magazine, or other periodical in which it is published as a fact anything known to said publisher or his responsible agents to be false shall be guilty of a felony, and on conviction thereof shall be fined not less that one thousand dollars nor more than ten thousand dollars, and shall be imprisoned for not more that two years."[9]

Publishers were infuriated. "Senator Minton's desire to curb newspapers reveals his intolerance for anything that does not coincide with his own views," shouted Frank E. Gannett. "Senator Minton's statements are indefensible. Fortunately, they will mislead only the stupid," cried Paul Patterson, publisher of the *Baltimore Sun*. The ANPA condemned intimidation of editors "in the exercise of their constitutionally guaranteed right" of free speech.

The unkindest cut of all appeared in an editorial in *The New York Herald Tribune* on April 30, 1938. The editorial snarled that "Sherman Minton, Democrat of Indiana, has become notable in Washington for several things: rudeness to witnesses, extravagant remarks on the floor of the Senate, and unbridled and often pointless loquacity, being a blind follower of all the dreams for the more abundant life. He possesses a total lack of that splendid quality known as the judicial temperament; this last notwithstanding (or maybe it is cause and effect) the fact that he has become mentioned as a possible appointee to the Supreme Court of the United States."

Minton later admitted that he did not think "it was going to backfire on me the way it did."[10] But the unexpected outcry from newspapers and their publishers did shake him and he permitted the bill to die in committee. "The only reason I introduced it was to attract the attention of the newspapers to my speech criticizing the American Newspaper Publishers Association," he explained. "Without the bill the newspapers probably would pay no attention to me."[11] Minton's action in this situation was typical of his impulsive reactions to attacks on Roosevelt from any source. His somewhat myopic view of Roosevelt and the New Deal coupled with his blind loyalty invited the dangerous wrath of the media.

Politics occupied much of Minton's time and effort in 1938. Roosevelt had made the decision to "purge" anti-New Deal Senators Walter F. George of Georgia; Guy M. Gillette of Iowa; Ellison D. Smith of South Carolina; Millard E. Tydings of Maryland; and four others. Following the lead of the President, Minton concluded that he could back only candidates for congressional seats who were one-hundred-percent New Dealers. The President had "a right to demand that the general pattern of his party be progressive" and to "urge election of congressmen and senators who are liberal-minded," according to Minton.[12]

Minton had little regard for Senator Van Nuys because he usually voted against New Deal legislation. He worked hard behind the scenes to deny Van Nuys the renomination of the Democratic party in Indiana in 1938. Minton wanted to get McNutt on the ticket instead of Van Nuys, but accomplishing that task was beyond his powers. Accordingly, he finally convinced himself to back Van Nuys in the interest of party unity.

Minton served as permanent chairman of the Democratic State Convention in 1938, and made an eloquent speech in praise of Roosevelt to the twenty-two hundred delegates assembled in Indianapolis.

After the convention, he conducted a vigorous campaign on behalf of the Democratic ticket in the Hoosier state. He made more than thirty-five speeches, traveling from the Michigan border to the Ohio River. Each speech was generally the same, with minor variations to suit the locale and the crowd. A local politician would give Minton a generous introduction, then Minton would list the good things that the New Deal had provided, such as the Securities and Exchange Commission, Utility Holding Company, Home Owners' Loan Bank with emphasis on the fifty thousand homes in Indiana saved by the bank. He beat the drum for the Bank Deposit Guarantee Law, Civilian Conservation Corps, Farm Credit Act, Soil Conservation Act, Wagner Act, Social Security Act, and the Works Progress Administration. Throughout the speech, Minton would lambast the Republican candidate for senator, Raymond E. Willis, and the entire Republican ticket. He would point with pride to the fact that farm income in Indiana had risen from $134 million in 1932 to $292 million in 1937. Finally he would pay tribute to "that eternal progressive Republican, William Allen White, and others of his ilk who know that Republicans dare not repeal the acts of the New Deal."[13]

Despite Minton's tireless work and the efforts of other Democrats, most Republicans won in Indiana in 1938. Van Nuys barely survived, defeating

Willis by only 6,535 votes (784,155 for Van Nuys to 777,620 for Willis). The election results in Indiana in 1938 reflected a national trend: that year Republicans gained eighty-two seats in the House and eight in the Senate. While the President retained his popularity, the vote reflected dissatisfaction over his strong-arm methods and increasing power.

Minton relaxed at his home in New Albany after the election and offered some predictable reflections. Roosevelt and his New Deal were "stronger than any other administration following a midterm election," suggested Minton. "I think the Democratic Party is the best in the country and that everyone should vote for it in order to save the nation."[14]

The year 1938 ended for Minton on a sad note. His seventy-six-year-old father suffered a heart attack in December. He remained bedfast at his home in Fort Worth, Texas, and died there on February 1, 1939. At the funeral in Georgetown, Minton caught a cold which developed such severe complications that he subsequently had to be hospitalized in Washington, D.C.[15]

The Democrats in the Senate broke precedent on April 18, 1939, when they unanimously elected Minton majority whip to succeed Senator James H. Lewis, who had died a few days earlier. Before this time this high post had been filled by a senator with seniority, who possessed years of experience in the procedure of the Senate and parliamentary law. Minton was starting the fifth year of only his first term in the Senate, a "youngster" as those things went.

In truth, however, for more than two years—since his appointment as assistant majority whip on January 10, 1937—Minton had been performing the job of majority whip, seeing that senators were notified of important pending business and marshaling members for important votes or arranging pairs for those absent from Washington. His was a *de facto* office: Lewis with his pink whiskers, toupee, eccentricities, and poor health had been unable to do the job of majority whip during that period. Though he obviously was senile, Lewis was tolerated by his colleagues. For example, on July 6, 1937, Lewis, on a "point of order," requested Robinson to silence the gallery, even though he could hardly hear the proceedings. Senator Robinson was curt: "The occupants of the galleries are not disturbing me in the least; and if the senator will excuse me, I will withdraw his point of order." Lewis, amid laughter, replied weakly and sheepishly, "As the senator is not disturbed, I will sit down quite content."

"That is right, that is the way to do it," agreed Robinson.[16]

Minton served as majority whip under Majority Leader Barkley for twenty-one months. In this capacity he helped enact much of the administration's continuing legislative program, including the extension of the Works Progress Administration and the Reciprocal Trade Agreements. His continued attacks on big business and defense of labor unions made him a prominent spokesman for the New Deal program. Additionally, in the face of the ominously deteriorating situation in Europe, the important national defense measures enacted during the time became law thanks in no small part to Minton: the Burke-Wadsworth Selective Training and Service Act, the repeal of the embargo provisions of the Neutrality Act of 1935, and the appropriations bills to fund the defense machine.

Many people, including news correspondents, liked his sincerity and candor even though some of them castigated him as a mouthpiece for the administration.

A March 1939 issue of *Life* magazine gave Minton a rating of 90 percent on "integrity" by asking newspaper correspondents in Washington, D.C., "Does Senator Minton have principles and stick to them regardless of political expedience?"[17]

Still, the abrasive, irrepressible enthusiasm which had characterized him from high school days, and which now manifested itself in dogged partisanship, earned him enemies. A slurring remark by a Washington columnist appeared on April 24, 1939, in a syndicated newspaper feature called "The Capital Parade." It said that "Minton is actively disliked by most of his other colleagues." This prompted the Fort Wayne, Indiana, *Journal-Gazette* to conduct a survey of United States senators. On May 20 William A. Kunkel, Jr., publisher of the *Journal-Gazette*, wrote to each senator:

> On April twenty-fourth of this year, a columnist in a column called "The Capital Parade" in a newspaper in Washington, D.C., wrote "Minton is actively disliked by most of his other colleagues."
>
> I think I am right when I attribute to you a high regard for the spirit of fair play and honesty in your relations with your fellowmen.
>
> Senator Sherman Minton was elected to the United States Senate from

the state of Indiana and every citizen in this state is entitled to know if this
statement of the columnist is right or wrong. America needs the combined
efforts of Republicans and Democrats alike to properly safeguard our liber-
ties in this country, and no man should be condemned among his colleagues
by a paid columnist, unless they themselves so desire.

Regardless of politics and in justice to Senator Sherman Minton, who is
regarded very highly in this state, I would like to have you answer the
question for yourself and to comment on it if you care to whether, in your
judgment, the observation is true.

Sixty-six of Minton's colleagues responded to the letter. None of them
admitted "any active dislike" of him. Many of them mentioned his selection
by the unanimous vote of the Democratic colleagues as the Democratic
whip of the Senate. Senator Robert F. Wagner of New York commented
that this election was an exceptional tribute to Minton, because as a rule
that office goes only to a senator having many more years of service in the
Senate that Minton. Senator Harry S. Truman of Missouri replied in his
usual blunt manner:

I read with a great deal of interest your letter of the twentieth, referring to
the column in the "Capital Parade" in which it was said that Minton is
actively disliked by most of his colleagues. This is just a plain barefaced lie.
That is about all you can call it. When Senator Lewis died, the Democratic
caucus unanimously elected Minton to succeed him. No one was even
nominated to oppose him in that election.

The senator is one of the ablest rough-and-tumble debaters on the Sen-
ate floor, and he usually takes them on as they come and handles them
without gloves, but he is well liked by all the members of the senate on both
sides of the aisle, whether they agree with him or not. Personally, I think he
is one of the ablest men in the senate and represents the state of Indiana
with honor to that great Commonwealth.

Senator Burton K. Wheeler of Montana replied that "I could not subscribe to that viewpoint at all. Senator Minton and I differed quite violently
with reference to the so-called packing of the Supreme Court, but it made
no difference with reference to my personal feelings concerning him, and I

am quite sure that it made no difference to his personal feeling toward me."
Wheeler noted that Minton was a member of the Interstate Commerce
Committee of which Wheeler was chairman. "In my judgment, he is honest, able and fearless. The fact that he has been elected whip of the Democratic party would indicate clearly that he is held in esteem by his colleagues."
Senator Prentiss M. Brown of Michigan observed that "Senator Minton and
I sit very close to each other in the Senate. Not only do I have the highest
regard for him, but I know that he is well liked by his colleagues. He is a
most able lawyer—I think one of the very best lawyers in the Senate—and
his legal ability is recognized by all. There is absolutely no justification for
the statement that Senator Minton is 'actively disliked' by his colleagues."

The letter from Mr. Kunkel to the senators and the sixty-six replies were
printed in the *Journal-Gazette* and were reprinted in the *Corydon Democrat*,
on June 28, 1939.[18]

How had the impression arisen in the press that Minton was disliked by
Senate colleagues? Perhaps it was because Minton was a hard-hitting fighter.
When Minton went into a debate the casual observer might think that he
and his opponent were bitter enemies. For example, on July 28, 1939, he
and Wheeler were in the midst of a debate. Minton accused Wheeler of
putting words in his mouth. Retorted Wheeler, "The senator's mouth is big
enough so that I can do it!"[19]

Minton created a furor in the McNutt candidacy for President in 1940
when he gave an interview in Washington on June 17, 1939, and proclaimed
that "Paul V. McNutt won't seek the presidency in the event President
Roosevelt wants a third term." The interview came as a surprise to Frank
McHale and other spokesmen for McNutt, who considered it clearly dam-
aging to the McNutt candidacy. Obviously no one would care about the
McNutt movement until Roosevelt broke his silence. Most Democrats
thought that Minton had made a serious mistake. Minton said the press
kept prodding him, demanding to know how he could be such a constant
Roosevelt booster and at the same time be favorable to McNutt.[20] The interview did produce sentiment among New Dealers that Minton would make
an ideal running mate for Roosevelt in 1940.

And then all political talk was suspended momentarily as the nation's
attention focused intently elsewhere. Germany had invaded Poland. On
September 1, 1939, Roosevelt called an emergency meeting of his top advi-

sors to discuss the European situation before he called a special session of the Congress on September 21. He needed to consider repeal of the arms embargo. It was a varied group which met in the President's office, because Roosevelt wanted to stress the bipartisan nature of the crisis. Accordingly, Secretary of State Cordell Hull, Vice President Garner, Speaker of the House William Bankhead, Senate Majority Leader Barkley, Minority Leader Charles McNary, House Majority Leader Sam Rayburn and Minority Leader Joe Martin were there. Governor Alfred M. Landon, titular leader of the Republican party, and Colonel Frank Knox, Landon's running mate in 1936, were invited. Senator Key Pittman, Chairman of the Foreign Relations Committee, attended, along with Senator James Byrnes, the Democratic moderate in the Senate, Senator Warren Austin from Vermont, and Senator Minton. Congressmen Sol Bloom and Carl Mapes also were present.[21]

Roosevelt shared with the group all of the information he had received on the last-minute negotiations between Germany and the other involved nations before the war commenced. He then asked for bipartisan action on repeal of the Neutrality Act. Minton was convinced after this meeting that the United States would ultimately be involved in the war in Europe.

The Neutrality Act, or the Nye Bill, enacted in 1935, placed a mandatory embargo on all arms shipments to any belligerent in any future war—even if one belligerent was a long-tested friend of America and another belligerent was the known and unforgiving enemy of the United States.

It was becoming difficult to remain neutral—very difficult. A month before the invasion of Poland, British Prime Minister Neville Chamberlain submitted a personal plea to Roosevelt requesting the secret Norden bombsight for use by England. Roosevelt was forced to reply that the request "could not be granted unless the sight desired by the British Government was made available to all other governments at the same time."[22]

On September 21 Roosevelt convened Congress in special session and asked for repeal of the arms embargo. It was a bitter fight. German interests began a campaign to stop repeal and congressmen were flooded with letters. Aviator Charles Lindbergh, by then considered an authority on foreign affairs, spoke against repeal on September 15 and October 13. The White House mounted an intense behind-the-scenes effort with Vice President Garner (this time on Roosevelt's side), the manager of the strategy.

A memorandum from Garner, dated September 21, 1939, revealed his plan: "Tell Barkley, Sherman Minton and Jim Byrnes to do two things: 1. To keep their mouths shut and to shut off debate. 2. Keep the ball going at least six hours a day for a week. If, at the end of a week, a filibuster starts, have night sessions and move the convening hour from noon to 11:00 and run it through to 10:00 or 11:00 every night. Tell them we are going to take care of neutrality first. Such other legislation as might be desired for emergency purposes might be considered after neutrality has been passed but NOT before."[23]

The isolationists fought repeal with rhetoric—Roosevelt planned, they said, "to send the boys of American mothers to fight on the battlefields of Europe." Amendments were offered to bar the sale of flamethrowers and poison gas.[24]

On September 22 representatives from Fort Wayne, armed with a petition containing five-thousand signatures against repeal, delivered their paperwork to Senators Minton and Van Nuys in Washington. Both senators declared that they were going to vote for repeal of the arms embargo. Minton was asked if he was willing to be a murderer. "No," replied Minton, "but I'm willing to supply a weapon to a man who is defending himself against a murderer."[25]

The Senate repealed the arms embargo provisions of the Neutrality Act on October 27, by a vote of sixty-three to thirty, and the House did the same on November 3. Roosevelt signed the joint resolution passed by Congress on November 4. Now England and France could buy ammunition and other implements of war they needed from America—on a cash-and-carry basis only. Roosevelt credited Senators Barkley, Minton, and Byrnes for steering the repeal of the arms embargo through the Senate.[26]

Minton had staunchly supported his chief because he knew that the President was right. The country would inevitably have to support its European friends or see them perish. Minton was to pay the price for his "war inevitability" views back home in Indiana. The Midwest historically had been a region where isolation was preferred over involvement in European affairs. Four generations of Scotch-Irish individualists, and others in the state, had come to feel that England, France, and the other countries in Europe couldn't be trusted. He was "on the wrong side of the crick" as far as many voters in Indiana were concerned, and the election was coming up.

But Minton's popularity was not in question in Washington, D.C. The year 1940 found him at the height of his power in the Senate and in the administration. Bills that were introduced needed not only his blessing but also his assistance as majority whip. Clearly, during this period, he was the ubiquitous prince of the New Deal, legislative custodian of the Democratic Party's progressive philosophy and one of Roosevelt's most trusted lieutenants. "When Minton rises to speak now, he is accorded more respect than he has enjoyed since his early days here."[27] Minton maintained that he was doing what he was supposed to do, "I am a lawyer," he said, "and a lawyer's duty is to represent his clients. When I was elected, the people of Indiana wanted to send someone here to uphold President Roosevelt. They were my clients and I have represented them as I said I would."[28]

As a member of the Senate Military Affairs Committee, Minton traveled some thirteen thousand miles to inspect military installations in the United States. He returned concerned, disheartened, and alarmed. America did not have an "army or the equipment to fit one out if we had one," he sadly concluded.[29]

Continuing to sound the alarm, Minton addressed the Young Democrats of Indiana at their state convention in Evansville on May 25, 1940. Emphasizing the nation's lack of preparedness, he predicted that Hitler would "induce Japan to attack us in the Pacific."[30]

In 1940 Minton aided General George C. Marshall, Chief of Staff of the United States Army, in his effort to streamline the Army, particularly the promotion system. He sponsored a bill which permitted a colonel to retire at age sixty instead of sixty-four, thus creating vacancies and permitting lower-grade officers to move up through the ranks. The measure passed the Senate in early June 1940, and on June 8 General Marshall wrote to Minton thanking him for his "leadership and assistance given to the Army." He stated that the bill was "one of the most important pieces of legislation in the interest of National Defense."[31]

On June 21 Minton made an impassioned plea in the Senate for military preparedness. "I have sons who are eligible to carry arms of their country today, and I am not a warmonger. I will turn my back upon my boys in shame if they turn their backs upon the flag of their country that my grandfather fought and died for in the Civil War and I offered my life for in 1917 and 1918. I saw war in Europe. I saw how towns were leveled and made shambles. I saw the victims of the war . . . the refugees, the wounded, the suffering and the dying. I do not want to see that condition come to America."[32]

Much of the administration-backed legislation introduced in the Congress in 1940 dealt with national defense and military preparedness. As the Battle of Britain raged in Europe, America inevitably prepared for a war that no one wanted to admit was coming:

> On June 13, 1940, the Military Supply Act was passed, allotting $1.8 billion for the military forces of the United States.
>
> On June 20 Roosevelt, seeking coalition, named Republicans Henry L. Stimson as Secretary of War and Frank Knox as Secretary of Navy.
>
> On August 9 the National Guard Service Bill was passed by a vote of seventy-one to seven.

In June, Roosevelt had requested authority from Congress to call members of the National Guard and reservists to active duty to "maintain our position of neutrality." The isolationists railed against the bill. Democratic Senator Rush D. Holt of West Virginia spoke against it in bitter terms. He stormed that this conscription program did not come from America but from foreign shores and was incubated in the banks and law firms on Wall Street. Minton responded, "I, for one, am supporting this legislation because I believe it is my patriotic duty to do so. I do not want to have to conscript boys. But we do not have any choice in the matter." Then he spoke of what Hitler's armies had done to the democracies of the world. Hitler's aim was to set up the rule of his own people over the rest of us. "I do not want to see the will of a foreign conqueror imposed upon the free people of America."

On September 16, 1940, the Selective Training and Service Act was signed and Roosevelt rejoiced; he had given the bill all of the quiet support he could.

The act required registration of all males in the United States between the ages of twenty-one and thirty-five. Those "selected" were to serve for one year in the Western Hemisphere. During the acrimonious debate on this act, Minton went so far as to impugn the patriotism of its opponents. "If we are not willing to go ahead and meet our obligations as citizens, then we deserve what we'll get."[33]

On October 16, registration day, 16.4 million young men signed up with a minimum of protest.

On October 29 Secretary of War Henry L. Simson drew the first number in the nation's first peacetime military draft lottery.

On November 25 the first draftees, 18,700 of them, entered the Army.

Minton was up for re-election in 1940. As international and national tensions escalated, he was forced to give some time to his own campaign for re-election. It was, of course, inevitably tied to that of Franklin D. Roosevelt.

Wendell Lewis Willkie, a lifelong Democrat who had opposed the New Deal, and who had switched to the Republican Party just the year before, had been nominated for President by the Republicans on June 28, 1940, defeating veterans Thomas E. Dewey and Robert A. Taft (the choices of the regulars). Minton told the National Colored Democratic Association on July 14 that Willkie had "changed his position as fast as Joe Louis."[34] Again, on October 17, at a Democratic party rally in Tomlinson Hall in Indianapolis, Minton chastised Willkie:

America's vital arms of national defense and mobilization for defense cannot be left to one who has never mobilized anything but high electric rates and watered utility stock. That is a job for which no leader in this country is so ably qualified as Franklin D. Roosevelt, who organized and built a section of naval defense. Here's a man who knows America's defense by heart and will not take four years to learn it. The Republican candidate may be a good soapbox debater; he may know how to win legal battles and force his government to pay dearly for obsolete and disconnected utility properties; he may even know what it takes of utility money to win Republican nominations and to influence votes in an election. But what does he know of answering diplomatic insults and of winning arguments with dictators who respect no other authority than national armed strength? When President Roosevelt began urging appropriations for national defense four years ago, the backers of Mr. Willkie were traveling in the ranks of the present fifth columnists. Because the President urged a big naval building program, the Willkie crowd charged him with offending the dictators and inviting war for America. Every step he has taken for the strengthening of national defense has been doggedly opposed by the appeasement bunch of

*the opposition. And now they reverse their tactics and accuse the President
of being dilatory in the building of national defense. We are preparing not
to go to war, but so others will not go to war against us.*[35]

The Hatch Act, sponsored by Senator Carl A. Hatch of New Mexico, had
been passed in 1939. It prohibited rank and file federal workers from engag-
ing in political campaigns. In 1940 Hatch proposed to extend this prohibition to include state employees who were paid in part by federal funds. Minton
opposed the measure from the beginning, and his opposition put him in the
rare position of opposing Roosevelt. Minton reported after a luncheon with
the President at the White House on March 5 that "the President listened
attentively to my squawks but was not very sympathetic to them."[36] The
extension was passed. Because the extension would prohibit these state
employees in Indiana from contributing to the Two Percent Clubs, Minton's
opponents suggested this was the reason he opposed the act. He was finally
having to choose between his loyalty to McNutt and Indiana Democrats
and his allegiance to Roosevelt, they alleged.

The international situation brought pressing legislative issues to the forefront almost weekly. Minton was concerned about the growth of subversive
influences in the country as early as 1938 and had urged the adoption of the
Smith Act. At that time, however, most legislators viewed the proposal in
the same light as the infamous Alien and Sedition Act of 1798. The Smith
Act, requiring that three and a half million aliens register and be finger-
printed and fined or imprisoned for anything written or spoken that could
subvert the armed forces, finally was signed by President Roosevelt in July
of 1940.[37]

But the clouds of the election had to loom even larger than those of the
war in Europe for Minton, who faced the re-election fight of his life. His
Republican opponent was Raymond Eugene Willis, a newspaper publisher
in Angola, Indiana. Willis was from Waterloo in northeastern Indiana's
Dekalb County, and had run unsuccessfully against Senator Van Nuys in
1938. Against the odds, Minton waged a vigorous campaign but lost. The
isolationist fear gripping this conservative section of the country and several bad years in the corn belt were factors in the loss.

On November 5, 1940, returns showed that Minton had lost by 23,267 votes (888,070 to 864,803). Though his idol Roosevelt won the national election, he lost Indiana to Willkie in 1940 by 25,403 votes (899,466 to 874,063). Harold L. Ickes later criticized Roosevelt for not doing more for Minton. "Toward the end of the campaign I was confident that the President would win, although I will admit that I was very anxious. Of these doubtful states, I believed that we would win in Pennsylvania, Ohio, and Illinois. I hoped that we would carry Indiana but I had been under such grave doubt that I had particularly urged the President to go to Indiana to make a speech. If he had done that, he would have carried Indiana and saved Senator Minton, who deserved this aid on the part of the President because he had been a fighting New Dealer during the last six years in Washington."[38]

Senator George W. Norris of Nebraska, a good friend, wrote to Minton on November 16 to express his condolences. His letter thoroughly analyzes the outcome of the recent election:

I feel very badly about your defeat. I do not know who the successful man is but your defeat is certainly a national loss. The successful candidate may be a very fine man but I do not understand why the people of Indiana defeated you. I have been very much dissatisfied over the outcome in my home State and also in the States of South Dakota, North Dakota, Kansas, and other western States. These States have received support from the Roosevelt Administration second to none in the United States. This part of the country would to a very great extent have been depopulated if it had not been for the Administration and yet these same men who have received so much assistance voted for Willkie in large numbers. I want to make a study of the German vote in this State. I have not as yet been able to do so because I have not received sufficient reports from the State. From what little I know about it, I do not believe the German vote was as bad as I anticipated it might be. It seems to me that, in this controversy, while there were several other things involved, the great weakness was that God was on the other side. He refused to let it rain for five or six years. Everyone became discouraged and I think unreasonable—yet it is probably perfectly natural that this should be so. Men who see their crops lost because of the burning winds, so hot that it is almost impossible to breath [sic], naturally become very discouraged. . . .

The utility people put up a great fight for Willkie and, of course, I knew they would. They had organizations which extended into every hamlet and every community in the United States—money was plentiful and flowed freely.

At your leisure, I wish you would write me a letter. Although you will not be in the Senate I do not want to lose contact with you. . . .

Of all the men in the Senate, President Roosevelt ought to have more regard for you than for any other.[39]

Minton replied to Norris on November 25 with his own analysis of his defeat:

Thank you so much for your good letter of the sixteenth, and above all, for your friendship and good will that prompted you to do so many fine things for me in the campaign. Words fail me to adequately express my appreciation. My defeat was softened by the realization that you approved of my efforts while I served with you in the Senate, for above all others, I have cherished that goal. Indiana, as I have often told you, is a peculiar State, politically. The cross currents are infinite. Had the President carried Indiana, I would have been elected, as I ran several thousand votes ahead of him. If the President could have found it possible to speak at Indianapolis, we would have won, but he couldn't go everywhere.

We expected to carry Indianapolis by 12,000 to 13,000, but we lost it by 3,000. Had we carried it, as expected, we would have won. Several things worked against us. We had organization difficulties. Our Catholic friends turned us down, and there is a larger German vote in Indianapolis and the well-to-do people voted in unprecedented numbers. Outside of Indianapolis all of the German communities went heavily against us. Had these communities voted by anything near the normal vote, we would have been elected. The best evidence of this was that the only man on our ticket elected was our candidate for Governor, Mr. Schricker, who was a German Lutheran. He squeezed through by 3,900 votes, and in every German community got the normal vote, except one, and there he ran way ahead of the rest of the ticket. Labor was solidly behind us in all except Fort Wayne and Indianapolis. Lewis hurt us some in the coal counties, which we lost, or had our majorities largely reduced. The rural communities, by

unheard of majorities, almost suspicious majorities in some places, wiped
out our fine showing in the industrial sections.

I think the Farm Bureau gave us a fine double-crossing. Secretary
Wickard told me before I went home for the campaign, that he had positive
information that Willkie's brother, and others, met with the President of
Farm Bureau and the head of the Farm Co-Operatives in Indiana, and
told them that if Willkie was elected and they carried Indiana, one of those
two would be Secretary of Agriculture. They each lived in good Demo-
cratic counties, but were Republicans, and we lost one of the Counties by
a large majority we should have had in our favor, and carried the other by
a majority of one-third of what it should have been.

The normal Republican rural counties rolled up such majorities as we
had never seen before. The use of money was lavish. The State Committee
has filed a report, admitting that they raised and spent $542,000. . . .

. . . I do not know what my future will be. I have had no intimation
from the President that he has anything in mind, so I suppose I will be going
back home to try and pick up my law practice. Though not there to follow
your lead in the Senate, I shall be watching you from afar and ready and
willing to do anything I can from my obscure position, and be sure that my
affectionate regards and best wishes go with you always.[40]

As he prepared to vacate his office and leave Washington, Minton was
discouraged by the silence from the White House. It seemed that now, when
he had lost the election, the administration for which he had labored so
diligently the past six years was ignoring its faithful defender.

On December 20 Minton and his daughter left Washington for New
Albany. As he was running to catch the train, his legs folded under him.
When they were safely aboard the train, Minton turned to his daughter and
said, "Mary-Anne, I don't know what happened." It may have been the
start of the pernicious anemia from which he suffered during the later years
of his life. Pernicious anemia is a severe, often fatal, form of anemia, characterized by a progressive decrease in the number of red blood cells; symptoms
include pallor, muscle weakness, shortness of breath, and disturbances of
the gastrointestinal and nervous systems.[41] Various health problems were
beginning to surface about this time for Minton and it is possible that the
anemia was the cause. Certainly, health problems were to be a major factor

in his life from the time he left the Senate.

The year 1941 dawned bleak and dreary for Sherman Minton. He had been defeated for re-election and was unemployed. His return to his law practice in New Albany with the firm of Stotsenburg, Weathers and Minton had its difficulties. He had been gone from the firm for more than seven years, and clients have a habit of disappearing when an attorney is absent for that long. Minton was at loose ends. On December 6, 1940, he lamented to his good friend, Senator Lister Hill of Alabama: "Nothing has developed. I had lunch yesterday with Tom Corcoran and he told me he thought some vacancies on the bench would develop in the District of Columbia that I might be interested in, and today I talked to Bob Jackson but he did not think any of them will develop until after the Inauguration." On this melancholy note, Minton continued "So, you see, I just drift along with the tide and nothing is happening that I know anything about. I have no doubt that there may be some developments later on, but just when they will materialize, no one seems to know and I suppose when I get back to Indiana my interests may be forgotten."[42]

The family was upset by the sudden change also. They were living at the Wardman Park Hotel where the rent was not cheap. Anxiety about finances was troubling; Sherman, soon to be twenty-two, was a student at the Indiana University School of Medicine. Mary-Anne would be entering college in the fall, while John, almost sixteen, was still in high school. Obviously they and their mother, who liked peace in her home, were going to need stability.

However, it was not long before Minton's anxieties were put to rest.

On Tuesday afternoon, January 7, 1941, President Roosevelt announced at a press conference Minton's appointment as a White House administrative assistant. Roosevelt said that Minton "will be legs, eyes, and ears for me." The President made it clear, however, that Minton would not be a liaison person between the White House and Congress because Congress "resents a White House lobbyist playing the buttonhole game on the Hill."

"Shay," said Roosevelt, "will have a passion for anonymity in this job as administrative assistant."[43]

Earlier in the day Minton had been summoned to the White House; he was all smiles when he left. His smile broadened after Roosevelt made the public announcement. His salary would be ten thousand dollars a year, the same he had received as a senator.

Although Minton undoubtedly welcomed the opportunity to serve his leader as a private assistant, the duties of this new position must have been somewhat deflating in actual practice. He had been in the forefront of every battle on every issue while in the Senate and now he was relegated to the ambiguous role of an unseen and unheard person behind the scenes in government. Lines of authority were uncertain. In fact, Minton did not possess any authority except such authority as Roosevelt gave him on a case-by-case basis. Publicly Minton referred to the four months he spent on this job as one of the "richest in my life,"[44] but it may be that he was being charitable and did not want to offend Roosevelt.

Whatever his feelings about the position, an event occurred while Minton was on the job which was significant. Not only had it had a profound influence on his own life, but also on that of his good friend, Senator Harry S. Truman.

With the country gearing for war production and national defense, it became apparent that Congress was going to investigate war contracts and other defense activities. Several resolutions to take a strong look at defense plants and related activities had been introduced in Congress by early 1941. Among these resolutions was one that had been introduced by Senator Truman, who had seen appalling waste in the construction of Fort Leonard Wood at Rolla, Missouri, in 1941. There were political implications, because the senator who introduced and sponsored the resolution to be eventually adopted would serve as chairman of the investigative committee. On February 27 Minton alerted Roosevelt with a "Memorandum for the President": "I just talked with Jim Byrnes. Unless you disagree he will report at once for passage the Truman Resolution to investigate defense activities. This is a matter of strategy to keep investigation in friendly hands in the Senate and away from unfriendly House fellows like Cox. Barkley agrees with Jim. I agree with them. The Truman Resolution is the best out. What shall I tell Jim?"[45] Roosevelt agreed with this strategy and at the bottom of this memorandum he scribbled "S.M. OK FDR."[46]

After Truman had been selected as the vice-presidential candidate to run with Roosevelt on the Democratic ticket in 1944, Minton enclosed this memorandum in a letter to Truman on October 11: "I enclose a little 'scrap of paper' that I thought you might be interested in seeing; and if you would like to have it to add to your papers, I shall be glad to give it to you. You can see from a perusal of it that your old seatmate was batting for you when he was down at the White House. You will recognize the pencil memorandum at the bottom of the sheet as that of the Boss himself."[47]

The exposure and publicity given to Truman during World War II as chairman of the Truman Committee—the group which became known for its careful investigation of defense spending—rocketed him into national prominence and secured for him the vice-presidential nomination. He did not forget the role Minton had played in thrusting him into the national limelight.

Although there is a hazard in reading too much into a little "scrap of paper" and in attaching too much significance to one event, the facts are that Truman became President on April 12, 1945, upon the death of Roosevelt, and that Minton was appointed by Truman as an associate justice of the Supreme Court four years later.

But of course other events had to intervene to qualify him—the most important and obvious of which was experience on the bench, and fate was about to intervene in that area. On April 27, 1941, Judge Walter E. Treanor of Bloomington, Indiana, died. Treanor had been a judge on the United States Circuit Court of Appeals for the Seventh Circuit in Chicago, recommended by Minton for appointment to the bench in 1938.

A few days later, as Minton was delivering a routine memorandum to the Oval Office, he exchanged a few words with the President. When he turned to leave, Roosevelt stopped him and asked almost as an afterthought, "By the way, Shay, would you be interested in that vacancy in the Seventh Circuit?"[48] Yes, the former senator from Indiana would!

Roosevelt nominated Minton for the federal judgeship on May 7. The nomination was referred to the Senate Judiciary Committee, of which Van Nuys of Indiana was chairman. Van Nuys promised that the nomination would receive prompt attention. On May 15 the nomination was confirmed by a unanimous vote. Minton took his oath of office as a member of the court on May 29.

A few days earlier, on May 12, Minton had written to his good friend W. A. Alexander, librarian at Indiana University, some thoughts about his elevation to the bench: "While I look forward with pleasure to my new assignment, I assume it with a tinge of sadness because my appointment was made possible by the death of our dear mutual friend, Judge Treanor. I only hope that my service on the bench may approximate in worth and distinction his service."[49]

Federal judges serve for life, and Minton and his family now had security. As a judge he would earn twelve thousand dollars a year, two thousand dollars more than he made in the Senate or the White House.

After his confirmation, Minton moved his family back to New Albany. They bought a large, stately house at 1540 Sunset Drive, on a hill overlooking the Ohio River in a part of the city known as Silver Hills. The only house that he and Mrs. Minton ever owned, they called this residence "Lone Oak." It would be the Mintons' home for the rest of his life, and one can only imagine his wife's joy, returning to these hills which she had left with such reluctance a decade earlier.

Chapter Six

Judge of the Court of Appeals and Appointment to the Supreme Court

MINTON WAS ENTERING A VENERABLE, COMPLEX, AND WELL ORGANIZED SYSTEM OF the judiciary. The Court of Appeals for the Seventh Circuit, located in 1941 at 1212 North Lake Shore Drive in Chicago, is the federal appellate court for the states of Illinois, Indiana, and Wisconsin, in which seven district or trial courts are located.

These circuit courts or courts of appeal review trial records from the district courts whose final judgments are appealable as a matter of right. The circuit courts also review trial records from the independent, regulatory commissions and some of the administrative agencies of the federal government, including direct appeals from specified ones such as the National Labor Relations Board and the Federal Trade Commission.

The Supreme Court of the United States, of course, is the court of last resort in the federal judicial system. An appeal to the Supreme Court is not a matter of right. The Supreme Court itself decides whether to hear a case from below. The only exception to that decision-making power is in those rare cases where a circuit court declares a federal law unconstitutional; then the Supreme Court must hear it.

Each of the circuit courts is "headed" by a justice of the Supreme Court— a carryover from the original practice of "circuit-riding," when a justice literally would travel by horseback in the course of fulfilling his judicial duties.

Since he had been sworn in in Washington, there was no ceremony when Minton assumed the bench in Chicago in October 1941. On arrival he was shown to his chambers, where he donned the customary black robe, after which he headed for the bench at that very hour with judges Otto Kerner and William M. Sparks. Judge Minton told reporters that he was "here to work."[1]

When Minton arrived, the Seventh Circuit included four other appellate judges: Evan A. Evans, Sparks, J. Earl Major, and Kerner. The senior judge of the five usually would assign one district judge and two appellate judges to a case. Drawing a district judge to hear a case at the circuit court was a common practice in those years, one which has become less common more recently, as Congress provides more judges to the circuit courts.

During Minton's term with the Seventh Circuit, the judges shared a warm and cooperative relationship, often meeting informally, with relaxed camaraderie marking their relationships. An advocate of close communication, Minton approved of this arrangement because he believed that camaraderie would permit the judges to resolve differences amicably, which in turn would smooth the work of the court.

However, Minton had been in his new position only a few months when Pearl Harbor shocked the world, ushering in the grim new era the former senator had predicted. Thereafter, he and other federal judges were inundated with cases without precedent and involving special wartime measures, selective service, price controls, rationing, and civil liberties in wartime.

During the eight years Minton served on the bench of the Seventh Circuit, he wrote 196 opinions, representing a full range of judicial subject matter. However, he wrote only twelve dissents. He apparently preferred to join the majority opinion unless he had strong feelings on a given issue. He also believed that the court should present a united front. If one or more of the judges were to write separate opinions, he thought, those dissenting opinions could confuse the judges in the district courts about the actual holding of the court and what the law was on an issue.

Minton's opinions were brief, simple, and orderly for the most part while he was on the Seventh Circuit. He stated the appeal issue as simply and as pointedly as it could be phrased. Then he proceeded to an examination of the arguments, answered each question in order, and summarized the conclusion. His composition was devoid of rhetorical tricks, his sentences were short and well composed, his language straightforward. It must also be said that his opinions were for the most part usually dry, seldom exciting, and sometimes even dull.

Occasionally, there would be a case where the facts stimulated his fancy and he would write a delightfully phrased opinion. One such case was *Modernistic Candies, Inc. v. Federal Trade Commission*. Modernistic Candies Com pany made a machine which would dispense a piece of gum when a penny was inserted. Most of the gum was one color. Once in a while a lucky boy or girl would receive a piece of gum of another color which entitled the recipient to a bonus from the house. The FTC issued an injunction against the company prohibiting the sale of these machines because the agency deemed it gambling in interstate commerce. The defense was that gambling was instinctive to man. The Seventh Circuit upheld the injunction in an opinion by Judge Minton, who wryly wrote:

> *Counsel for the petitioner discussed at great length from a sociological point of view, the age-old problem of the gambling instinct in the human being. According to his analysis, gambling pervades our entire economic system; thus insurance contracts are gambles, stock and grain exchange transactions are gambles, and the farmer's dependence on the weather is a gamble. Counsel's attempt to apply this analysis to the present case left us cold and unimpressed. He even reminded us that our great idol, Mr. Chief Justice John Marshall, in his day attended the horse races and wagered with his clergyman. In fact, they ran a book. As indicating how times have changed, and how even our coarse nature has yielded to the protecting care of governmental policy, we confess we do not even know a bookmaker, clerical or otherwise, and our passes to the beautiful race tracks around Chicago lie in our desk unused. 145 F. 2d 454, 455 (7th cir., 1944).*

Minton often stated his position that as a judge he would "pronounce the law as it was written, but on no occasion would he make the law."[2]

Shortly after he assumed the bench on the Seventh Circuit, a case came before him which shows how difficult it sometimes is for judges to decide a case in which the facts are unpleasant or painful.

The case was *Nellie B. Wigginton v. The Order of United Commercial Travelers of America*, an insurance company, 126 F. 2d 659 (7th cir., 1942). The insured was killed when a shotgun he was cleaning discharged. The beneficiary of the life insurance policy claimed the benefits of the policy. A provision in the fraternal benefit certificate insuring against accidental death stipulated that in the event of a self-inflicted death, the company was not liable unless an eyewitness was present at the time of the event to attest to the involuntary nature of the act. No one had been in the room when the shotgun discharged. There was testimony from witnesses present immedi-ately before and immediately after the accident. The district court had ruled in favor of the beneficiary. Minton, writing for the court, started with the proposition that insurance contracts are to be construed against the com-pany in order to protect the insured if that can reasonably be done. And what about the "eyewitness" requirement? He held that it was ambiguous—did "eyewitness" refer to the shooting or the dying of the insured? The lan-guage would be construed against the insurance company, he wrote. There was an "eyewitness" to the dying. The requirements of the policy were met and the judgment of the lower court was affirmed.

Judge Minton relied upon the doctrine of precedent, supporting the con-tinuity of the law. His opinions usually contained long citations of past de-cisions. Also, from his experience as a practicing attorney, he knew how important it was for a lawyer to be able to research the applicable law on the matter and advise a client.

He also was convinced that a judge should never substitute his opinion or his will for that of the legislature. He remembered from his days in the Senate that the Supreme Court had struck down one by one the economic and social acts of the New Deal. Thus, as a judge, he scrupulously avoided injecting any of his own ideas into his interpretation of acts of Congress. "It is not necessary for us to justify the policy of Congress. It is enough that we find it in the statute," he wrote in an opinion while on the Supreme Court.[3]

His respect for the untrammeled legislative process was almost as strong as his respect for our federal system of government. He considered it "indeli-cate" for a federal court to interfere with proceedings in a state court.[4] Be-fore any interference was justified, all state remedies first had to be exhausted. In *United States ex rel. Feeley v. Ragen*, he expressed his personal philosophy on federal courts *vis-à-vis* state courts:

> We should not lose sight of the fact that the federal courts are being used to invade the sovereign jurisdiction of the States, presumed to be competent to handle their own police affairs, as the constitution recognized when the police power was left with the States. We are not super-legislatures or glo-rified parole boards. We as courts look only to the violation of Federal Constitutional rights. When we condemn a State's exercise of its jurisdic-tion and hold that the exercise of its power is not in accordance with due

process, we are in effect trying the States . . . 166 F.2d 976, 981 (7th Cir., 1948).

As a judge, Minton was most reluctant to overturn a decision of the lower court. He believed, as do many jurists, that the trial court is closer to the facts in a case. Minton, in most instances, would not vote for reversal unless the district court acted without or beyond its jurisdiction. In one case, he dissented from an opinion by the Seventh Circuit that had ordered a new trial where the trial court knowingly had admitted perjured testimony.[5]

Minton often invoked the rule of "harmless error" to keep from having to reverse the lower court. Harmless error holds that improprieties made in the course of a trial are not grounds for reversal if they neither prejudiced the substantive rights of the losing party nor affected the outcome. He was willing to overlook errors in a trial if he thought the proceedings had been fair overall.[6]

Minton's term in the Senate had given him a profound respect for an act of Congress and the need to apply it with an accuracy that would not thwart the legislative intent or engraft upon it language that was not there. He would not grant judicial review of an administrative action by an agency of the executive branch of the government unless Congress expressly provided for such review. Congress had provided that the ruling of certain administrative agencies were "final" and their review by federal courts was thereby precluded. Minton wrote in such cases in this manner:

United States v. Daily, 139 F.2d 7,9 (7th Cir., 1944), majority opinion, "The District Court has no authority to review the proceedings of the Draft Board."

Bowles v. Lizak, 142 F.2d 787, 789 (7th Cir., 1944), "The [District] Court had no right here to control by its order the manner in which the Administrator [Office of Price Administration] might conduct his investigation."

Schreiber v. United States, 129 F.2d 836, 840 (7th Cir., 1942), was an action to recover a refund for excess postage which plaintiffs were required to pay for mailing certain items as first-class mail instead of the third-class rate. Plaintiffs won in the trial court, but the judgment was reversed by the Seventh Circuit. Minton wrote in a dissenting opinion: "Congress did not provide for judicial review. On the contrary, it left the decision to the discretion of the Postmaster General. It is his discretion and not ours that has received the sanction of Congress. The Postmaster General has decided against the appellees [Schreiber]. That exhausts their remedy. No resort to the courts is authorized. If we had the right to act in this case, I would agree with the conclusion of the majority. I do not think a right of action within the jurisdiction of the District Court is stated."

His decisions in the field of civil liberties could be seen as somewhat surprising in view of his well-known personal progressivism. While on the bench at the Seventh Circuit from 1941 to 1949, Minton wrote opinions in thirty-two cases where there was an alleged violation of one or more civil rights guaranteed by the first ten amendments to the Constitution—the Bill of Rights. He ruled in favor of the state in twenty-seven of these cases.

Minton apparently decided these civil rights cases according to the doctrine of "fundamental fairness" enunciated in 1937 by Mr. Justice Cardozo writing for the Supreme Court in *Palko v. Connecticut*.[7] This case held that the requirements of due process were met where the defendant in a criminal case has received fair treatment by the state in light of all the facts and circumstances of the case. Minton also balanced conflicting rights. "The right of free speech . . . is not an absolute right. It is a relative right that may be modified in its interplay with the rights of others," he wrote in one case.[8] In the area of prohibition against unreasonable searches and seizures guaranteed by the Fourth Amendment, Minton, writing for the Seventh Circuit, wrote an opinion upholding a search of an automobile[9] without a warrant. He relied on the authority of a prior decision of the Supreme Court. This decision held that police officers might search moving vehicles without a warrant when they had probable cause to believe that the vehicles were instruments for illegal activity and when it appeared probable that the vehicles otherwise would escape before a warrant could be obtained.[10]

In cases involving the rights of aliens, Minton usually held against the noncitizens. In affirming the denial of habeas corpus to a resident-alien by the district court in one case, he wrote: "In a proceeding of this kind but one question is open to the relator [alien], and that is whether he is an enemy alien . . . if he is that ends the proceeding."[11] It was his position that in a deportation proceeding, the alien did not have any legal rights—his status was a political decision to be made by officials in government.

Minton wrote a particularly strong opinion in *United States v. Knauer*, a case in which the government had instituted action under the Naturalization Act of 1940 to revoke and cancel the certificate of naturalization issued to a German sympathizer and a member of the German-American Bund. He wrote:

> *This was no beer drinking, song singing gab-fest in Deutsch by a group of nostalgic old burghers. This organization had a serious purpose, a tragically serious and sinister purpose. It was, as defendant said, "Hitler's grip on America." It was the instrument chosen to lay the ground work for the Nazi infiltration into this country . . . 149 F.2d 519,522 (7th Cir., 1945).*

This case was affirmed on appeal to the Supreme Court. In his opinion, Justice Douglas paraphrased extensively the language of Minton.[12]

Labor cases under the National Labor Relations Act, the Federal Employers' Liability Act and the Fair Labor Standards Act were numerous while Minton was a judge on the Seventh Circuit. He authored thirty-four opinions and ruled in favor of labor or the worker in twenty of them. The opinions show an obvious desire for fairness on the part of the judiciary. "As a judge," he stated, "you are responsible for the law in each case, with no leaning over fences. I have decided cases against labor and against corporations, according to the law—the law must be nonpolitical."[13]

Minton accorded the National Labor Relations Board, as he did all agencies, the freedom in which to perform its duties. In order to establish an unfair labor practice interfering with, restraining and coercing the employees in their right to organize, he did not consider it necessary to show duress, but only interference on the part of an employer. Neither was it necessary to show that the interference by the employer was successful. In his view the slightest interference, intimidation or coercion by the employer in the exercise of the worker's right to self-organize constituted an unfair labor practice. In *Western Cartridge Co. v. National Labor Relations Board*, 139 F.2d 855 (7th Cir., 1943), he held the company guilty of intimidation of its employees in an anti-union campaign.

Yet, Minton would not tolerate violence or coercion on the part of the workers. If the workers participated in wildcat strikes or if a strike in any way threatened the efficiency of a company involved in the war effort, he would rule against labor in the disputes.

In a landmark labor law case, Minton held that pensions were a part of wages and hence a legitimate subject of collective bargaining. The ruling further held that the anti-Communist affidavits required by the Taft-Hartley Act were constitutional. *Inland Steel v. National Labor Relations Board*, 170 F.2d 247 (7th Cir., 1948). This holding was affirmed by the Supreme Court after Minton became a member in *American Communications Association v. Douds*, 339 U.S. 382 (1950). Justice Minton did not sit in the Douds case, but he later indicated his position in *Osman v. Douds*, 339 U.S. 846 (1950).

More in keeping with his earlier stated views were Minton's opinions on restraint of trade. In the field of unfair business practices—usually actual or threatened monopolies—Minton sided with the public interest and against the alleged monopolizer in eighteen out of twenty cases in which he wrote the majority opinion or dissented. He had "monopoly-phobia," according to one law review article.[14]

During his last year on the Seventh Circuit in 1949, Minton took on two corporate giants—the New York Great Atlantic and Pacific Tea Company (A & P) and Standard Oil of New Jersey.

The FTC, ruling that the A & P chain stores had violated the Sherman Antitrust Act by combining and conspiring to restrain the food trade in interstate commerce, had issued cease-and-desist orders. As was its right, A & P appealed to the Seventh Circuit. A & P—then the largest retail food chain in the country—was using its economic power to obtain favors in price from wholesalers, and then would undercut competitors in price and eventually force them out of business.

In *United States v. New York Great Atlantic & Pacific Tea Co.*,[15] Minton wrote one of his best-regarded opinions. First he reviewed the facts in the case. He described the highest echelon of the A & P hierarchy as a maze of interlocking directorates in a tight corporate structure. Company executives denied they had acted to further a conspiracy, but Minton was not convinced. "Byoir [one of the high officers] was thoroughly familiar with the policies of A & P. Byoir is no babe in the woods, likely not to understand what goes on around him." Then Minton waxed Shakespearean to address the price advantage: "This price advantage given A & P by suppliers was, it is fairly inferable, not 'twice blessed' like the quality of mercy that 'droppeth as the gentle rain from heaven.' It did not bless 'him that gives and him that takes.' Only A & P was blessed." He ruled against the company on the charge of restraint of trade, warning against the power of a large corporation to take unfair advantage of its competitors. 173 F.2d 79, 83, 89 (7th Cir., 1949).

Next came a controversial ruling on a case against Standard Oil Company. Again, the FTC charged the company with price discrimination and issued its cease-and-desist orders. Those orders were appealed by *Standard Oil Company v. Federal Trade Commission*, 173 F.2d 210 (7th Cir., 1949). Minton found that Standard had been selling gasoline to wholesale distributors, known in the industry as "jobbers," in the Detroit area at a lower cost than that charged to its retail customers. This action gave the jobbers a price advantage which they used to undersell retail outlets. The result was that competition in the Detroit area was diminished.

Standard Oil argued that it had adjusted its prices through necessity, in order to meet the same low price charged by other producers in the area. The company's defense was that these lower prices were charged in good faith to meet competition.

The Clayton Act, passed in 1914, provided that a company could discriminate in its prices if by so doing it was meeting competition in good faith. This loophole enabled large corporations to gobble up their small competitors. In 1936 Congress passed the Robinson-Patman Act, amending the Clayton Act and designed to tame the competitive jungle created by it. "Meeting competition in good faith" apparently was not now a complete defense but only a factor to be considered in these cases. But in 1949 it still was not clear what Robinson-Patman required.

After reviewing its legislative history, Minton concluded that by including the phrase "meeting competition in good faith," in the act, Congress did not intend for the corrective provisions of Robinson-Patman to be circumvented. He was convinced that the actions of Standard Oil were but local manifestations of a national pattern of collusive trade restraints. Writing for the court, Minton held that Standard Oil's defense could not stand—the company was, indeed, practicing injurious price discrimination.

Two years later, in 1951, when Minton was on the Supreme Court, the same *Standard Oil Company v. Federal Trade Commission* case came up on appeal. Justice Burton wrote the majority opinion, which reversed the earlier decision by Minton and held that, under Robinson-Patman, a price differential made in good faith to meet competition was a complete defense to a charge of price discrimination. Justice Minton did not participate in the case, *Standard Oil Company v. Federal Trade Commission*, 340 U.S. 231 (1951).

Interestingly, considering his Senate career as a no-holds-barred scrapper, the judicial Minton seems tough, stern, and conservative. And the latter-day Minton was dignified. With his tall stature, broad-shouldered and square-faced look, he projected a staid, proper air. He possessed an innate concept of judicial propriety, and he was careful to conduct himself to conform to this concept. Yet, underneath the judge's robes was a man who retained his sense of humor—at least from what we can read in his opinions, and he manifested the same sense of humanity he had shown in the Senate.

In *E. Edelmann and Co. v. Auto Parts and Gear Co.*, 127 F.2d 897 (7th Cir., 1942), his explanation for the denial of a patent to an alleged inventor showed the same wry humor with which he'd often assailed Senate colleagues:

> *What was the discovery of this alleged inventor? He discovered that when trying to read the hydrometer, the fluid and the float in the barrel needed to be stabilized. He conceived the brilliant idea that if you want to stabilize something without a base, you put a base on it. Could anything be simpler than that? If something without a base will not stand upright and steady, what is the first thing one would think of? A base, of course. Is that invention? If it is, then the human family has not understood what has been perfectly apparent ever since the first baby sat upright upon its own bottom. The stabilizing influence of that stance cannot be considered novel in the year 1942. 127 F.2d at 898–9.*

The patent was denied because it had been anticipated by the prior art; it was not novel and did not rise to the dignity of invention.

The opinion in *Tovar v. Jarecki*, 173 F.2d 449 (7th Cir., 1949), reveals the judicial Minton as the same kind and sympathetic man who had earlier crusaded for the rights of the unrepresented. Tovar was a Mexican, an alien laborer who spoke no English and who, when working steadily, earned fifty-five dollars a week in a steel mill in Chicago. With these earnings, the man supported a large family and made payments on a small house that he was purchasing. Tovar discovered marijuana growing in the alley behind his house and was smoking it when police officers burst into his home and made an illegal raid. Tovar was jailed and interrogated at length by a federal narcotics agent. A report was made to the Internal Revenue Service, whose officers immediately filed an assessment of more than seven thousand dollars on Tovar's home. The assessment was computed on the basis of a one-hundred-dollars-per-ounce tax on marijuana which the Internal Revenue Service could levy on any person found using marijuana without having first registered and paid a prescribed tax.

In most of his opinions, Minton confined himself to facts of the case as contained in the record. But in the Tovar marijuana case he did not. He looked beyond the record:

> *Even on this meager record, a proper conclusion could be reached that the state officers, the Federal Narcotic bureau, and the Internal Revenue bureau acted in close liaison, to put it mildly, from the time the plaintiff's home was illegally searched and he was arrested and incarcerated, to the alleged interview the narcotic agent had with him in jail, which was followed sometime later by the proceedings in the federal court and not in the state court. 173 F. 2d at 452.*

The IRS collector contended the procedure (without notice to Tovar or a hearing) was proper in this case because the assessment was authorized by a civil or taxing statute and not a criminal statute. Minton did not buy this argument. He held that the assessment was a penalty for use of the marijuana, not a tax within the ordinary meaning of the word.

The government also argued that Tovar had an adequate remedy at law, i.e., he could pay the tax of seven thousand dollars and sue to recover. This argument, too, fell on deaf ears. Minton wrote: "In this case it is clear on the whole record that this laboring man, struggling to buy a cheap home that cost four thousand dollars, and which he had only half paid for, could not pay this tax of over seven thousand dollars and sue in the normal course to recover. To insist upon such procedure is, as the District court said, 'unrealistic.' " 173 F. 2d at 451–2.

Judge and Mrs. Minton lived in a rented apartment in the Lake Shore Drive Hotel during his tenure in Chicago with the Seventh Circuit. They continued to enjoy family life as a closely knit group, supervised by a mother who enjoyed giving full time to her children's growth and progress.

The war affected the family, of course, as it did countless others across America. Their older son, Sherman, had received two degrees from Indiana University, an A.B. in 1939 and an M.D. in 1943. He promptly joined the Navy, and was stationed at San Diego, California. On October 10, 1943, Dr. Sherman Anthony Minton, lieutenant junior grade, married twenty-three-year-old Madge Alice Shortridge Rutherford, the daughter of Elmer Virgil and Irene Shortridge Rutherford of Greensburg, Indiana. Madge had joined the military service after graduating from Butler University in 1941, and was stationed at Long Beach, California.

The wedding was held at the First Baptist Church in San Diego with a few service friends in attendance. No one from either family could come because of wartime restrictions on travel. The couple was lucky enough to be granted a five-day leave; so they drove south of the border as far as the road went in those days—to Ensenada, then a little fishing village—where they spent three lovely days. Eventually, three daughters were born: Brooks on May 14, 1945; Mary April on April 8, 1951; and Holly Susan on July 14, 1952. Brooks, as first grandchild in the family, received a lot of attention from her grandfather Minton. When she was almost eight, Grandpa Minton wrote to tell her how proud he was of her in her Easter hat in a photograph which appeared in the newspaper in her hometown. The family reports that while Brooks was in college (about 1966), an instructor in her government class made a disparaging remark about the late Justice Minton and Brooks took the instructor to task right in front of her classmates.

After his tour of duty with the Navy, Dr. Minton joined the faculty of the Indiana University School of Medicine in 1947. As an assistant professor of microbiology, he taught the subject to medical students and to students in the allied health fields. He retired as a full professor in 1984.

Minton's only daughter, Mary-Anne, graduated from Indiana University in June 1944 with a B.S. degree. On June 12, 1945, she married dentist John H. Callanan in Holy Trinity Church in New Albany. They had five children: Patrick, born in 1947; Thomas in 1949; Charles in 1951; James in 1952; and Janet, born in 1959.

Judge and Mrs. Minton lived a quiet and unpretentious life in Chicago, with Gertrude staying in New Albany as much as possible, in order to be with the friends and family she loved. If she were "back home," Judge Minton would stuff his briefcase with pleadings and briefs and take the Monon train to southern Indiana as often as he could, working on the way there and back.

Although his residence was in the Midwest, affairs in the nation's capital were only as far away as the latest copy of *The Chicago Sun-Times*. In 1942 Minton was boosted by his former associates in Washington and mentioned prominently as the likely successor to Henry L. Stimson as Secretary of War in the event that Stimson retired.[16] He also was mentioned seriously as the vice presidential nominee to run with Roosevelt in 1944. Truman, of course, was selected and Roosevelt, by now tragically worn down by the war efforts and in ill health, was re-elected.

Minton's own health problems were clearly becoming noticeable by 1945. On March 16, 1945, he bemoaned to then Vice President Truman, "I think I am making some headway with my health. I am on a strict diet & I haven't had a tasty morsel of food in three weeks. Eating was one of the things I lived for! The other one is about gone too!"[17] Ill health did not prevent him from kidding and teasing Truman as he had when they had sat in the back row as freshman senators. In the same letter to Truman, he continued:

> I read all the newspaper accounts of your comings and goings. I hope you don't get the gout or delirium tremens with so much social this & that. Lew Schwellenbach was a bit worried about the Lauren Bacall picture but I wasn't, knowing you as I do. I still don't see how in the hell they ever got the picture. I would have been looking up those legs but you had your head turned as usual![18] [At a National Press Club party in February, 1945, a picture had been taken of Truman seated at a piano with Lauren Bacall sitting on top of the piano in a rather sexy pose. This photo-

graph was carried by many newspapers in the country.]

In early 1945, following widespread complaints about court-martial sentences given in cases overseas, President Roosevelt appointed Minton to a board of inquiry to review the entire system of court-martial proceedings. Roosevelt convened a board in Washington consisting of three circuit judges (including Minton), the Judge Advocate General of the Army and the Judge Advocate General of the Navy to review a great number of cases. If the board concluded that the sentence in a case was too severe, it could recommend that the President commute the sentence. Minton traveled between Washington, D.C., and Chicago for several months while working on this assignment—he still had his judicial duties to perform.

Roosevelt's association with Minton, which had now stretched over a decade and a half, was brought to an abrupt end on April 12, 1945, when the President died. Just as the war was ending, Harry S. Truman became the President of the United States. On April 13 his good friend Sherman Minton, in a "My dear Harry" letter, expressed his affection and concern. "In the hour of our greatest sorrow my heart goes out to you in deepest affection & with the most earnest wish that God will protect you and sustain & help you in these momentous years that lie ahead." Then asserting his complete confidence in the new President, Minton continued, "Would that all the world knew you as I do, then all would face the future with confidence in your assurance that the nation continue to be consecrated to the task to which President Roosevelt had set it until his purpose shall be consummated." Perhaps with an eye to the future (the hope of a position in the new administration), Minton concluded, "I need not tell you I am always ready to do anything I can to serve you. I hope I can come down soon to see you."[19]

In the rush of events, it took the new President some time to reply. He did so in a "My dear Shay" letter on May 16: "I am deeply grateful for the kind and sympathetic expressions which your letter conveys to me. To know that I have your confidence and your prayers strengthens me immeasurably." As a kind of postscript to this typewritten letter was a note in Truman's handwriting, "I've been one hell of a long time getting this done—but there just are not enough hours."[20]

Apparently Minton had written to Truman again, shortly after his first letter on April 13, but this time he sent the letter to Les Biffle, Secretary of the Democratic majority in the Senate, for personal delivery to Truman. On May 11 Truman replied with mock seriousness to Minton, "Received your letter from Biffle and bear in mind, you don't have to get at me thru any secondhand route. As far as you are concerned I am just as approachable as I was when we sat together in the Senate. The first time you are in Washington I hope I won't have to have you arrested to have you come to see me."[21]

Truman did have Minton "arrested" shortly thereafter. On May 30 Truman recorded in his diary:

> Took a day off Memorial Day (May 30) and went down the Potomac on the "Potomac." Had Steve Early, George Allen, Ed McKim, John Snyder, Harry Vaughn, J. K. Vardaman, Russell Stewart of Chicago Times and Shay Minton along. Don't think I ever had a more pleasant holiday. Found out Minton was in town so I had the Secret Service round him up and bring him aboard. We had a grand time discussing old Senate days and planning future good times for the country. Wish Minton were physically fit, I'd have him in the "family"—political family to help run the country.
>
> We organized a low limit poker game and the wisecracks would make Bob Hope laugh. My sides are sore. We made George Allen a "whipping boy" most of the time—and can he take it.
>
> Think I'll organize a road show out of this gang after I'm out of the White House and I won't have to go to the Soldiers' Home to retire.[22]

On August 10 President Truman noted in his diary that "Minton came to see me about an appointment to the Supreme Court."[23] This seems to have been the first broaching of the subject by Truman. Minton later said that he and the President talked over appointments to the Supreme Court for others but never discussed an appointment for himself.

A vacancy on the Supreme Court occurred shortly. Associate Justice Owen Josephus Roberts retired in September. Minton's friends, including Associate Justice Hugo Lafayette Black, immediately asked Truman to appoint Minton to fill this vacancy. But it was not to be. On September 19 Black sent his condolences to Minton:

I went and did my best but it was not enough as you now know. Whether it would have been more effective had I gone earlier will remain unknown, but I wish that I had. While the party believes that the selection is a good one, the reason given why it did not go another way was "health." Unquestionably you stand very high in the respect & affection of the gentleman. You may entertain regrets but I doubt whether your regret equals mine. When you come back to Washington I want you to have dinner with me.[24]

Instead of Minton, President Truman nominated his close friend, Harold Hitz Burton, of Ohio, to replace Roberts. Burton was a Republican who had served three terms as mayor of Cleveland and then was elected to the Senate. The friendship between the President and Burton had been cemented when Burton was the ranking Republican on the famous "Truman Committee" investigating defense contracts during World War II. Moreover, Justice Roberts was a Republican and when he retired, there was a nationwide demand that his replacement be a Republican. (Chief Justice Harlan Fiske Stone, who had been appointed an associate justice by President Coolidge and named chief justice by Roosevelt, was the lone Republican on the court when Burton was appointed.) By naming Burton, Truman sought to improve his relationship with Republican congressional leaders. Truman sent the nomination to the Senate on September 19, 1945, and Burton was confirmed by a unanimous vote on the same date.

It was reported in the press on September 15 that Truman had asked Minton to become Secretary of War to succeed Stimson, who had just retired. Minton declined for reasons of health (again, the pernicious anemia which was affecting his general health seriously by now). Truman instead chose Robert P. Patterson to replace Stimson.[25]

The long tour of duty in Washington reviewing court-martial proceedings, in addition to his duties on the Seventh Circuit bench, further taxed Minton's health, which was already strained by the anemia and other troubles. He had a heart attack and was confined to Walter Reed Hospital from October 1945 to January 1946. When he was released from the hospital, though, he had recovered almost fully from the ordeal.

Chief Justice Stone died on April 22, 1946. On May 22 Minton offered some suggestions to Truman as the President prepared to fill the vacancy.

"Now 'I make bold' to suggest Justice Black as Chief and [Secretary of Labor Lewis B.] Schwellenbach as Associate. Even by his former enemies, Justice Black is admitted to be the ablest man on the bench. He is capable of doing and does the bulk of the work. He is liberal, and is to that Court a breath of fresh air in a musty, damp cellar."[26] Truman did not accept this suggestion from his old friend. Instead, in June 1946, he appointed another close associate, Fred Moore Vinson, then Secretary of Treasury, as Chief Justice of the United States to succeed Chief Justice Stone.

For the first time in eighteen years, as a result of the off-year election on November 5, 1946, the Republicans captured both Houses of Congress. The group became what Truman labeled as the famous "do-nothing" 80th Congress. With Richard M. Nixon and Joseph R. McCarthy as two of its new members, this 80th Congress was the most ultraconservative one since the Fighting 69th Congress in the 1920s.

The electorate had given control of both the Senate (51 to 45) and the House (246 to 188) to the Republicans, and with New Hampshire Senator Styles Bridges gloating that "the United States is now a Republican country," an interesting exchange of letters between Minton and Truman ensued. Minton wrote on November 6:

I feel as though I had been hit by a hurricane—and I suppose you feel the same. Here's my thought after the storm.

Carroll Reece has asked you for your cooperation. I would give it to him one hundred per cent. I would announce at a press conference that I would accept the will of the people so plainly made manifest and the offer of Mr. Reece for complete cooperation. I would state that if Congress passes a law I do not like, I will not veto it; neither will I sign it. In this way, the Republican majority will have complete responsibility for the legislation they pass. . . .

This will prevent the Republicans from shifting their responsibility. They will not be able to say, "If we had passed a bill, the President would have vetoed it. . . ."

As a further evidence of your willingness to cooperate, I would have Jim Byrnes resign (although he has done a good job) and I would appoint John Foster Dulles Secretary of State so that the Republicans would have complete charge of our foreign affairs. I think it good for the country and

*for the Party that the Republicans be prevented from avoiding this clear call
to responsible action. You will remember that after the Congressional Election of 1918 President Wilson very seriously considered resigning and turning
over the responsibility of the Government to the Republicans for the remaining time. You need not do that, but you can hold this incoming Congress to its responsibility.*[27]

President Truman replied on November 14:

*You don't know how very much I appreciated your letter of November
sixth, and I don't expect to knuckle under to the Republicans.*

*As far as the foreign policy is concerned, we have been cooperating all
the time on a bipartisan policy; but when it comes to domestic policy you
know, and I know, the Republicans are a "special interest" party and I
certainly can't expect to join them on that sort of proposition. John Foster
Dulles has an appointment from me as an Alternate of the United Nations
Assembly Delegation from the United States. Vandenberg, Eaton and Austin are my appointments too.*

*Wilson did not consider resigning when he thought Hughes was elected
President. He was proposing to turn the Presidency over to Hughes four
months ahead of March fourth. That situation, of course, has been remedied by constitutional amendment.*

*The only sane proposal that has been made to meet this present situa-
tion is the one proposed by Senator Hatch which would cause the House of
Representatives to be elected for four years and to be elected with the President—that is practical and proper. If you will read the constitution carefully you will find the President is elected for four years and he has a job to
do for four years. I was elected in 1944 with the President, and was elected
just as much as the President himself—in fact the campaign was made on
me because they anticipated the succession and I expect to carry out that
mandate just as thoroughly and completely as I possibly can. As you know,
I never hunted a fight, but I have never in my life run from one and I don't
expect to run now.*

*Between you and me I don't expect this Congress to be any worse than
the one I had to deal with the last two years.*

I am enclosing you [sic] copy of the statement which I issued Monday on the subject of cooperation. As you know, cooperation is a two-way street and it depends all together on who wants the cooperation.[28]

On April 3, 1948, the United States District Court for the District of Columbia issued an injunction against the International Union, United Mine Workers of America, ordering an end to a strike in the nation's bituminous coal industry. On that same day Truman appointed Minton chairman of a fact-finding board or board of inquiry to perform such functions as might be required under the Labor Management Relations Act of 1947.

After the Republican sweep of the off-year elections, President Truman's popularity, which never had been high anyway, continued to decline. All the political experts voiced the belief (reinforced by public opinion polls) that if Harry Truman ran for President in 1948 he would meet his political Waterloo. The Gallup Poll showed that between October 1947 and March 1948 the percentage of Americans who thought Truman was doing a good job had sunk to 36 percent and that if he ran he would lose to Dewey, Stassen, MacArthur, or Vandenberg.

The nadir of his popularity was reached in April 1948. Clearly, the sincerity, competence and dedication recognized by those around him were not being communicated to the American public. Then a miraculous discovery was made. His staff conceded that Truman could never read a speech. They remembered that his extemporaneous remarks, however, were interesting, effective and well received. Why not have him deliver an improvised speech before a sizable audience? Truman liked the idea. On April 17, after reading a prepared text before the American Society of Newspaper Editors, he talked offhand without notes for a half-hour on American-Soviet relations. The editors loved it and cheered him at the end. More off-the-cuff speeches followed and on May 14, Truman gave a political talk to Young Democrats at the Mayflower Hotel. He brought them to their feet at the end when he vowed, "I want to say to you that for the next four years, there will be a Democrat in the White House and you're looking at him!"[29] The papers reported that it was a fighting speech delivered in the new Truman manner. President Truman and his staff now were ready to try this new style in a coast-to-coast campaign.

On June 3, the "Presidential Special" train left Washington and headed for the west. The last car was the "Ferdinand Magellan," a luxurious, walnut-paneled car built for President Roosevelt by the Association of American Railroads. The car had a large platform in the rear which was protected by a striped canopy and equipped with a public address system. The "off-the-cuff remarks" show was going on the road. The presidential train stopped in dozens of towns to let Truman speak to the people—a group he trusted and understood.

While Truman was on this campaign trip, Senator Taft spoke to the Union League Club in Philadelphia, lamenting that Truman was blackguarding Congress at "whistle-stops" all over the country. Taft unwittingly coined a word which he later regretted. Democratic headquarters in Washington telegraphed the mayors of all the little towns and cities at which Truman had spoken that Taft had referred to them derisively as whistle-stops. The mayors and the people were angry and upset with this slur and so informed the President, who was delighted to give their replies to the press. A huge crowd was on hand for Truman in Los Angeles, where he grinned and announced merrily, "This is the biggest whistle-stop!"

The "Presidential Special" returned to Washington on June 18. During this span of two weeks, Truman had covered 9,504 miles and delivered seventy-three off-the-cuff speeches in sixteen states.

Back home in Washington, on June 22, Truman conveyed to Minton his satisfaction with the results of the trip and the political hay gained from it. "I rather think we did stir up the animals on this trip—evidently the shoe is beginning to pinch. They [the Republicans] have gone to Philadelphia [for the Republican National Convention at which Dewey was nominated] to put a lot of hooey in a platform, which certainly can be made to backfire on them because their only excuse for election is their record in Congress." Truman then gave his strong opinion of that record, an opinion which he would offer whenever the opportunity presented itself: "I don't think there has been a Congress in my recollection that has a record that is as poor."[30]

The Truman miracle occurred on November 2, 1948—a victory at the polls which was one of the major upsets in American political history. All of the national polls, all of the political experts, all the pundits of the press, and all of the seasoned observers of the national scene predicted a victory for the Republican Party and its standard-bearer, Thomas E. Dewey. Only Truman himself believed that he had a chance to win.

Win he did! Ohio went for Truman by 7,000 votes at 9:30 A.M. on November 3, which put him over the top with 270 electoral votes. Later Illinois and California fell into the Truman camp. Dewey conceded at 11:14 A.M. Truman's plurality over Dewey was 2,136,525, but his victory in the electoral college was even more astonishing—303 to 189 (39 went to the States Rights or Dixiecrat ticket headed by J. Strom Thurmond of South Carolina). Truman also carried a Democratic Congress with him: 54 to 42 majority in the Senate and a 263 to 171 majority in the House.

Minton sent a telegram to Truman at Independence, Missouri, the day after the election, "God Bless Your Righting Heart, Your Devoted Friend." Truman thanked him by letter, dated November 23: "Dear Shay: I am especially happy to have your good wishes. My warmest thanks come to you for that splendid message of yours." In his own handwriting Truman added, "Talked to [Senator Carl A.] Hatch last night & he said you and he had been celebrating. Hope to see you soon."[31]

On August 5, 1949, Minton tripped and fell over a stone in the front yard of his home in New Albany and broke his right leg. He was admitted to St. Edward's Hospital for observation and treatment. Truman sent a wire to him at the hospital on August 8: "Sorry to hear of the accident which has sent you to the hospital. Hope you will not be detained there long. Best of luck always."[32]

Truman would soon have an opportunity to demonstrate his affection, support, and admiration of his longtime friend. Wiley Blount Rutledge, Associate Justice of the Supreme Court, died suddenly at the age of fifty-five from a massive cerebral hemorrhage on September 10. Truman did not take long to choose a successor. Apparently in the final analysis he chose to ignore Minton's health problems and appointed his good friend to a position that he believed both experience and character had fitted him to fill. In reality, the appointment was a matter of confidence and the appreciation of party and personal loyalty more than anything else.

On the day of the memorial service for Rutledge, Thursday, September 15, Truman called Minton at 7:00 A.M. at his home in New Albany. Miss Frances Kelley, Minton's secretary for many years, answered the telephone. She was told that it was the White House calling. Truman had called on other occasions, but this time Miss Kelley sensed something momentous.

Excitedly she informed her boss that the President wished to speak with him. "Shay, I was figuring on naming you to the Supreme Court today. Will you accept?" asked the President.

"I told him I would and then we talked for a few minutes. But I don't recall now what else we chatted about," Minton told reporters later.[33]

At 10:30 A.M. on the same day Truman read to the press the public announcement of the selection of Minton to the high court.

Minton, responding to the announcement, said "I'm proudly grateful for the President's confidence in me. I hope I shall prove worthy and I shall endeavor to the best of my ability to do so."[34]

The public announcement, predictably, turned the Minton household upside down. Minton spent that day and the following day opening congratulatory telegrams and mail, answering seemingly endless telephone calls from relatives and well-wishers, talking to reporters and posing for photographers.

A local bakery sent a cake to the home which was decorated with the words "Congratulations, Shay." Friends sent three dozen red roses and a simple white one delivered by Ben Bryant, a twenty-seven-year-old World War II veteran from Georgetown, Indiana, whose father had gone to grade school with Minton. The card with the roses did not explain the significance of the lone white rose, but one theory was it showed that the judge was a "standout."[35]

Henry F. Schricker, Democratic governor of Indiana, sent a telegram to Truman on September 16, 1949:

THE PEOPLE OF INDIANA ARE VERY PROUD AND DEEPLY GRATEFUL FOR YOUR APPOINTMENT OF THE HONORABLE SHERMAN MINTON TO THE UNITED STATES SUPREME COURT AND I WISH TO VOICE MY PERSONAL GRATITUDE IN THIS CONNECTION. YOU HAVE HONORED ONE OF OUR MOST BELOVED SONS AND THROUGH HIM THE ENTIRE CITIZENRY OF INDIANA.[36]

Among the callers to offer congratulations was Paul V. McNutt, the person largely responsible for the nomination and election of Minton to the Senate in 1934. McNutt was now practicing law in Washington, D.C. Minton, keenly aware of the vast debt he owed to McNutt for past political favors, expressed his gratitude and appreciation in a letter to McNutt on

September 19, 1949: "I never forget that you were in the position to have checked my career, but you didn't and you gave me your blessing—without which I could not have succeeded. It is a long ways from the hills of Southern Indiana to the Supreme Court of the United States, and I know I have not traveled that road alone, and I hope if I get there to see old friends like you oftener."[37]

Not everyone was pleased with the President's selection. For example, Indiana's Republican Senator Homer E. Capehart was disappointed. He said: "I was in the hopes the President would appoint a Republican to the Supreme Court bench as a means of retaining a true balance of bipartisanship in the judicial branch of our government. However, since he did not choose to appoint a Republican I am delighted that the appointment went to a Hoosier, Judge Minton."[38]

There were cries of cronyism and rule by friends from the press, who had not forgotten Minton's fight in the Senate to support Roosevelt's court packing scheme. Opponents cited his role in the episode as concrete evidence that Minton lacked any respect for the Supreme Court and that he had tried to degrade it.

But Minton was used to being derided in the press, and he determined to ignore their negative comments. It was a time for reflection and a certain anxiety. In a letter to a friend, Winfried K. Denton, member of Congress from Indiana, Minton wrote

The President had so often passed me by that it had gotten to be a habit. [Minton also remembered his own limitations as a lawyer and a judge.] *But he is a great guy to remember his friends, and whether I deserve it or not, he always thought, when we served together in the Senate, that I was a good lawyer. Well, the woods are full of lawyers better than I, I know, and judges far abler and more deserving, but I am gratified to know that the President of the United States has enough confidence in me to think I might measure up to this great responsibility."*[39]

Minton's nomination was referred to the Senate Judiciary Committee which scheduled a public hearing for Tuesday, September 27, 1949.

The committee met at 10:30 A.M. on that day in Room 424 of the Senate Office Building with Senator Harley M. Kilgore (D–W.Va.), ranking member and acting chairman, presiding. Present also were committee members Senators Warren G. Magnuson (D–Wash.); Herbert R. O'Conor (D–Md.); Bert H. Miller (D–Id.); Alexander Wiley (R–Wis.); William Langer (R–N.D.); Homer Ferguson (R–Mich.); Forrest C. Donnell (R–Mo.); and William E. Jenner (R–Ind.).[40] Senator Scott W. Lucas (D–Ill.), majority leader of the Senate, and Indianapolis attorney Henry J. Richardson, Jr., representing the National Bar Association, appeared before the committee and spoke on Minton's behalf.

Members of the committee were not much interested in the nominee's record for the preceding eight years while he was on the bench in Chicago. The committee's primary focus and the members' concerns were on Minton's political record as a New Deal senator, particularly his speeches and work on behalf of the court packing bill and his bill to "throttle the press."

Senator Jenner, although from Indiana, was a staunch Republican and an opponent of all New Dealers. The Indianapolis newspapers reported as late as September 18 that he had not made up his mind with respect to the confirmation of the appointment. At the hearing he read a formal statement into the record which questioned Minton's early radicalism.

He went on: "I believe, however, that time and his judicial experience have tempered his judgment, and there is every indication he has abandoned his radical beliefs."[41] Jenner concluded, "I have balanced his political record against that which he has made as an Appeals Court judge, adding the weight of honor that comes to Indiana in his present appointment. I am inclined to favor his confirmation."[42] Senator Ferguson, also a Republican, seized on this comment, declaring that Jenner's favorable view seemed to depend on the fact that Minton had abandoned his radical beliefs, and that Minton "should be given the opportunity to explain how he feels about this; whether there has been an actual change of mind, or whether there has not been."[43]

The committee adjourned at 12:15 P.M. on September 27 to go into executive session where it was voted (five to four, with Jenner casting the deciding vote) to invite Judge Minton to appear before the committee.[44]

In response to the invitation of the committee to appear before it and to explain his present views on the court packing bill, his proposal to require a seven to two decision by the justices of the Supreme Court to declare a law unconstitutional, and his timeworn and much quoted "You can't eat the

Constitution," Minton sent this letter, dated October 1, 1949, to acting chairman, Senator Kilgore:

> *I have received your request to appear before the committee.*
>
> *I, of course, desire to cooperate fully with the committee at all times, but I feel that personal participation by the nominee in the committee proceedings relating to his nomination presents a serious question of propriety, particularly when I might be required to express my views on highly controversial and litigious issues affecting the court. I am informed that the principal question with which the committee is concerned is my position with regard to the bill presented in 1937 to increase the membership of the Supreme Court.*
>
> *You will recall that at the time the bill in question was under discussion, I was assistant majority whip and, understandably, I strongly supported those legislative measures recommended by the administration. As assistant majority whip of the Senate, I was a strong partisan and supported the administration. I do not deny this. The record was made and I stand upon it. . . . When I was a young man playing football, I strongly supported my team. I was then a partisan. But later, when I refereed games, I had no team. I had no side. The same is true when I left the political arena and assumed the bench. Cases must be decided under the applicable law and upon the record as to where the right lies. I have never approached a case except to try to find the answer in the law to the question presented on the record before me. . . .*
>
> *In conclusion, I should like to refer to a statement submitted by Justice Frankfurter when he was asked to appear before the Senate Judiciary Committee in 1939, and read to the committee last Tuesday by you.* [Justice Frankfurter had written: "I suggest that neither an examination of my record nor the best interests of the Supreme Court will be helped by the personal participation of the nominee himself."][45]

The letter was read in a closed session of the committee on October 3, after which the committee reversed its earlier decision to ask Minton to appear for questioning by a vote of eight to three and then voted nine to two in favor of confirmation.[46] Jenner was absent from the meeting because of the serious illness of his father.

The nomination of Minton as associate justice was reported favorably to the floor of the Senate on October 3 by the Judiciary Committee. The Senate took up the nomination the next day and, after a marathon session that lasted nearly to midnight, the nomination was confirmed by a vote of forty-eight to sixteen.[47]

Senators Ferguson and Donnell, joined by Senator Wayne Morse (R–Ore.), had led a last-ditch fight on the floor to recommit the nomination to the Judiciary Committee. Their argument was not over the qualifications of Minton but was on the ground that a precedent had been set in permitting a nominee to the court to avoid appearing before the committee. A motion to recommit by Senator Morse lost by a vote of forty-five to twenty-one. After the motion to recommit was defeated, confirmation by the Senate came quickly and easily.[48]

The Indiana senators did not help Minton very much in his confirmation. Capehart, an ardent anti-New Dealer, was silent during the proceedings.[49] Although he voted against sending the nomination back to the committee and in favor of confirmation, he said that he believed Minton should have appeared before the committee for questioning but that he saw no use to return the nomination to the committee.[50]

Jenner, one of the most conservative members, was ambivalent about the nomination. In the hearing before the Judiciary Committee, he charged that "it is deplorable that this Senate is asked to consent and advise on appointments by the President of the United States whereby we are destroying the equitable ratio of the third arm of our government, the judiciary, by what I term as purely political appointments."[51] He finally—somewhat reluctantly— voted in favor of confirmation primarily because Minton was from Indiana.[52]

The day after his confirmation, reporters surrounded the new associate justice for statements about his aims. Minton said that he would never attempt to be a strict rule book justice but that "on the Supreme Court I would have a tendency to give leeway to Congress, and yet work fiercely for the enforcement of the Bill of Rights."[53]

Again with that keen awareness of his own limitations, Minton confided to his friends that he "did not intend to write for the ages" but rather that he would "decide the cases clearly and let it go at that."[54]

CHAPTER SEVEN

ASSOCIATE JUSTICE
OF THE SUPREME COURT

THE SUPREME COURT BUILDING IS A MAGNIFICENT STRUCTURE.[1] NEARLY SQUARE, it stands ninety-two feet high and stretches three hundred and eighty-five feet on its longest side. Four courtyards divide the building into a cross-shaped center core with offices and corridors surrounding the courtyards. The portico contains eight Corinthian columns which support an entablature and a sculptured pediment. Set as it is, with its stark simplicity contrasting with its distinguished neighbors on Capitol Hill, the bone-white building calls to mind the temples of ancient Greece.

This grand building was designed by architect Cass Gilbert. When he submitted his design to the building commission in May 1929, his aim was "a building of dignity and importance suitable for its use as the permanent home of the Supreme Court of the United States."[2]

The building is made almost entirely of marble from both domestic and foreign quarries. Vermont furnished one thousand rail carloads of flawless white stone for the exterior walls—24,700 blocks and slabs ranging in weight from two hundred pounds to sixty-three tons. Georgia provided the marble for the outer walls of the four courtyards. Alabama marble was used to face the interior corridors and walls.

On October 13, 1932, President Herbert Clark Hoover laid the cornerstone. Chief Justice Charles Evans Hughes spoke. (He had succeeded William Howard Taft, who resigned in early February 1930 because of ill health. After days of intense debate, Hughes was confirmed by the Senate as chief justice on February 13, 1930. Opponents had argued that Hughes would only deepen the already conservative hue of the Supreme Court.)

At the cornerstone laying, Hughes had observed: "The Republic endures and this [building] is a symbol of its faith."[3]

The courtroom stands opposite the main entrance at the end of the impressive main hall, a chamber eighty-two feet by ninety feet walled by "ivory vein" marble from Spain. The interior contains twenty-four massive Ionic columns which support the ornate ceiling. Gilbert had insisted that these columns be made of marble of a particularly delicate tint, a stone called "silver gray" or "light sienna old convent," from the Montarrenti quarry in Italy. Heavy red draperies and the dark luster of the bench made from solid Honduras mahogany, contrasting with the rare marble, give the courtroom a unique richness.

The Supreme Court sat for the first time in its new home at the opening of the term on October 7, 1935.

Each associate justice and his or her staff is assigned a richly carpeted, oak-paneled suite of three rooms in which to work and conduct business. Each associate justice is permitted a personal staff of two law clerks, a secretary, and a messenger. However, an associate justice has to make do with his or her own automobile.

On the other hand, the chief justice rates larger chambers, three law clerks, an additional secretary (or more if need arises), and a government limousine with chauffeur.

In contrast to the Periclean splendor of these chambers where he spent his daytime office hours, Minton's private time was spent in a rented one-bedroom apartment in the Methodist Building on Maryland Avenue, just across from the Supreme Court Building. With his health stabilized a bit, the new justice could walk to and from his work. He and Gertrude settled into the quiet and secluded life they had always favored. Minton would often have dinner with Justice Black, and occasionally he would host a dinner for the entire Court at a hotel in downtown Washington, but seldom, if ever, did they entertain at the apartment. Minton soon developed a work routine, usually arriving at his chambers each morning about nine-thirty and leaving around six in the evening. In an odd way, Jenner and the others who had commented on Minton's change were right. As an associate justice of the Supreme Court, Minton was not the same person he had been as a senator. In the Senate, his liberal views had painted him as a radical—even a socialist—who possessed an almost pathological partisanship which enabled him to espouse and defend all of the economic and social reforms of the New Deal administration. Now he was much more circumspect and deliberate. Most of the new moderation no doubt was attributable, in part, to his experiences in his eight years as a judge on the second-highest court in the land. Shortly after he was elevated to the Supreme Court, one writer described him: "Today his face seems a bit battered, like that of a man who has come through storms which have left their mark on his personality and made him sadder and warier than in his flamboyant political heyday."[4] Certainly his poor health had taken a toll. Perhaps also he now realized that he needed to act and look like a Supreme Court justice.

However, his political heart was as strong as steel, and forever bound to the Democratic party. Beneath the black robes was the competitive soul of the youthful football star, and he would not be denied participation in the political process. Soon after he took his seat, Minton attended a Jackson Day dinner held by the Democratic Party. He wanted to visit with old friends and shake the hands of men he had not seen since his Senate days. Afterwards, another justice asked Minton if he did not think it might be embarrassing for a disinterested and impartial jurist to attend a political gathering of that kind. With a big grin and a twinkle in his eye, Minton turned to his fellow justice and asked, "What is political about the Democratic party?"[5]

Later, in August 1956, and just weeks before he retired from the Supreme Court, Minton was asked by reporters about the candidate of his choice in the forthcoming election for President. "I have great confidence in Adlai E. Stevenson," he answered without hesitation. He then remarked that he hoped his Democratic candidate would win in November and added that he was afraid President Eisenhower was "terribly handicapped physically." [Eisenhower had suffered a heart attack the previous September, and eight months later underwent surgery to relieve an intestinal obstruction.] These remarks brought him criticism from the media for his partisanship, which provoked this forthright response: "Hell, I wasn't speaking judicially."[6]

Minton was gregarious by nature. He also was a politician who liked people and liked to win votes. Instinctively, he sought to make people like him. These attributes remained, and when he joined the court he brought with him courtesy, charm, and openness. The employees of the court regarded him as a personal friend. One sentimental lady on the secretarial staff recalled, with deep feeling, that Minton was never so hurried that he did not blow kisses to the ladies as he met them in corridors.

The justices themselves regarded him as a friend. Minton served under two chief justices, Fred M. Vinson and Earl Warren, and with eight associate justices: Hugo L. Black, Stanley F. Reed, Felix Frankfurter, William O. Douglas, Robert H. Jackson, Harold H. Burton, Tom C. Clark, and John Marshall Harlan. He managed to get along well with each of them despite the diversity of temperaments and the range of personalities. He was as well-liked as any justice and may have been the only justice who was welcome in the chambers of every other justice. Clark recalled that when Minton walked down the corridors in the Supreme Court Building, everyone from fellow justices to maintenance personnel turned to greet him.[7]

The camaraderie in the halls and chambers did not extend to further social contacts, however. When he arrived at the Supreme Court, Minton encouraged his fellow justices to eat together each day in the dining room provided for them, but only a few of his comrades decided to accept the new justice's invitation. Chief Justice Vinson tended to preside at the table, where he was joined by Justices Reed, Burton, Clark, and Minton. Both Minton and Vinson had a semipro background in baseball, so the conversation was usually about sports. Frankfurter regarded the conversation as boring and somewhat beneath him and thus declined to join the group. Douglas generally lunched in his office. Black usually went to lunch with his law clerks in the public cafeteria, and Jackson lunched alone.[8] Therefore, the easy comradeship that Minton had felt on the bench at the Seventh Circuit was not to be repeated.

Minton was an enjoyable companion because he was eclectic in his interests. "Shay could talk about anything," according to Black, "just anything."[9] He had a hundred humorous anecdotes. Once, Black recalled, Minton told the story of a trip he and Mrs. Minton took through the South on the road which General Sherman used on his infamous march through Georgia from Atlanta to the sea. A burly policeman stopped the justice and his wife, put his head through the window, and said, "I think you were speeding. What's your name?"

"Sherman Minton," was the answer. "I don't believe I heard you correctly," said the policeman with a nasty look. "I said my name is *Herman* Minton," the justice shouted back. The policeman then permitted the Mintons to continue on their way.[10]

Minton remained unabashedly Hoosier, and in fact was often quite earthy. Once in 1953, while the justices were in conference, discussing a challenge to the exemption of baseball under antitrust law, Frankfurter in his usual positive (if not pompous) manner told his colleagues that since Holmes wrote the decision which granted the immunity in 1923 Holmes would know when to change his mind. "Bullshit, Felix!" Minton said in a loud voice. "Baseball is a sport. It's the all-American sport, our national pastime, like motherhood and apple pie. So I say to you, bullshit, Felix." The brethren thought it was very funny and they laughed long and loud.[11]

Minton frequently entertained his fellow justices by holding an open house in his chambers in the late afternoon. Tea was served in fine china cups to his guests. Frankfurter appeared frequently to savor this good tea and to visit. Other beverages served were decaffeinated coffee for Justice Burton and straight whiskey for Justice Douglas.[12]

When he took his place on the Supreme Court on October 12, 1949, Minton was seated at the extreme left of the chief justice, in the seat reserved for the most junior justice. Minton was very close to Vinson and Clark, both of whom had been appointed by Truman, as he himself had been. The three of them were of like mind judicially; in a letter to Truman, dated June 3, 1953, Minton wrote, "Fred, Tom and I meet before lunch each day and discuss the State of the Union. Your judgment is vindicated every day in naming them to this Court. Fred is a champion in every way."[13]

The new justice had plunged into his work with his usual vigor. During his first term, 1949 to 1950, he wrote twelve opinions. That output would have been reasonable for a seasoned justice, but it was a remarkable production for the newest justice. These twelve cases represent the range of litigation that reaches the Supreme Court, such as search and seizure, composition of a jury, admission to the United States of the war bride of a veteran of World War II, patents with antitrust implications, peaceful picketing, income tax, criminal procedure, statutory interpretation of federal statutes dealing with commerce and labor relations, and judicial review of administrative findings.

The practice of assigning cases has varied throughout the Court's history. When Minton was on the Supreme Court, a case was assigned to a particular justice, who then prepared a draft of an opinion to circulate among the other justices. After reading the draft opinion, each justice either returned the draft or a separate note to the justice responsible for the opinion, noting agreement or making suggestions for revisions.

The opinions written by Justice Minton and later donated to the Truman Library by his widow contain revealing notes from the other justices. Frankfurter almost always had comments on the proposed opinion. Black frequently did. Chief Justice Vinson, and after him Chief Justice Warren, simply returned the draft opinion with a noted "I agree," as did Burton, Reed, and Douglas. Jackson and after him his successor, Harlan, varied their responses.

The first opinion authored by Minton was on *Commissioner of Internal Revenue v. Connelly,*[14] decided November 7, 1949. The issue was whether the taxpayer was entitled to a fifteen-hundred-dollar exclusion from gross income as a civil service employee in the legal division of the Coast Guard because he was an officer in the Coast Guard Reserve. Minton held that the taxpayer was not entitled to the exclusion, because he was paid as a civil service employee and not as a reservist in the Coast Guard. His draft opinion prompted a laudatory note from Black: "It manifests a keen form of analysis to hit the jugular as you have in this case. This is good writing that follows the classical rule Aristotle laid down in his Rhetoric—Start-Continue-Finish."[15]

On opinion day in the Supreme Court, the justice responsible for the majority opinion usually delivered the opinion by reading it from the bench to the audience in the courtroom. Minton, however, varied that custom by condensing the opinion and speaking the contents. This technique brought him high praise from Frankfurter, Jackson, and Clark.

An important opinion by Minton during his first term was *United States ex rel. Knauff v. Shaughnessy,*[16] decided January 16, 1950. Mrs. Knauff, an alien, married an honorably discharged World War II U.S. Army veteran in Frankfurt, Germany. Soon after their marriage, the couple left for the United States, where Mrs. Knauff planned to become a naturalized citizen. When they arrived in New York Harbor on August 14, 1948, she was denied entry without a hearing and without explanation. Mrs. Knauff instituted *habeas corpus* proceedings, maintaining that she could not be excluded from the United States without a hearing. The lower courts summarily dismissed her action. The Supreme Court granted *certiorari*, a writ whereby the Court brings a case up from a lower court for review and decision, to decide whether the attorney general could exclude Mrs. Knauff without a hearing for security reasons. The answer depended on the resolution of two apparently contradictory policies enacted by Congress. The first was an act of June 21, 1941, which authorized the President to issue reasonable rules, regulations, and orders to govern the entrance of aliens for the duration of a national emergency. A regulation under this statute authorized the attorney general to order exclusions without a hearing. The other statute was the War Brides Act passed in 1945 to assist war veterans in bringing their wives to America. The War Brides Act specified that the alien brides must be "otherwise admissible" under the immigration laws; it was this provision, according to the attorney general, which authorized the screening of Mrs. Knauff and her exclusion without a hearing. Minton, writing for the majority, held that the War Brides Act did not in specific language say that the exclusion provision in the 1941 Act did not apply. Hence, the War Brides Act was immaterial and Mrs. Knauff properly was excluded under the 1941 Act.

The press castigated the Supreme Court and particularly Justice Minton for the decision in Knauff. Typical of the criticism was an editorial in the *Chicago Sun-Times* on January 23, 1950. "It seems a pretty raw deal to hand a soldier's bride. Congress passed a War Brides Act for the purpose of relaxing certain immigration restrictions. . . . Justice Minton in his first opinion on civil liberties after he replaced Justice Rutledge lined up with Chief Justice Vinson and Justices Burton and Reed who were the opponents of Justice Rutledge on civil liberties."

Stung by this criticism, Minton wrote to Russell Stewart of the *Sun-Times*, on January 28, 1950: "Where I line up is not of much importance, but it is important as to whether I am right in what I decide. That I try to be, irrespective of which line I get in. If it was a 'raw deal,' it is something Congress fully authorized. I have always believed that this court has no power to legislate, and I certainly believe it now as strongly as when I fought the old court because we thought it was using its power to legislate. I considered it then and still consider it an usurpation of power to do so."

Minton also wrote to Mark F. Ethridge, publisher of the *Courier-Journal* in Louisville, Kentucky, on January 23, 1950, because that paper had printed a similar editorial critical of the decision: "Another error in the editorial is the assumption that the activities in Czechoslovakia [Mrs. Knauff had fled to Czechoslovakia from her native Germany and remained there until 1939, when she went to England as a refugee] were before the Iron Curtain fell.

Quite the contrary, she was reported to be an informer to the present Government of Czechoslovakia. This is not for publication. I just didn't want the paper I consider the Country's best going off half-cocked."[17] Interestingly, Minton, and presumably the other justices, were privy to classified information which does not appear in the text of the opinion. In a personal memorandum in the Knauff file in the Truman Library, this note by Minton appears: "Soldier may not bring in spy as a wife."

If the vigor of the dissent constitutes a criterion, another important case was *United States v. Rabinowitz*,[18] decided February 20, 1950. It was a search and seizure case and it may have been the most important opinion written by Minton during his first term. Federal agents knew that Rabinowitz had sold forged postage stamps and they obtained a warrant for his arrest. The agents went to his one-room place of business, which was open to the public, and arrested him. Over his objections, the agents then proceeded to search the room and found many forged stamps. After a summary of the many cases on searches and seizures, Minton focused on the central issue: "What is a reasonable search is not to be determined by any fixed formula. The Constitution does not define what are 'unreasonable' searches and, regrettably, in our discipline we have no ready litmus-paper test." Minton then discussed the test enunciated in an earlier case: whether the agents had time to obtain a search warrant. Though "appealing from the vantage point of administration," Minton found objections to a rule of this sort. On balance, Minton held, the factor of time was outweighed by the necessities of police administration. "The relevant test is not whether it is reasonable to procure a search warrant, but whether the search was reasonable," he held. "That criteria in turn depends upon the facts and circumstances—the total atmosphere of the case," he continued. "Law officers must justify their conduct before the courts which have always been, and must be, jealous of the individual's right of privacy within the broad sweep of the Fourth Amendment."[19] Thus, the court, declaring through Minton, who also spoke for Chief Justice Vinson and Justices Reed, Burton, and Clark, upheld the search of the premises of the stamp dealer because it had been a reasonable search incidental to a lawful arrest. Black, Frankfurter, and Jackson dissented.

Another well respected opinion by Minton during his first term was *Eugene Dennis v. United States*,[20] decided March 27, 1950. Dennis, general secretary of the Communist Party of the United States, had been convicted by a federal district court in Washington, D.C., of willfully refusing to obey a subpoena served on him by the House Committee on Un-American Activities. On appeal, Dennis argued that, in view of the loyalty program of the United States, an important Communist on trial in the District of Columbia could challenge all government employees as potentially biased jurors. The issue had been narrowed a couple of years earlier in a case in which the Supreme Court had ruled that, barring special circumstances, government employees as a group could not be disqualified from jury duty in Washington, D.C., in a case to which the government is a party. Minton held that argument was irrelevant, noting that the earlier case arose before the loyalty program went into operation. He upheld the conviction, refusing to assume without proof that all employees of the government were so likely to fear for their jobs that they automatically should be excluded from the jury. While concluding that the right of a member of an unpopular minority to an impartial trial must be protected scrupulously to the same extent as any other defendant, he reasoned, "While one of an unpopular minority group must be accorded that solicitude which properly accompanies an accused person, he is not entitled to unusual protection or exception."[21] Then he concluded with a ringing affirmation of faith in the fundamental fairness and integrity of the men and women who serve as jurors:

> In this case, no more than the trial court can we without injustice take judicial notice of a miasma of fear to which Government employees are claimed to be peculiarly vulnerable—and from which other citizens are by implication immune. Vague conjecture does not convince that Government employees are so intimidated that they cringe before their Government in fear of investigation and loss of employment if they do their duty as jurors, which duty this same Government has imposed upon them. There is no disclosure in this record that these jurors did not bring to bear, as is particularly the custom when personal liberty hinges on the determination, the sense of responsibility and individual integrity by which men judge men.[22]

Documents at the Truman Library show that Minton wrote a note, apparently to himself, that "Dennis is really being tried for being a Communist—not for refusing to appear." Despite his personal belief that Eugene Dennis was prosecuted for political reasons, Minton held that the man had not been deprived of an impartial trial.

When the first draft of his opinion in Dennis was circulated, Justice Jackson on December 15, 1949, sent this note to Minton:

> *Dear Shay:*
>
> *I concur in the result. I shall probably need to say a few words in view of my dissent in Frazier [Frazier v. United States, 335 U.S. 497 (1948), decided January 3, 1949]. But what I say will not disagree with your reasoning. Maybe if I wait until the dissent is out I can take care of a few of its points that you would not want to take a shot at.*
>
> *You have done a good job and I don't think they can poke any holes in what you have written.*
>
> Bob [23]

Writing for the majority in the troublesome case of *United States v. Alexander Lawrence Alpers,*[24] decided February 6, 1950, Minton reiterated his determination as a justice to discover the intent of Congress and to uphold, if possible, an act of Congress. (The case involved the interstate shipment of obscene phonograph records. A federal criminal statute forbade the shipment of any "obscene book, pamphlet, picture, film or other matter of indecent character."[25])

Minton held that the Supreme Court must not "defeat the manifest intent of Congress" which was "to prevent the channels of interstate commerce from being used to disseminate any matter that, in its essential nature, communicates obscene, lewd, lascivious or filthy ideas."[26] So, even though phonograph records were not included in the statute, they were included, according to the opinion, because it was the obvious purpose of Congress to prevent the dissemination of "any matter" of the forbidden type.

His opinion in *Automatic Radio Manufacturing Company v. Hazeltime Research, Inc.,*[27] decided June 5, 1950, showed Minton's passion for precedent and reluctance to make new law. It involved a patent license arrangement in which the licensee agreed to pay the licensor a royalty on all sales whether or not any of the patents were used. The licensee urged that this arrangement was analogous to "tie-in" sales (a means by which licensors extended their patent monopoly beyond the mere collection of a payment for the use of the patent)—a practice earlier held illegal by the Supreme

Court in a number of similar situations. Minton found that the challenged practice was not dissimilar to the other "tie-in" sales. If the practice in the case at bar did not fit a specifically defined practice condemned in prior cases, Minton was unwilling to extend the condemnation to a new, even if similar, practice. He would not legislate; the case would be decided by precedent and established law. Jackson responded to Minton's first draft of the opinion: "Please note that I took no part. P.S.: But that does not stop me from saying I like your opinion."[28]

Even after he ascended to the Supreme Court, Minton continued to write warm, personal letters to his friend President Truman, for whom he had a deep and abiding affection. Some of these letters were written as favors to friends of Minton. One such letter was written by Minton to Truman on January 9, 1950. He enclosed a copy of a letter from Judge J. Earl Major, chief judge of the Seventh Circuit Court of Appeals in Chicago, about the need for an early appointment of a federal district judge to replace the retiring judge in Indianapolis.[29]

The warmth and affection that Minton had for Truman was reciprocated in kind. On January 28, Truman wrote back to Minton, thanking him for his note about the need for a new judge in Indianapolis. He also penned at the bottom of the letter this earthy note: "Shay, if the Pres. didn't have to make appointments to office he could spend all his time kissing horses' asses to make the gov't run and he could have a grand time! Maybe?"[30]

On July 3, 1950, a few days after the outbreak of the Korean conflict, Minton wrote to Truman from his home in New Albany: "In the hinterland your brave stand on the Korean situation has called forth only approval all around. It was a characteristic move & one in keeping with your sterling character and stout heart. More power to you. I am taking it easy here in the shade with three grandchildren running me ragged but I love it."[31] He was speaking of Brooks, April, and Holly Minton, his son Sherman's daughters.

Minton's Hoosier ties remained strong, and the affection he felt for Indiana was reciprocated by the folks back home. On September 13, 1950, a group of neighbors and friends honored him with the dedication of a bronze plaque set into a stone wall in front of the one-and-a-half-story frame house in Georgetown where he was born. The idea for the plaque came from F. Shirley

Wilcox, Treasurer of the State of Indiana, and Robert C. Bulleit, a New Albany attorney. Justice and Mrs. Minton spent the Supreme Court's summer recess in New Albany and thus were able to attend the ceremony. Homer E. Capehart, the Republican senator from Indiana running for re-election in 1950, also was there. Indiana Governor Henry F. Schricker was the main speaker and unveiled the plaque, and President Truman sent a telegram to Wilcox, who read it to the local folk:

> IT IS A SATISFACTION TO KNOW THAT FRIENDS AND FELLOW TOWNSMEN OF JUSTICE MINTON ARE TO REGISTER THEIR ADMIRATION OF A HOMETOWN BOY BY PLACING A MARKER AT HIS BIRTHPLACE IN GEORGETOWN. AS HIS COLLEAGUE IN THE SENATE I ADMIRED SHERMAN MINTON'S STERLING CHARACTER, WISDOM, LEGAL LEARNING, AND HIS GREAT CAPACITY FOR HARD WORK. HIS OUTSTANDING SERVICE AS A MEMBER OF THE HIGHEST COURT IN THE LAND HAS JUSTIFIED MY ACTION IN APPOINTING HIM TO THAT DISTINGUISHED BODY. . . .[32]

When the court's new term opened on Monday, October 2, 1950, the Korean conflict was boiling. United Nations forces had landed at Inchon, the port city of Seoul, on September 15, and General MacArthur had returned in triumph to Seoul on September 29. United Nations troops recaptured the capital of South Korea three months after it fell to the Communists.

Minton plunged into the work of the Court with his usual enthusiasm. He was not quite as productive during this term as he had been in the first, authoring just nine majority opinions.

One of Minton's important opinions during this term was *Panhandle Eastern Pipeline Co. v. Michigan Public Service Commission*,[33] decided May 14, 1951. It held that Michigan constitutionally could require a certificate of convenience and necessity for interstate sales of natural gas directly to the consumer, sales not covered by the Natural Gas Act, which applied only to "sales for resale." Panhandle Eastern's position was that even in the absence of federal legislation, a state requirement of this nature was forbidden by the Commerce clause of the Constitution itself—the position Justice Frankfurter took in his dissent. But Minton reasoned, "It does not follow that because [Panhandle Eastern] is engaged in interstate commerce it is free from state regulation or free to manage essentially local aspects of its business as it pleases. The course of this Court's decisions recognizes no such license. Such a course would not accomplish the effective dual regulation Congress intended and would permit [Panhandle Eastern] to prejudice substantial local interests. This is not compelled by the Natural Gas Act or the Commerce Clause of the Constitution."[34]

Minton wrote ten opinions during the 1951 term, which opened on Monday, October 1. Writing for the majority during this term, he authored the controversial opinion in *Adler v. Board of Education*,[35] decided March 3, 1952.

The State of New York had passed the Feinburg Law prohibiting employment of public school teachers who advocated the violent overthrow of the United States government, or who were members of organizations which they knew advocated such overthrow. Adler challenged the Feinburg Law.

Adler had created controversy by the time the case reached the Supreme Court. Some writers and commentators were persuaded that if the law were upheld, learning in the classroom would be smothered under a blanket of censorship. Others were equally convinced that if the law were struck down, Communist traitors would contaminate the minds of innocent children in the classroom.

The principal contention of the opposition was that the Feinburg Law violated First Amendment rights.

Minton's opinion sustained the Feinburg Law. He did not agree that the law denied the rights of teachers under the First Amendment. Such persons have the constitutional right "to assemble, speak, think and believe as they will," but "it is equally clear that they have no right to work for the State in the school system on their own terms."

Minton continued:

If they do not choose to work on such terms, they are at liberty to retain their beliefs and associations and go elsewhere. His freedom of choice between membership in the organization and employment in the school system might be limited, but not his freedom of speech or assembly, except in the remote sense that limitation is inherent in every choice.[36]

As Minton saw it, the decisive inquiry was whether loyalty to the government was a reasonable standard for employment of teachers. In answering in the affirmative, he made his opinion very specific:

> A teacher works in a sensitive area in a schoolroom. There he shapes the attitude of young minds towards the society in which they live. In this, the state has a vital concern. It must preserve the integrity of the schools. That the school authorities have the right and the duty to screen the officials, teachers, and employees as to their fitness to maintain the integrity of the schools as a part of ordered society, cannot be doubted.[37]

If loyalty to the government is a reasonable standard for employment of teachers and others in the school system, does membership in a subversive organization constitute *prima facie* evidence of disloyalty? Again, Minton was very definite when he answered in the affirmative:

> One's associates, past and present, as well as one's conduct, may properly be considered in determining fitness and loyalty. From time immemorial, one's reputation has been determined in part by the company he keeps. In the employment of officials and teachers of the school system, the state may very properly inquire into the company they keep, and we know of no rule, constitutional or otherwise, that prevents the state, when determining the fitness and loyalty of such persons, from considering the organizations and persons with whom they associate.[38]

After the Adler opinion came down, Kurt F. Pantzer, an attorney in Indianapolis, on March 6, 1952, sent Minton a copy of an editorial from *The Indianapolis Star* (a Republican newspaper) expressing approval of the decision and his opinion. In reply, Minton wrote to Pantzer: "I am grateful to have *The Star* approve of something I do. This is a rather unique experience for me—and therefore all the more acceptable."[39]

On Saturday night, March 29, 1952, the Democrats held their annual Jefferson-Jackson Day dinner in the National Guard Armory in Washington, D.C. Some fifty-three hundred faithful were in attendance. After sharing his intention only with his family, during his after-dinner remarks President Truman told the stunned audience that he would not seek another term. The Democrats were not prepared to find a new leader—standouts in the party were few. Minton sent a note to the President to which Truman responded on April 8, 1952:

Dear Shay:

—Your note about my quitting is one I more than appreciate. You and I have been through the mill. Most politicians never know when to quit. All this "weeping and wailing and so forth" convinces me that no mistake was made.

Some of our friends? in the Senate had told the National Democratic Chairman that "we" could not win with me. After Saturday night the same "friends" said "Well what will we do now? The S.O.B. has run out on us!" This human animal has no equal.

Had a letter from Carl Hatch. He expressed the same opinion you did. Remember when we sat behind him in the Senate and cussed the Hatch Act? It needed and still needs cussing.

I am most happy that I'll have lunch with the Big Court today. We'll have a good time.

My very best to Mrs. Minton.

Sincerely, Harry[40]

Any commentary about the decisions of the Supreme Court during the 1951 term would not be complete without discussion of the controversial and politically explosive case of *Youngstown Sheet & Tube Company, et al. v. Sawyer*,[41] decided on June 2, 1952.

The case was the culmination of a long and bitter dispute between the steel companies and the United Steelworkers of America, CIO. On December 18, 1951, the union gave notice that it would strike on December 31. The Federal Mediation and Conciliation Service was unable to resolve the controversy. On December 22 President Truman referred the dispute to the Federal Wage Stabilization Board, and this board made an award which offered higher wages to workers but did not allow for an increase in steel prices. On March 20, 1952, the steel companies refused to accept or abide by the award. Truman did not invoke the provisions of the Taft-Hartley Act, which would have provided for a "cooling off period" before a strike; the union announced on April 4 that it would call a nationwide strike on

April 9. On April 8, just a few hours before the strike was to commence, Truman directed Secretary of Commerce Charles Sawyer to seize most of the steel mills in the country and to operate them as government property. Sawyer issued the necessary orders for such a seizure, and Truman reported the action to Congress on April 9 and again on April 21. But Congress, exploiting Truman's "lame duck" status as President, declined to act. The steel companies complied with the orders under protest and filed an action in the federal district court in the District of Columbia, seeking a temporary injunction to halt the seizure.

On April 19 Congressman George Bender of Ohio called for the impeachment of President Truman for the steel seizure.

David Pine, judge of the District Court, calling the seizure unconstitutional, issued a preliminary injunction in the case on April 30. On the same day the Court of Appeals for the District of Columbia Circuit issued a "stay order" for the ruling of Judge Pine.

The Supreme Court, expeditiously acting on its well-established precedents, bypassed the Court of Appeals on May 3 and issued a writ of *certiorari* to the District Court and brought the case to its docket.

The decision of the Supreme Court came down on June 2, 1952. The Court, dividing six to three with Justice Black writing for the majority, held that the seizure violated the Constitution by usurping the power of Congress. Only Congress, according to the majority, can authorize the taking of private property for public use. The President, according to Justice Black, must confine himself "to the recommending of laws he thinks wise and the vetoing of laws he thinks bad."

The complexity of the case is evidenced not only by the fact that the justices split six to three, but that seven justices wrote separate opinions which covered one hundred twenty-eight pages.

Chief Justice Vinson wrote the dissenting opinion, in which Minton and Reed joined. This dissenting opinion held that the seizure was instituted to keep the supply of steel continuing, and so avert a national emergency. *Woods v. Miller*[42] decided in 1948, had held that the war power of Congress could be employed after hostilities had ended to deal with problems generated by the war. This is not "a time for timorous executive action," wrote Vinson. "Faced with the duty of executing the defense programs which Congress had enacted and the disastrous effects that any stoppage in steel production would have on those programs, the President acted to preserve those programs by seizing the steel mills." He concluded: " . . . judicial, legislative and executive precedents throughout our history demonstrate that in this case the President acted in full conformity with his duties under the Constitution."

The decision in this case was a bitter setback to Truman. He later wrote: "[T]he Supreme Court's decision . . . was a deep disappointment to me. I think Chief Justice Vinson's dissenting opinion hit the nail right on the head, and I am sure that someday his view will come to be recognized as the correct one."[43]

No less an authority than William H. Rehnquist, chief justice of the United States (1986–), agrees with Truman and Vinson. He writes:

> The law on the equitable issues was clearly in favor of the government, and while the law on the constitutional question was more or less up for grabs, the whole trend of the Court's decisions in the preceding fifteen years leaned toward the government. Why, then, did six members of the Court vote against the government in this case? I think that this is one of those celebrated constitutional cases where what might be called the tide of public opinion suddenly began to run against the government, for a number of reasons, and that this tide of public opinion had a considerable influence on the Court.[44]

Although Truman decided not to seek another term, he did plenty of barnstorming for the Democratic candidate, Governor Adlai E. Stevenson of Illinois, in the fall of 1952.

Minton wrote a "My dear Harry" letter to Truman on October 13:

> First, I want to thank you for the book, Mr. President, and especially for the autograph. I shall cherish it not only for this and the book's content, but because of my personal knowledge of the courage, high integrity and great ability of the subject thereof.
>
> I wanted to see you before you went barnstorming, but I got back to Washington too late. You have been doing what had to be done, namely, keep the record straight on the General [Eisenhower] who has been talking out of both sides of his mouth. . . .

I know you will keep up the fight. You are doing a great job. Whenever you hear the Republicans complain that Truman's "Whistle-Stopping" and Stevenson's "Humor" are making votes for Eisenhower, you know you have each hit the quick. I am surprised that Senator Nixon's act was accepted by the press and commentators. He was far from frank. You and I know that, because of his statements as to a Senator's expenses and what he can charge to the Government. He has been in Congress just six years. In the six years I was there, I never saved enough money to buy $54,000 worth of houses and furnish them. It seemed timely to me that Jim Farley demanded on the radio the other night that Nixon reveal all, and I don't mean about the dogs![45]

When President Truman returned to the White House from the campaign trail on October 15, he responded to Minton: "I am sorry I didn't get to see you before I started on my barnstorming tour. It turned out to be a most successful one. I believe we are going to hang the hide of the Republican party on the tree to dry on November fifth. We will do the hanging on the fourth but it won't dry until the fifth. I hope everything is going well with you." The President added in longhand: "I know you must be itching to get into the fray."[46]

As his term of office drew to a close, Truman made a farewell speech by radio. Afterward, Minton sent a handwritten letter, dated January 16, 1953:

It was a grand speech and so like you in every respect. I know the country loved it as Gertrude and I did. When Mrs. Truman & Margaret walked on the scene it was much too much for the emotions of your old friend and unabashed the tears rolled down my cheeks. It was a moment of great triumph for those of us who love you & know you so well, as you closed the book on what we confidently believe to be one of the greatest eras of achievement in our nation's history. While our lips were uttering "well done thou good & faithful servant" our hearts were sad with the thought of your going. It is going to be pretty lonesome for some of us around here when you have gone. I hope to get down to the train to see you off, but if I don't you will know it was because my legs were weary & my heart too heavy. As the Hoosier Poet said "Good bye Harry! Take keer yourself."[47]

Truman replied to Minton with a letter in his own handwriting, dated January 18, 1953:

Dear Shay:
—I've never received a letter that I appreciated more than yours of the 16th. You know me as well as anyone alive and your reaction to the broadcast was all I could want. It was my topnotch effort to leave a good taste with the people and from your letter I guess it succeeded. Now I'm going to be a fish out of water—nothing to do, nowhere to go, no one to fight with— just whittle and ponder my errors. What a boresome outlook! How long do you think it will last? The boss says I'll have plenty to do to unpack the nine car loads of junk which went to Independence. She says I'll have to do it too. Maybe that will keep me busy for several days. If you come our way look me up and if I come to the capital city I'll try to mooch a meal and rehash some good stories.[48]

Minton, along with five thousand other well-wishers and faithful followers, gathered at Washington's Union Station on Tuesday afternoon, January 20, to say good-bye to former President Truman as he, Mrs. Truman, and Margaret left Washington, D.C., on the Ferdinand Magellan for Independence, Missouri. A page was closing in Minton's life as one of his earliest colleagues and best political and personal friends went into retirement.

During the 1952 term of the Supreme Court, which opened on October 6, 1951, Justice Minton wrote eleven opinions for the court.

One of these was *Lutwak v. United States*,[49] decided February 9, 1953. The case involved a conspiracy by honorably discharged veterans of World War II. The veterans had contracted spurious, phony marriages in Paris with Polish refugees. The women, of course, were hardly driven by romantic impulses; they were planning to deceive the immigration authorities by becoming "women married to honorably discharged veterans." One item of hearsay evidence was improperly admitted at the trial, a possible cause for reversal. Minton, writing for the court, however, affirmed the veterans' convictions and held that "a defendant is entitled to a fair trial but not a perfect one" and that the error was harmless.[50]

Barrows v. Jackson,[51] decided June 15, 1953, is considered by some legal scholars to be one of the most skillful opinions Minton wrote while on the court. A white owner of real estate had signed a restrictive covenant agreeing not to sell her property to any person who was not a member of the Caucasian race. This owner later sold the property to a black family; whereupon the remaining co-signers of the covenant sued the property owner in a state court for damages for breach of contract. Legal issues of the most knotty kind were in the case—the meaning of "state action" under the Fourteenth Amendment, the definition of "persons" as this term was intended in the Fourteenth Amendment, and the ever troublesome concept of "standing to sue." Minton framed the question in the case: Can a racially restrictive covenant be enforced at law by a suit for damages against a co-covenantor who allegedly broke the covenant? Writing for the court, Minton said "no," thereby pleasing civil libertarians in attaining a desirable social result and evolving a judicial solution acceptable to his brethren (except Chief Justice Vinson) by his skillful craftsmanship. The case files show Minton spent an inordinate amount of time on this opinion, drafting different versions and memoranda and assembling research materials gathered by his clerks.

Minton's opinion in *Barrows* evoked this note from Frankfurter: "Shay, this is a fine, lawyer-like job. Greater praise is not in my vocabulary."[52] And from Burton came this note: "Congratulations upon a difficult constructive job admirably done."[53]

Truman celebrated his sixty-ninth birthday on May 8, 1953. It was his first birthday in Independence, Missouri, since Eisenhower won the 1952 presidential election. Minton sent a handwritten letter, dated May 5:

Happy Birthday! I am glad you are back home to celebrate it and I would like to join you. Some of us here at the Court will lift a "cup" to you anyway. I hope you and the family had a good vacation in Hawaii. This town hasn't been the same since I saw the B & O train pull out January 20th with you standing on the back platform. I try to be charitable to this new bunch. You can imagine that is not too easy for me! I have never seen an outfit march up the hill and down again like this one. It is a dull day when Dulles doesn't make it duller! And Ike doesn't repudiate himself of some of the team. I thought they knew all the answers and when they got to

Washington everything would suddenly snap to attention before the General and the forces of the great Crusade would move in with the precision of a West Point Cadet Company and take over from the people who didn't know how to run the government. But—we can't balance the budget; we can't reduce taxes. We can't stop the war in Korea. We have to appease in Laos and Indo-China. We don't know whether to extend the reciprocal trade agreements so on ad nauseam. What a mess!!

I just wanted to welcome you home and wish you the best of everything for your birthday. Mrs. Minton joins me in affectionate good wishes to all the Truman family.[54]

Upon his return from a vacation in Hawaii, Truman replied to Minton with a long letter in his own handwriting on May 21:

We had a grand time in Hawaii. Ed Pauley [a California oilman who had been treasurer of the Democratic National Committee] and some of his friends own an island in Kaneohe Bay which is on the Pacific Ocean side north of Honolulu. There are 10,000 coconut trees, oleanders, orchids, hibiscus, spiders, toads, lizards, just a few mosquitoes, a lovely climate, and a grand quiet time. The island contains 18 acres and was improved by a fellow named Holmes who married Fleischmann Yeast. He spent 2 1/2 million on it and used up 56 barrels of hooch while he was doing it and finally passed on by the sleeping pill route.

It really is a place to dream about and we had it under ideal conditions. An oriental cook, a major domo who had managed top hotel dining rooms, and native Hawaiian maids (all married with copious offspring) and a manager who works for Pauley all the time.

I reviewed the Marines and received 21 guns in a salute for doing it. I told the tough old 3-star general in command that he'd probably be court-martialed for doing that for me and he said 'By God the Marines and the Navy will always give you 21 guns.' And believe it or not, Radford [Admiral Arthur W., Commander in Chief, Pacific] confirmed it!

Margie and the Boss had a grand time sleeping and sunning themselves and so did I. The only social function was a formal dinner with Gov. King. He came to Washington as Delegate in 1935 when you and I did. Mrs. King and Bess [Mrs. Truman] are members of the 74 Club as is Mrs.

Minton. *The daughter went to Guniston Hall with Margie. The function was a grand one and "a good time was had by all" as the Indiana weekly paper would say.*

Then I borrowed a C47 from the Navy and flew off to the island of Hawaii which is 200 miles southeast of Honolulu to inspect the biggest volcano in the world—Mauna Loa. It is 13,700 feet high and 18,000 feet down into the sea to its base. Its twin, Mauna Kea, is 13,800 feet above sea level and both are snow capped all year. In the eruption of 1950, it put out 200 million cubic yards of lava—more than all the other volcanoes in the world have put out in a 1000 years. Most of it went into the sea and killed a million or so fish some of which the smart boys haven't classified yet! You know I'm rated an amateur volcanologist (which means a dumb one) so I had a grand time with a real one. He showed me colored pictures of the eruption of 1949–50 and by asking nutty questions I obtained a lot of useless information with which I can floor anyone who knows nothing about the subject.

They say we've had a Square Deal, New Deal, Fair Deal and now a Raw Deal. The chairman of our party in Oregon came in to see me yesterday and told me that a man came into his office the other day with his pockets turned inside out and said he was flying the new Ike flag.[55]

As the term of the Supreme Court was about to end, Minton wrote to his old friend Truman on June 3, 1953:

I was delighted to have your letter. It read like a chat with you which I wish I could have right now. I am "craw" full on the great Crusader and all his motley crew. I think the people are trying to wake up to the fact that Ike is just another Grant—another misfit Army man in office. From what I hear, he is running true to form. They say he could not make a decision in the Army. His Chiefs of Staff gave him the answer and he issued an order and that was that. It was obeyed or court martial, etc. Not so now. He may issue an order and maybe a half dozen Congressmen don't agree and even his cabinet members. He doesn't understand that kind of "Army" and he is frustrated and has to get away for golf. I was out to Chicago last week to the judicial conference of my Circuit and one lawyer who had been trying a case out in Iowa said the farmers out there were seething. The

Judge from Danville, Illinois, who you appointed said if you want to hear gripes, go down to the grain elevator and listen to the farmers. Another friend told me Dan Rice, the big broker on the Board of Trade at Chicago, told him if he had a friend running on the Democratic ticket in the farm belt next year bet on him. "There won't be a damn Republican elected in the farm belt." He says the farmers are hot. . . .

We will get away from here June 15th I hope. I shall go to Indiana for the summer. If you come our way or I yours, I shall see you. Mrs. Minton is out in Indiana but I know she would want to be remembered to Mrs. Truman as I do.

Fred & Tom & I meet before lunch each day and discuss the State of the Union. Your judgment is vindicated every day in naming them to this Court. Fred is a champion in every way.

Your comment about the information you got out of the scientist about the volcano which will enable you to stump the guys who don't know much about volcanoes reminds me of Booth Tarkington's visit to Vesuvius. He sent a big box of lava to one of his rich friends collect. His comment was "It wasn't much lava but it was a good deal for a fellow that had no lava at all."[56]

On July 13 Truman wrote:

Dear Shay:

Wasn't that a party at Frank McKinney's [former chairman, National Democratic Committee] house? The high-light for me was your being there. For some reason my old associates of the Senate pull a heartstring none others can pull. Even Republicans like Taft and old John Townsend of Delaware and Warren Austin of Vermont can make me homesick for the old Senate. But when it comes to colleagues like yourself and Hayden, Joe Guffey and John Garner, Carl Hatch and Mon Walgren, well I'm really a damned sentimentalist. When you think of Lew Schwellenbach, Nate Bachman, Joe Robinson, Alva Adams, Charlie McNary, Wallace White and a dozen others who have passed on it makes you want to go wherever they are come hell or high water. And I think you and I will do just that. [Truman had visited the Senate recently and had been invited to go on the floor.]

*Well, I went in, took old Bob Taft by the hand and he almost wept, said
my little say after an ovation bigger than I ever had as President and then
had a reception Democrats and Republicans shaking hands like I was still
at the other end of the Avenue or had risen from the grave.*

*What a day! It was worth the trip as were many others—but I thought
you'd enjoy my reaction.*

My best to Mrs. Minton. Send me a note when the spirit moves you.[57]

The spirit soon moved Minton, who was at his home in New Albany
while the Supreme Court was in recess. He responded on July 27 with more
than a note:

*It was good to see you at Frank McKinney's party. When I saw that B &
O taking you away January 20th, I wondered when, if ever, I would see
you again and I am glad it wasn't long. I wish I could have been in Washington while you were there. You had a grand reception even if you did
have to swallow the hospitality of Nixon. Like you, I use to enjoy my visits
to the Senate but there are so few of the old bunch left and some of the new
ones so disagreeable I don't enjoy my visits like I use [sic] to. And within
the last week, old Tobey [Senator Charles] passed to his reward. He was
a bit of the psalm singing hypocrite but he had a lot of good in him too.
Tonight's radio had another unfavorable report on Taft's condition. I fear
poor Bob is about to reach the end—a leader the party would sorely miss*
["Mr. Republican," Robert Alphonso Taft, died of cancer on July 31,
1953, at the age of sixty-three]. *One of my neighbors has just returned
from Nantucket, Mass., a place lousy with Republicans, and she reports
that there is much regret now being expressed that Taft wasn't elected. I
have about lost any respect I had for Ike. I really started slipping when Ike
came to Chicago and joined that cry of "Thou shalt not Steal." Whatever
else you may say about Taft he isn't a thief. I have come to believe that Ike
will say or do anything for a political advantage. Just recently he made a
speech in South Dakota in which he claimed credit for his administration
for the decision of the Supreme Court in which it outlawed segregation in
Washington restaurants. No one in his group had a damn thing to do with
bringing about that decision. He either knew it or he didn't. In either case,
he was shown a bit short on integrity. I have heard considerable expression*

of disappointment by folks who voted for him last fall. The reaction is setting in.

Mrs. Minton hasn't been well and is giving me much concern. She has lost a lot of weight and looks bad. The doctor reports no organic trouble so I have hope that she will pick up a bit. I was pleased to note Mrs. Truman looked well and very happy. You have earned the right to do as you damn please so don't let anyone inveigle you into doing anything you would rather not. I know you can say "No" so don't get out of practice.

We could not refuse a truce in Korea but if it took two years to get a truce I fear it will be a long time before we get a peace treaty during which time the "Bring the Boys Home" crowd will get in their licks and down will come our guard and our security will disintegrate and then the Commies will move in. Ike's trip to Korea now appears as phony as a three dollar bill. It looks like every time Ike is confronted with a real problem he looks for a "Caddy"—and so far the best he has turned up yet is that colored boy in Georgia called "Cemetery" Jones!

I hope all goes well with you. Don't build any round stables![58]

When the fall term of the Supreme Court opened on Monday, October 5, 1953, few people suspected that it would hand down a historic decision during the term. The case was *Brown v. Board of Education of Topeka*,[59] decided May 17, 1954.

The doctrine of "separate but equal" enunciated in the case of *Plessy v. Ferguson*,[60] decided by the Supreme Court in 1896, had been followed in cases dealing with black segregation without any re-examination. However, by the fall of 1952, the Supreme Court had cases on its docket from four states (Kansas, South Carolina, Virginia, and Delaware) and from the District of Columbia—all of which challenged the constitutionality of racial segregation in public schools. In each case, the facts showed that the black and white schools involved had been equalized, or were being equalized, with respect to buildings, curricula, qualifications and salaries of teachers, and other tangible factors. Now, nearly sixty years later, the Supreme Court was faced squarely with the question of the constitutionality of segregation *per se* and whether the doctrine enunciated in *Plessy v. Ferguson*[61] should be affirmed or reversed.

These five cases were argued together and the arguments were concluded on December 11, 1952. Two days later, on the morning of Saturday, December 13, the nine justices gathered in their conference room on the first floor, just behind the courtroom, to discuss together for the first time their disposition toward these school segregation cases. The session was marked with the customary informality of conference times; the justices wore business suits instead of robes.[62]

Chief Justice Fred Moore Vinson took his seat at the head of the conference table, a rectangular table about twelve feet long covered in green felt. The senior associate justice, Hugo Black, sat at the far end of the table. To the right of the chief justice, on one side of the table, sat Stanley F. Reed, Robert H. Jackson, and William O. Douglas. Across from them sat Felix Frankfurter, Harold Hitz Burton, Tom C. Clark, and Sherman Minton. Since he was the most junior of the justices in length of service, Minton, in keeping with the custom, sat nearest the door to receive or send messages because no one else was permitted in the conference room when the justices were assembled.

As a senator, Minton had supported and worked for the antilynching bill of the National Association for the Advancement of Colored People. When someone suggested that the antilynching bill trespassed on states' rights, he responded, "I am interested in states' rights; but I am much more interested in human rights."[63]

There was little in his record as a federal judge to link him with the social commitments for which he had worked so diligently in the Senate. In fact, his prior record on the bench earned him low grades as a civil libertarian. His law clerks were fond of saying that he was so ultraconservative that he would not even consider acting favorably on a writ of *habeas corpus* unless it reached him with blood on it.[64] So, his position on segregation was not known until he spoke that Saturday morning.

Again, as the junior justice, Minton was the last one to speak. His position was unmistakable. "It is true," he said, "that a body of constitutional law has grown up to surround the separate-but-equal doctrine with an aura of legitimacy, but the court has been chipping away at the protective covering for some time now. Classification of American citizens on the basis of race is unreasonable," he said. "Segregation in and of itself is unconstitutional," he added.[65] And he was ready to vote that way that day.

Years later, in 1968, Douglas disclosed that Minton had joined with Black, Burton, and himself to grant *certiorari* in these cases.[66] At least four justices must vote in favor of the grant of *certiorari* before a case will be heard by the Supreme Court.

As the end of the 1952 term neared, the justices could not agree on a disposition of the cases. Finally, it was agreed to hold the cases over until the new term with some questions for discussion.

On June 8, 1953, the cases were restored to the docket for reargument in the fall. At the same time, the court issued a list of questions upon which the reargument was to be based. The court asked for help on two main points: First, was there historical evidence which showed the intentions of those who framed and ratified the Fourteenth Amendment with respect to the impact of that amendment upon racial segregation in the public schools? Second, what kind of decree could and should be issued to bring about an end to segregation if the court should hold segregation unconstitutional?

Summer passed and the time for reargument neared. But Chief Justice Vinson died of a heart attack in his Washington apartment on September 8. He was sixty-three. On September 30, President Eisenhower named California Governor Earl Warren as the fourteenth chief justice. Almost at once Minton formed an attachment for and a strong bond with the new chief justice even though Warren was liberal and Minton conservative in his judicial philosophy. In a letter to Truman dated January 18, 1955, Minton wrote, "I still miss old Fred Vinson, but the best thing Ike has done was to appoint Warren."[67] These feelings and this affection were reciprocated and the two formed a friendship which lasted through Minton's retirement and until his death.[68]

On December 9 the reargument in these school segregation cases was concluded. Elaborate briefs were filed in response to the court's questions. The NAACP and its scholarly counsel, Thurgood Marshall (himself a graduate of Jim Crow schools and later an associate justice of the Supreme Court), refused to deal with the form of decree by which segregation might best be ended should the court hold it to be invalid. In their view, segregation, if held invalid, should be abolished completely and without delay.

Three days after the reargument, on December 12, the justices convened in their conference room to discuss the school segregation cases. Unlike the year before, Warren, a liberal, presided instead of the more conservative

Vinson, who was inclined to favor segregation.

Minton, again the last one to speak, agreed with Warren and Douglas that segregation in the public schools had to end. "The concept of a separate equality had been read into the Constitution by the Court in *Plessy*, 'a weak reed today,' and now it should be read right out of it. The world in 1953 was very different from that of the 1860s," said Minton, "and no justification remained for racial barriers except, as the chief justice had said, an avowed belief in Negro inferiority."[69] In terms of remedying the practice, he would just as soon leave that up to the District Courts to settle, in keeping with local conditions.

Still the Court moved with deliberation; its decision was not handed down until May 17, 1954. The Court was unanimous. Segregation in public schools was unconstitutional—against the law. Associate Justice Robert H. Jackson, who was convalescing from a heart attack, left his hospital bed that morning so that the full court, including its three Southerners, would be on the bench when the case came down. One opinion, by Warren, was written:

> *We conclude that in the field of public education, the doctrine of "separate but equal" has no place. Separate educational facilities are inherently unequal. Therefore, we hold that the plaintiffs and others similarly situated for whom the actions have been brought are, by reason of the segregation complained of, deprived of the equal protection of the laws guaranteed by the Fourteenth Amendment.*[70]

Again, the Court set for argument in the fall of 1954 the complex problem of formulating an appropriate decree for the implementation of its antisegregation decision. In a companion case from the District of Columbia (under congressional jurisdiction), the court issued a separate opinion which held that the due process clause of the Fifth Amendment forbade racial segregation by the federal government.

On August 19, from his home in New Albany while the court was in recess, Minton wrote to a friend about this important case: "I suppose we will need the wisdom of Solomon and the patience of Job in the resolution of our remaining task. But having put our hand to the plow, we must follow through in justice to all."[71] Most of the nation was surprised, many shocked, by the decision which affected schools with a total population of twelve million children. There was gloom in the white South. Public school segregation was required by law in seventeen states and the District of Columbia, and four other states permitted it. Senator Richard Russell of Georgia fumed that racial matters were in the jurisdiction of the legislative, not the judicial, branch of the government. He accused the Warren Court (as he and some others were already calling it), of "a flagrant abuse of judicial power."

Other issues were, of course, brought before the court. During the 1953 term, October 1953 to June 1954, Justice Minton wrote seven opinions, one concurring opinion, and five dissenting opinions.

Probably his most far-reaching opinion during this term was in *Phillips Petroleum Co. v. Wisconsin*,[72] decided June 7, 1954. This decision held that the Federal Power Commission had jurisdiction over sales to an interstate pipeline company by an independent natural gas producer, despite the fact that the FPC had decided that it lacked such jurisdiction. The applicable provision of the Natural Gas Act exempted "the production or gathering of natural gas" from FPC jurisdiction. The activities of Phillips in the production and transmission of natural gas ended with the sales to the pipeline companies and did not extend to its interstate transportation or local distribution. Minton, writing for the court, held that the sales of Phillips to the pipeline companies were separate and apart from its production and gathering activities and therefore not within the claimed exemption. The Natural Gas Act had contemplated regulation by the FPC of "rates of all wholesalers of natural gas in interstate commerce, whether by a pipeline company or not and whether occurring before, during or after transmission by a pipeline company."[73] Minton refused to weaken the "protection of consumers against exploitation at the hands of natural-gas companies [which] was the primary aim of the Natural Gas Act . . . by a strained interpretation of the existing statutory language."[74]

The Phillips case was decided by a five to three vote (Jackson abstained because he had not heard the argument). Clark was one of the dissenters. After Minton's death, Clark wrote: "At one time, we dissenters had hopes that the Justice [Minton] might change his mind after studying the case and before writing the opinion. This would make the vote four to four and would, we hoped, require a reargument with Justice Jackson taking part. One morning, Justice Minton dropped by my chambers while on the way to his, stuck his head in the door, and said, 'Tommy, if I were a senator, I might agree with you on that gas case, but being a judge, I have to declare the law, not make it.' "[75]

Consideration of the serious issues did not preclude lighter moments. Minton's personal file in the Truman Library regarding *Remmer v. United States*,[76] decided March 8, 1954, shows his wry sense of humor. Remmer had been convicted by the jury of purposely evading payment of federal taxes. Some person had made contact with a certain juror during the trial. Minton was designated to write the opinion. Frankfurter sent a note to Minton after he had received the first draft of the opinion: "I made a vow never to agree to an opinion that uses 'contact' as a verb." Minton sent this note in response:

> *My dear Felix:*
> *I have your comments on my circulation of No. 304, Remmer v. U.S.*
>   *I have made the following addition, at the end of the opinion:*
>   MR. JUSTICE FRANKFURTER *concurs in the judgment of the Court and in the opinion, except that he disagrees with the use of the word "contact" as a verb.*
>   *But, on second thought, to save the printing of this concurrence, I'll change the verb "contact."*[77]

A consideration of Minton's opinions during this period would be incomplete without a discussion of his dissent in *Terry v. Adam*.[78] It is regarded as one of his best opinions. The pre-primary, private elections of the Jaybird party in Texas had excluded blacks. The court held the elections violated the Fifteenth Amendment that "No state shall deny any person the right to vote on the basis of race, color or previous condition of servitude." Minton was the lone dissenter. The Supreme Court had decided in 1883 that private discrimination, however offensive, was not forbidden by the Fourteenth and Fifteenth Amendments, which by their language apply only to "state" action.[79] Minton meticulously analyzed the three majority opinions, discussed the cases in these opinions relied upon and concluded that the activities of the Jaybird party did not bring state action into play. He wrote:

I am not concerned in the least as to what happens to the Jaybirds or their unworthy scheme. I am concerned about what this Court says is state action within the meaning of the Fifteenth Amendment to the Constitution. For, after all, this Court has power to redress a wrong under that Amendment only if the wrong is done by the State. . . ·

What the Jaybird Association did here was to conduct as individuals, separate and apart from the Democratic party or the State, a straw vote as to who should receive the Association's endorsement for county and precinct offices. It has been successful in seeing that those who receive its endorsement are nominated and elected. That is true of concerted action by any group. In numbers, there is strength. In organization, there is effectiveness. . . .

I do not understand that concerted action of individuals which is successful somehow becomes state action. . . .

The propriety of these practices is something the courts sensibly have left to the good or bad judgment of the electorate. It must be recognized that elections and other public business are influenced by all sorts of pressures from labor unions, from the National Association of Manufacturers, from the Silver Shirts, from the National Association for the Advancement of Colored People, from the Ku Klux Klan and others. Far from the activities of these groups being properly labeled as state action, under either the Fourteenth or the Fifteenth Amendment, they are to be considered as attempts to influence or obtain state action.

The courts do not normally pass upon these pressure groups, whether their causes are good or bad, highly successful or only so-so. It is difficult for me to see how this Jaybird Association is anything but such a pressure group. . . .

In this case, the majority have found that this pressure group's work does constitute state action. The basis of this conclusion is rather difficult to ascertain. Apparently it derives mainly from a dislike of the goals of the Jaybird Association. I share that dislike. I fail to see how it makes state action. I would affirm.[80]

In the 1954 term (October 1954 to June 1955), Minton wrote seven opinions for the court, one concurring opinion, and nine dissenting opinions.

Writing for the court, he authored opinions that

- Sustained a conviction in a case which the United States attorney had presented to the grand jury without securing the approval of the attorney general. (Approval was required by an unpublished order.) Minton held the attorney general's approval was simply a necessity for the internal housekeeping rule for the Department of Justice and was not for the protection of the defendant.[81] This case was another instance where "A defendant is entitled to a fair trial but not a perfect one" which Minton had held in an earlier case.
- Reversed the Court of Appeals and held that the judgment of the District Court was not "clearly erroneous" on the factual issues in the record.[82] Minton was willing to give great weight to the factual conclusions of the trial court.
- Gave priority to the federal tax lien for unpaid federal tax over a garnishment lien in Texas[83] and an attachment lien in Ohio[84] (which under state law was perfected at the time of attachment). The court held the garnishment lien in Texas and the attachment lien in Ohio were "for federal tax purposes inchoate liens" because, at the time the garnishment and attachment issued, the fact and the amount of the lien were contingent upon the outcome of the suit for damages. It is interesting that during his tenure on the Supreme Court, Minton wrote all the opinions for the court concerning the priority of federal tax liens.
- Held that the existence of the landlord's lien in South Carolina which under state law was in the nature of a judgment did not make the landlord a judgment creditor within the meaning of the federal statute which created the federal tax lien.[85] Justice Minton emphasized the need for uniformity in the federal tax scheme and held that a competing lien under state law was perfected only when the amount of the lien, the identity of the lienor, and the property to which it related were established with certainty and the continued existence of the lien was no longer contingent on the outcome of subsequent litigation with the debtor.
- Affirmed the decision of the Court of Appeals upholding the conviction of a person for violating a federal statute requiring every

person engaged in wagering in the District of Columbia to register and to pay a "Gambler's Occupation Tax" of fifty dollars.[86] Another federal statute in the District made gambling a federal crime. Defendant claimed that the statute was unconstitutional because the registration requirement compelled him to incriminate himself in violation of the Fifth Amendment. Justice Minton reasoned that the statute did not violate the Fifth Amendment because it applies to acts committed in the past and not to future acts. "The only compulsion under the Act is that requiring the decision would-be gamblers must make at the threshold. They may have to give up gambling, but there is no constitutional right to gamble. If they elect to wager, though it be unlawful, they must pay the tax," he wrote.[87]

- Held that a 1948 law gave the federal district court in which an action is brought broad discretion to transfer a case to any other federal District Court where it might have been brought initially.[88] Before the law, the court was required to dismiss the case. This ruling significantly improved the administration of justice.

But the big issue loomed, unsolved. The justices convened on April 16, 1955, to decide how to form the decree for the implementation of *Brown v. Board of Education of Topeka*.[89] Minton was adamant that the court take a firm and decisive approach: "Sherman Minton, like Hugo Black, said he thought it vital that the Court remain unanimous in this phase of the case. He felt it important that they not talk big in the opinion and small in the decree—that would be weasling," he said. "The Court's main goal should be to get the desegregation process started without, in the process, revealing its own impotence to make it happen."[90]

It was not until the last day of the 1954 term, May 31, 1955, that the opinion came down implementing the decision in *Brown v. Board of Education*. Again Warren delivered the opinion and again the decision was unanimous. The opinion contained only seven paragraphs and the words "segregation" or "desegregation" did not even appear in it. It concluded with the now famous "with all deliberate speed" language:

> . . . *the cases are remanded to the District Courts to take such proceedings*

and enter such orders and decrees consistent with this opinion as are necessary and proper to admit to public schools on a racially nondiscriminatory
basis with all deliberate speed the parties to these cases.[91]

On June 4, 1955, Justice Minton wrote to a friend in Indiana about the
decisions in Brown v. Board of Education:

This Court has spoken clearly as to the illegality of and unconstitutionality
of segregation. We have, by our latest opinion, given the parties a fair
opportunity to work it out. The reaction to our last opinion is good on the
whole. For instance, the editor of The Atlanta Constitution was enthusiastic about it, and he is not a hard-shelled segregationalist. Maybe it would
have been advisable in the early days to have followed the lead of the Quak-
ers and returned all the slaves to Africa. But it wasn't done, and I personally have grave doubts as to its wisdom. So we had the problem, and we
must live with it and work it out, and that we will do as we have in days
gone by. Perhaps you may feel that we did not act strongly enough and
forthrightly enough. Courts are awkward institutions and it is difficult to
enforce their decrees if there isn't reasonable acceptance. I think it was
Churchill who said that the first thing a democracy must learn is never to
reveal its weakness, that is to say, never enter an order that you cannot
enforce.[92]

And, as ever, the affectionate correspondence with Truman continued.
On January 18, 1955, Minton wrote:

I was delighted to get your letter and to have some first hand information
about you. The latrine rumors were thick and fast about the time you were
in the hospital and I was worried for a time. Believe it or not, I say a little
prayer for you every night. Maybe it doesn't get above my heathen head,
but I start it in the right direction.

I thought you had your gall bladder removed, but from what you say,
they might as well have done a little nut cuttin' as Sam Rayburn would
say. Well, it is comforting to know you are on the road to recovery.

Ike's message was like the old Mother Hubbard dresses the women used
to wear, it covered everything and touched nothing. It was all sweetness

and light with not a cloud in the sky. Even in peace time they can't balance the budget! Now defense expenditures have gone up a half a billion dollars. That was where the fakers were going to save all the money to reduce taxes and balance the budget. Saving was not to be made at the expense of our security and that is the only place they have cut appreciably. . . .

Mrs. Minton doesn't improve. She weighs about 85 pounds. Nothing seems wrong except she has to live with me![93]

Gertrude Minton was always petite and probably never weighed more than a hundred pounds. At the time of this letter, she had what her son Sherman believed was a severe depression. Son John thought that she did not like living in Washington, D.C., and longed for her friends and home in New Albany. She recovered after she and Justice Minton made a trip to Europe. She said Dutch beer helped her regain her appetite, the younger Sherman recalled.

Again on April 21, 1955, Minton wrote to Truman about the affairs of state and other matters:

The plain fact [is] that he [Ike] doesn't know what it is all about and passes the buck in good old Army style.

Your handling in your speech of the "leashing" and "unleashing" of Chiang and the role of the Seventh Fleet is what I am talking about. Pure fraud and political crap as you pointed out.

I am sure Lyndon Johnson would never have kept us still in the time I was in the Senate. We can't win by talking about Ike's popularity and overlooking his gross errors. We can't beat him by saying what a great man he is but he just belongs to the wrong party. I would assume he is going to run. That old soldiers never die and old politicians never quit. He is an old politician but a damned poor one. . . .[94]

When the Supreme Court convened on October 3, President Eisenhower was recovering from a "mild coronary thrombosis" which struck in his sleep on September 24. This was to be Minton's last term of service on the court. He wrote nine opinions for the Court and two dissenting opinions during this 1955 term.

Writing for the Court in United States v. Anderson, Clayton & Co.,[95] decided November 7, Minton held that a corporation did not realize any gain on the sale of its own treasury stock. This result was codified in the Internal Revenue Code of 1954.[96]

In *Local Union No. 25 v. New York, New Haven and Hartford Railroad Company*,[97] decided January 9, Minton wrote the opinion of the court holding that a state court in Massachusetts did not have jurisdiction over a suit involving a labor dispute by the railroad against a trucking union. The truck drivers had objected to the railroad's practice of hauling trailers on railroad cars (the piggyback system) thereby depriving truck drivers of work. The officers of the local teamsters union had directed its membership to persuade other truckers not to deliver trailers to the railroad for shipping. The state court enjoined the local union from these actions. On appeal, the Supreme Court held that the state court did not have the authority to enjoin the local union from interfering in the railroad's business. Jurisdiction, in this dispute, the Court held, was exclusively vested in the National Labor Relations Board and federal authority had preempted any state regulation.

Minton accorded little weight to the administrative interpretation of a statute. Thus, writing for the court in *Shields v. Atlantic Coast Line Railroad Company*,[98] decided February 27, 1956, he rejected the contention of the Interstate Commerce Commission that the Safety Appliance Act[99] did not apply to dome running boards on trains. Shields, the plaintiff, had been injured while working on a dome running board of a railroad car when the car was standing still in the yard. He sued the railroad for his injuries. The Interstate Commerce Commission held that only appliances designed to protect a worker while the train was moving came within Section 2 of the act and therefore the railroad was not liable for the injuries. Minton's opinion extended the coverage of the Interstate Commerce Act when he wrote: "There is no reason to import such a distinction into Sec. 2 in order to deny the humane benefits of the Act to those who perform dangerous work on train cars that are not moving."[100]

Remmer v. United States,[101] decided March 55, 1956, made its third and final appearance in the Supreme Court. This was the case involving an outside person's contact with a juror named Smith during the trial of the case. On the previous remand, the District Court decided that Remmer had not been prejudiced. Minton again wrote for a unanimous court, reversing the conviction, holding that: "We think this evidence, covering the total picture, reveals such a state of facts that neither Mr. Smith nor anyone could say he was not affected in his freedom of action as a juror. . . . He had been subjected to extraneous influence to which no juror should be subjected, for it is the law's objective to guard jealously the sanctity of the jury's right to operate as freely as possible from outside unauthorized intrusions purposefully made."[102]

Normally a federal court will not decide the constitutionality of a state statute until the highest court in the state has passed on its constitutionality and has interpreted its meaning. In *Doud et al. v. Hodge*,[103] decided March 26, 1956, Minton, wrote for a unanimous court. He held that a federal District Court had jurisdiction over an action based on a claim that a state statute unconstitutionally denied claimant equal protection of the laws, although the highest court in the state had not yet interpreted the statute.

The validity of migratory divorces and related questions of alimony and custody create problems. It happens when a husband or wife leaves the state where the couple lives and goes to Reno, Miami, or Sun Valley where, after a short "residence" period, he or she obtains a divorce. When, following the divorce, alimony or some other aspect of the decree becomes an issue in litigation in the home state, the question arises whether the home state is required to give full faith and credit to the decree in the first state. Justice Minton, writing for the court, avoided deciding whether an *ex parte* divorce decree obtained by the husband (a decree by the court where the wife did not appear) must be given full faith and credit in a subsequent action for alimony by the wife in her home state by holding that the first state had not ruled on alimony so that the home state of the wife was free to do so.[104]

Minton usually deferred to the judgment of an administrative agency if possible. The adequacy of the findings of the Civil Aeronautics Board were challenged in *American Airlines v. North American Airlines*,[105] decided on April 23, 1956. Minton, writing for the court, upheld an order of the Board which directed North American Airlines to cease using that name because of its similarity to American Airlines.

In two cases, *Southern Pacific Company v. Gilco*,[106] decided June 11, 1956, and Reed v. Pennsylvania Railroad Company,[107] decided on the same day, Minton writing for the Court, extended the coverage of the Federal Employers' Liability Act. He held that an amendment to the act in 1939 brought an employee engaged in the construction of new railroad cars in one case and in the other case an employee working as a blueprint file clerk were covered by the act. The rationale was that their duties "furthered" and "closely and substantially" affected the interstate transportation operations of the railroad concerned.

In his unpublished dissent in Cole v. Young,[108] decided June 11, 1956, Minton showed his genuine concern about, if not fear of, subversives or those whose political loyalties were suspect. Kendrick Cole, who allegedly associated with Communists and belonged to a subversive organization, was an obscure food and drug inspector in the Department of Health, Education and Welfare. In 1953 he was suspended from his job without pay while an investigation of his activities was pending. After Cole waived his right to a hearing at which he could answer the charges against him, the Secretary of the Health, Education and Welfare Department, acting on an executive order of the President, summarily discharged him. Justice Harlan, writing for the majority, held that only civilian employees in sensitive positions could be discharged summarily, meaning that Cole could be terminated only through established procedures of the civil service. Minton wrote the dissent which underwent a number of painstaking revisions. He joined in the dissent of Justice Clark at the last minute, apparently because he did not want to lessen the impact of Clark's opinion by the publication of his own dissent. However, Minton's dissent is still on file at the Truman Library. In it, Minton wrote:

> There is no reason to believe that Congress intended that disloyal persons were to be free from the provisions in the Act wherever they were. I do not believe that Congress intended that any place in the federal government should be a "snug harbor" for Communists. If I have understood the purpose and intention of Congress it was to root out communists in government as summarily as possible. The construction of the Security Act now advanced by the Court thwarts that purpose. . . .
>
> Even if we admit that the Act applies only to sensitive agencies, who is the judge of what is sensitive? Congress has surely left it to the President. The Court has taken unto itself that judgment. Should we dispute the President's determination that all agencies are sensitive to all machinations of Communists and the disloyal as of today? If we have learned anything

from the hot and the cold war it is that old procedures to oust the disloyal were inadequate for this fast moving day.[109]

Even in the final opinions of his tenure on the bench, Minton never wavered from his conviction that the Supreme Court should interpret the law and not make it.

The health problems which had troubled Minton for a long time had not lessened. He had simply borne his troubles and continued to work. Now they were catching up to him. On December 27, 1955, he wrote to his friend and confidant, Truman:

I think I should tell you in confidence my plans. I think I shall retire next fall. I am slipping fast. I have to carry a cane now all the time. I find my mental health keeps pace with my physical health. I find my work very difficult and I don't have the zest for the work that I used to have. So I am firmly convinced that I should retire under the new act which permits retirement at sixty-five if you have had fifteen years on the Courts. I am past sixty-five and my fifteen years will be up next spring. You know I have had pernicious anemia for ten years & it has sapped my vitality, especially mental.[110]

By letter, dated September 7, 1956, Minton informed President Eisenhower of his intention to retire on October 15, 1956. He pointed out that he was over sixty-five and had served continuously on the federal bench for more than fifteen years and that his retirement was authorized by 28 United States Code, sec. 371 (b), 1952.[111] President Eisenhower acknowledged receipt of the letter on the same date and in his reply told Minton: "I trust that you will find your life in retirement to be filled both with contentment and good health."[112]

When Minton announced his retirement, he told reporters: "Time was when they waited on an elderly Justice and told him he wasn't doing his work right. I don't want that to happen to me. It's hard for me to walk more than a block, and this last term I had to take to a cane. My knees buckle and I lose my balance. It's pretty depressing. This thing keeps pecking away at me. Worst of all, it's gone to my brain. It affects my power to concentrate and think and retain arguments in my mind. It is not an easy place to leave," he said sadly, and added, "I hate to go." Then he thought of the future and the past and added: "There will be more interest in who will succeed me than in my passing. I'm an echo."[113]

Eisenhower promptly nominated William Joseph Brennan, Jr., a member of the Supreme Court of New Jersey, to succeed Minton.

Minton was correct. His retirement did go almost unnoticed by the press. Much more attention was paid to the nomination and confirmation of his successor.

Brennan was an Irish Catholic and a Democrat. Eisenhower, a Republican, hoped that Brennan's nomination would help undermine the liberal challenge of Democrat Adlai E. Stevenson, whom Eisenhower faced in his bid for a second term as President in November 1956.

Minton during two Senate-related trips to American military installations. In August 1935, he toured Fort Knox *(above)*, and in May 1936, he visited the U.S. Military Academy at West Point *(below)*, taking time to pose with three Indiana cadets, *from left:* John O. Frazier of Elwood, Joseph S. Lester of Salem, and Arthur D. Poinier of Indianapolis.

Minton's fun-loving nature, nurtured in his youth, continued during his tenure in the Senate. During a break in the floor action (*above*), Minton cups his ear to hear a World Series broadcast along with a group of Senate colleagues, including fellow "Young Turk" Harry Truman (*second from right*). At left, he and Texas Democrat Tom Connally team up to give Kentucky's Alben Barkley a ride in a cart.

Minton took his role as assistant Senate majority whip quite seriously, despite this whimsical pose.

Good friends Truman and Minton *(far left)* with a group of their Congressional colleagues. (Acme)

Minton's disappointment with his loss in his 1940 re-election bid seems obvious in this photo taken at New Albany with young Sherman and daughter Mary-Anne.

In 1948, as judge of the U.S. Seventh Circuit Court of Appeals in Chicago, Minton was appointed chairman of a federal fact-finding board empaneled to bring an end to a national coal strike. Here he shows reporters a defiant letter from United Mine Workers leader John L. Lewis. (Acme)

With Gertrude smiling in the background, Minton takes a congratulatory call after his appointment to the U.S. Supreme Court in September 1949. (Louisville *Courier-Journal*)

A year later, on September 13, 1950, this commemorative plaque was erected in Georgetown, Indiana, Minton's birthplace.

The Supreme Court in its 1950 term (*from left*): Felix Frankfurter, Tom C. Clark, Hugo L. Black, Robert H. Jackson, Chief Justice Fred M. Vinson, Harold H. Burton, Stanley Reed, Sherman Minton, and William O. Douglas. (Photo by Harris and Ewing, Collection of the Supreme Court of the United States)

The Supreme Court in its 1954 term (*from left*): Felix Frankfurter, Sherman Minton, Hugo L. Black, Harold H. Burton, Chief Justice Earl Warren, Tom C. Clark, Stanley Reed, J. Marshall Harlan, and William O. Douglas. (Photo by Harris and Ewing, Collection of the Supreme Court of the United States)

After Minton's retirement from the high court in 1956, he and Gertrude did some traveling, including an around-the-world trip in 1959 that included a visit with their son Sherman in Karachi, Pakistan. While there, cake was served in honor of Mrs. Minton's birthday.

On Dec. 21, 1956, a bust of Minton was dedicated at the Indiana Statehouse. The likeness, created by University of California sculptor Merrill Gage, stands today in the Statehouse Rotunda, a tangible reminder of one of the most prominent names in Indiana law and politics.

CHAPTER EIGHT

RETIREMENT

—— ◄►◄═►►◄ ——

AFTER THE SUPREME COURT RECESSED IN JUNE 1956, JUSTICE AND MRS. MINTON took a trip to Europe. It was a sorely needed vacation for both of them. As earlier mentioned, Mrs. Minton had been in a state of depression for months and had lost weight. The pernicious anemia to which Minton had alluded in the letter to Truman was truly taking a toll. The couple needed to get away, and from early July to late August they toured England, France, Germany and the Netherlands.

Truman also was abroad, though their paths did not cross. Oxford University conferred an honorary doctorate of law on the former President on June 21, 1956. The recipient was greeted, dined and honored by his hosts as befitted the award. Truman wrote to Minton:

> When I walked into the Sheldonian Theater, the ovation was so great it was almost like walking into a Democratic National Convention. Lord Halifax told me that there were more eggheads present on this particular occasion than had ever been assembled there in his memory, and after the degree was conferred, I got another ovation equal to anything I have ever had anywhere. At the Pilgrims Society dinner in London the next night there was a repeat performance. Lord Halifax and Clement Atlee and Prime Minister Menzies of Australia each made a speech of introduction. They preached my funeral, buried me and dug me up again before I had a chance to reply.[1]

Upon Minton's return to New York on August 21, he told reporters that he had "great confidence" in Adlai Stevenson, who four days earlier had been named the Democratic presidential nominee, and he hoped that

Stevenson would win the election.[2] These comments disturbed some who thought that an associate justice of the Supreme Court should remain above the political fray.

Minton reported this incident and other matters in a letter to "My dear Harry" on August 24:

> Harry Truman went to Londontown
> Just to ride a pony,
> They stuck a feather in his hat
> And called him macaroni.

They really did put a feather in your hat, for the cheers were still echoing for you in London when I passed through shortly after you had been there. One of my English friends sent me a copy of Sir Oliver Frank's speech about you that was published in The Listener. *It was music to my ears and confirmed me in my faith, which did not need any confirmation. I am sure you had a great trip to Europe.*

I would like to have heard Prime Minister Menzies' speech about you because I am sure it was a good one. We had him here for lunch one day and he is one of the most attractive, forceful personalities I have ever met. We just got back on Tuesday. We enjoyed ourselves thoroughly, although we were much handicapped by my inability to get around. I am sorry I missed all the doings at Chicago [Democratic National Convention at which Stevenson and his running mate, Tennessee Senator Estes Kefauver, were nominated], *but I think we have nominated a good ticket and with a vigorous campaign the Democrats can yet win.*

I enclose a little squib that appeared in the papers upon my landing in New York and this morning I received a couple of nasty postcards. I seem to have committed some sin or other against the deity Ike by suggesting that he might be handicapped by his physical condition. It seems to be profane for anyone to even suggest that Ike isn't God. I am afraid I must be a pretty profane man because I haven't the least bit of a deity complex pertaining to that fellow. . . .

As I told you before, I feel compelled to accept retirement, which I will do in October. I assure you I would not take this step if I were not con-

vinced that my condition of health compels it. It is not an easy thing to leave this attractive place where I have served a short time with great satisfaction, and, again, my deepest appreciation to you for giving me the opportunity. [Minton added in his own handwriting: "I have received two postcards and two letters giving me hell for not recognizing Ike as God!"][3]

On August 28 Truman responded with a "Dear Shay" letter:

I cannot thank you enough for your good letter of the 24th. The jingle is a crackerjack. I think you had a perfect right to say whatever you pleased. A jurist is not to be muzzled any more than anyone else in this great country. When I have the time, I'll sit down and tell you something about the convention in Chicago. At the moment, I am trying to get ready for a campaign tour for the [Democratic National] *Committee. I go to Iowa on Saturday and to Milwaukee for Labor Day. After that I do not know what will happen. The Boss joins me in best wishes to Mrs. Minton and to you.*[4]

In his letter to Eisenhower Minton had designated October 15, 1956, the effective date of his retirement. So when the Supreme Court opened its October 1956 Term on Monday, October 1, he was robed and ready and with the other justices filed to his customary seat on the bench as the traditional "*oyez, oyez, oyez*" were cried out in the hushed room. Plans then were made by Chief Justice Warren to swear in Brennan, Minton's successor, on the same day Minton would step down.

A surprise retirement party was given by Minton's former law clerks at the Mayflower Hotel on Saturday night, October 6. Seventeen young attorneys attended, including seven from Indiana: Raymond W. Gray, Charles E. Kelso, Thomas M. Lofton, Alan T. Nolan, and Richard S. Rhodes from Indianapolis; Gerry Levenberg from Gary; and Marshall E. Hanley from Muncie. They presented the retiring jurist with a handsome gold watch.[5]

On Monday, October 15, Minton formally retired without ceremony. Fifteen minutes after the court convened, he turned to his nearest colleague, Burton, shook hands, and left the bench. During his last fifteen minutes on the bench, Minton witnessed the swearing in of the usual quota of attorneys admitted to the bar of the Supreme Court. Among those admitted was his old friend from Princeton, Indiana, A. Dale Eby, judge of Gibson Circuit Court. Mrs. Minton was present for the retirement ceremony.[6] She and her husband soon returned to their home in New Albany.

Although there was no formal ceremony, tribute was paid to Minton when he retired. Chief Justice Warren said, "With the concurrence of all my colleagues, I announce with regret the retirement from the Court of Mr. Justice Minton. He has been more than our associate. He has been our companion. We are reconciled to his departure only because it is in the interests of his health. We all wish for him in his retirement a restoration of his vigor and the satisfaction to which his distinguished services to his country so justly entitle him. Our appreciation of his services and our personal regard for him are more adequately expressed in a letter to him which, together with his warm reply, will be spread upon the Minutes of the Court."[7]

The letter from his colleagues read:

> *Supreme Court of the United States*
> *Chambers of the Chief Justice*
> *Washington 25, D.C., October 15, 1956*

DEAR JUSTICE MINTON:

> *As the day of your retirement from service on the Supreme Court arrives, the realization of our loss bears down upon us. If considerations other than your health had prompted your decision, we would have joined in urging you to remain with us in active service. We appreciate, however, the sacrifice that your adherence to duty has already occasioned you. Both our admiration for you and our concern for your well being have increased as you have so faithfully carried on your duties without the loss of a single day in recent years, either from the Bench or the Conference.*

> *You have earned retirement—a long and satisfying one. Your distinguished services to your country as an Infantry Captain overseas in World War I, as a Senator from your native State of Indiana, as an Assistant to the President of the United States, as a member for eight years of the Court of Appeals for the Seventh Circuit, and for the past seven years as a Justice of the Supreme Court justly entitle you to the opportunity which retirement will afford you to recover your health.*

We shall miss both your wise counsel and our constant companionship with you. While you no longer will be with us daily, you will continue to be one of us.

Sincerely, EARL WARREN
HUGO L. BLACK
STANLEY F. REED
FELIX FRANKFURTER
WILLIAM O. DOUGLAS
HAROLD H. BURTON
TOM C. CLARK
JOHN M. HARLAN[8]

Justice Minton warmly replied:

Supreme Court of the United States
Chambers of Justice Sherman Minton
Washington 13, D.C., October 15, 1956

MY DEAR CHIEF JUSTICE AND COLLEAGUES:

I am deeply grateful to all of you for the considerate and more than generous comments contained in your letter concerning my retirement.

My stay here has been a happy and rewarding one, sweetened always by the many acts of kindness and friendship you have shown me. It is with much regret that I take my leave of the Court and you, but it is comforting to know that I am still accepted as one of you.

I shall often think of you as I watch from afar. My fondest recollections will be of the Court and each of you with whom I have served.

Faithfully yours, SHERMAN MINTON[9]

On October 16 Brennan took his oath of office and assumed Minton's place on the high court. Minton retired at full pay of thirty-five thousand dollars a year because of his eight years on the Court of Appeals and his seven years on the high court.

Honors came to Minton after his retirement. A Hoosier tribute was paid to him on December 21, 1956, when a bronze bust of him executed by Merrill

Gage, University of California, was dedicated and placed in the rotunda of the Indiana Statehouse. Republican Governor George H. Craig said in dedicating the bust: "Indiana has never produced a son greater than we honor here today."[10]

Minton kept up his warm correspondence with Truman during his retirement. On February 8, 1957, he wrote :*

I was frightened when I saw in the paper where you had a fall but as a friend of mine once said to me when he heard I was in an automobile accident & got a bump on the head he was not alarmed when he heard I was hit on the head that I couldn't have suffered more than a flesh wound!!!

It is bad business for old people to be stumbling around. When I was in Washington I called on Matt Neely at Bethesda Hospital where he was convalescing from a broken hip he received in a fall. I got the hardest fall in my house a few weeks ago but fortunately I broke nothing.

Speaking of stumbling how about that stumble from Dulles? [The Secretary of State had blamed the British and French for Egypt's attack on the Suez Canal.] *If you & Dean Acheson had been caught in such a predicament the kept press & the Republican trigger men would have had a field day. It looks like that halo can't be knocked off of Ike's brow. I have a feeling that it is a bit tilted now. . . . I am having a good time doing nothing. The worst part about retirement is you have the very real feeling that you are not doing anything worthwhile. This Spring we are going again to Europe tho I can't get around except with the greatest effort & the most limited way. I can sit & ride & see.*[11]

Truman was on vacation at the Olney Inn in Islamorada, Florida, when Minton's letter arrived. On February 18 he replied: "When I get home I will write you a long-hand letter that you better not let your secretary read!"[12]

The Harry S. Truman Library in Independence, Missouri, was dedicated on July 6, 1957. It had been built and furnished, without cost to the government, by the Harry S. Truman Library, Inc., a foundation, from funds donated by thousands of individuals and organizations in all parts of the country. Truman wrote to Minton on July 1:

---

* NOTE: Original spellings and wording have been maintained in the "Dear Harry" and "Dear Shay" letters, even when misspellings occur.

I cannot tell you how very much I appreciated receiving your card from Munich. It is always good to hear from you, and I wish it were possible for you to be here on the 6th for the library dedication. The first time you have the opportunity, please come out for a look at the new building and its contents. I think you will like it very much.[13]

Justice and Mrs. Minton returned from their second European trip on July 8 to their home in New Albany. On July 10 he wrote to Truman:

I just got back Monday from Europe. We had a wonderful trip and I stumbled through with good luck. We were in London, South France, Nice, Italy, Switzerland, Germany, Denmark & Finland.

The most interesting thing that came to my attention was the amazing spectacular recovery of Germany & the success of the Social Reform States in Scandinavia. We are fifty years behind them in our program so valiantly fought for by you & Roosevelt & so vigorously opposed by organized industry.

The Germans show the great possibilities of the Marshall Plan & have gone to town in places like Frankfurt, Dusseldorf & the whole of West Germany, especially the Ruhr Valley. As you know, they are so prosperous that they are now loaning France money. Twenty years from now they won't have to whip France (or try to) they will own it! You hardly notice the scars of war in Germany outside of Berlin. The prettiest farm country I ever saw—the best kept farms—were near Munich as we came in by rail from Zurich. Every farm had new tractors & new machinery. Surely there is no more industrious intelligent people than the Germans. If they have that "Superior Race" complex knocked out of them, which I doubt, they will fight the next war from the factories & the commerce lines. From what I have seen of them I am inclined to agree they are a "Superior Race"!! Certainly they have no peers. That small car the Volkswagen is running all over Europe like the lice of Egypt. The American big car will have to reckon with them and the Italian Scooter Motorcycle. I expect to be dead when the Scooter takes over! I don't see how old decrepit coots like me could survive them!

I hear you are a grandpa! Wonderful. There is nothing like it. Grandchildren can do nothing wrong. You get damn tired of them sometimes but they aren't gone five minutes until you wish they were back.

I wish I could have been to the dedication of the Library. I am sure Warren did you justice because he not only likes you but appreciates what you have done for the Country. I never have contributed to that worthy cause. No one ever solicited me & I just keep putting it off. Will you see that this little check gets to the right place?

I would love to see you & get your reaction to what goes on. I hope it won't be long until I may have that opportunity.

Gertrude (Grandma Minton) joins me in affectionate good wishes to you & Grandma Truman.[14]

Truman responded to the letter and enclosed check from Minton on July 17:

I do not know when I have received a letter I appreciated more than yours of the tenth with the check for the library enclosed. . . . The $200 check was very welcome, and I am grateful to you for sending it. I wanted your name on the list, but I didn't have the nerve to ask you to put it there."[15]

In early 1958 journalist Edward R. Murrow did a series of television programs with the former President. On February 7 Minton wrote to Truman:

I just had to write and tell you what a wonderful appearance you made with Ed Murrow. Your grasp of the present situation and your excursion in the history recent and ancient was marvelous. Coming at this time it shows just what is wrong in the White House—no leadership! Why? Because the President doesn't know where he is going. He says the nice things his staff prepares for him to say but there is no execution because he doesn't understand what is going on or what went on in the world before. . . .

I would like to talk to you so we could take our hair down. I write so poorly & it is an effort to write.[16]

On March 27 Truman replied:

Dear Shay:
What a prompt and efficient correspondent I've turned out to be! My in-

ability to say No! with exclamation points has put me in a bad fix with my friends. Good thing I wasn't born with a split tail—no telling what would have happened.

I'm very happy you liked the Ed Murrow program. I spent 3 weeks and fourteen hours making 50,000 feet of film with no rehearsal. It seems to have gone over on the first hour all right.

I had about 1500 or 2000 letters and wires on it—all favorable but four. That four turned out to be Baptist and Methodist preachers who didn't like damn and hell. That's what they scare their members with when they are trying to increase their paying customers. But no farm boy should use those Biblical terms for educational purposes.

Since the Murrow show I've tried my best to stir up the baby elephants. They are screaming their trumpets off. So I guess what we said was right.

The old Republican National Chairman said he'd give $1000.00 to any charity I'd name if I could prove that Tricky Dickie had called me a traitor. I proved it and suggested that he send his thousand to the Korean Red Cross. It was more than he could stand. He quit. But the thousand is still unpaid!

When I called Ed Murrow and told him his show was a flop he almost had a fit. "Why," said he, "All my returns have been favorable." I told him so had mine and that was what was wrong. When the press and the public don't raise hell with a public figure he's bound to be wrong! We both know that. Always glad to hear from you.

I've some more unprintable comments on the present halo wearers. Let me have your comments.

Sincerely, Harry[17]

Truman wrote a letter to Minton in the early part of 1958 marked "Personal & Confidential." Minton already had left for Europe when the letter arrived in New Albany. The postmaster at New Albany returned the letter to Truman who thanked him for his kindness. Minton wrote to Truman on September 2:

When I came home from Europe this spring the postmaster showed me your letter. Was he ever proud of that letter! I was sure when you got around to it you would send the letter back to me. I was delighted to get it.

Again I say that Murrow interview was the best I ever saw or heard.

I am sometimes ashamed of myself for my low opinion of the President. Not since Buchanan has there been such a woeful lack of leadership in the White House. Ike was so right in 1948 when he said a man trained in the military was not fit for political office. Gen. Sherman & Gen. Lee supported that view. Ike proceeded to demonstrate it. His lack of fitness & ability were kept covered up by the press that made him into a mythical god. It was profane to say anything about him. The Democrat leaders in Congress kowtowed to him and at a big dinner in Washington the feature of the evening was the presentation to the President of a blooded Hereford heifer by Lyndon Johnson & Sam Rayburn!! I said to Johnson six months after Ike took over that the Democrats should end the honeymoon & take after him. Lyndon replied "Oh! It's too early." Far as I can see it is still too early for him. . . .

Ike talks now about integrity & honesty—his own honesty—his integrity has been missing more & more from the day he came from Colo to Chicago in 1952 to the Republican Convention & embraced that phony campaign slogan against Taft "Thou shalt not steal." Then he put his arms around [Indiana Senator] Jenner and [Wisconsin Senator] McCarthy and when Ike was going to make a speech in Milwaukee & say something good about Gen. Marshall to whom he owed so much McCarthy made him take it out! Then he piously vetoed the gas bill because of the money spent to further its passage forgetting all about the hundreds of thousands he accepted because he advocated the tidewater oil bill. . . .

I will be at Fort Wayne for your speech. I wish you could stay over with me a day or two. We would sure get that "cussin" done.[18]

Truman replied immediately:

September 6, 1958

Dear Shay:
You'll never know how much I appreciated your good letter. Your postmaster is a gentleman and one of very few in public positions. I'm glad you had a good visit abroad. I took a trip myself in Southern France. I've tried for five years to return to my position of anonymity that I had in 1935 when you and I had such grand times together in the Senate of the United States

with Joe Guffey, Nate Bachman, Pinkwhiskered Ham Lewis, Louis Swellenbach, and a lot of others including that man Bilboe, Hughie Long and Tom Connolly. What a galaxy!

Your statements on the present situation at 1600 Penna Ave. are so right. Why I don't know. Had a message from General Marshall the other day. He's been snubbed by the White House Bonehead just as I have. If Franklin Roosevelt were alive he'd be treated the same way. It is fantastic. How could a man be that way?

The people around the halls of the Great White Jail have succeeded in making General Grant and Warren Harding great Presidents!

The Dickson-Yates giveaway [on October 5, 1954, the Atomic Energy Commission approved a contract under which a West Memphis power plant would be built for the TVA by a Southern utility group headed by Edgar H. Dixon and Eugene A. Yates], the atomic power debauchery, and the giveaway of our forest reserves for fake mining claims rank almost with off-shore oil in the use of public assets for payment of political debts to the special Republican interests.

I can't help but explode once in awhile on what has happened. I reduced the national debt by 27 billion dollars, balanced the budget for six of my eight years, met Tito, Stalin et al. in Yugoslavia, Persia and the near east, kept Stalin out of Greece and Turkey and Berlin and put the United Nations into Korea and saved that Republic. Also kept crooked old Chiang Kai Chek from being mopped up by placing the 7th fleet between him and danger.

Then what happened, they surrendered in Korea, unloosed Chiang by moving the 7th fleet from Formosa Strait and like the 50,000 Frenchmen at Agincourt they put it right back again! Lied to Indochina, Britain and France on Suez and forgot the near east and now where in hell are we? Landed in Lebanon, probably at war with terrible Red China, lost all our Western Hemisphere friends and searching desperately to blame Truman for the whole fantastic business!

Even Grant, Harding and Coolidge were not quite that bad.

Well to hell with it. I'm going to paste their hip and thigh in this 58 go around and then try to smash them in 1960—if we can find a candidate to do it with.

Take care of yourself and get into a position to help.[19]

On November 4, 1958, the Democrats gained fifteen seats in the Senate and forty-eight in the House, Nelson Rockefeller was elected governor of New York, and John Fitzgerald Kennedy was reelected senator from Massachusetts.

Truman had campaigned vigorously for the Democratic Party and its candidates. Minton wrote to him on November 18:

You deserve a lot of credit for that victory a week ago. You have been working & speaking among the Democrats for months & you helped to keep them up.

The election to me means a vote of no confidence in Eisenhower and all his works. The people that I hear talking don't spare the President. The people are just beginning to learn that this man on the pedestal, so carefully served & built up by the kept press, has feet of clay. . . .

We had a great victory in Indiana. Handley [Harold W., who was then in the middle of his term as Republican governor of Indiana] *was the most vulnerable candidate ever to run in Indiana in my time. I do hope Hartke* [Vance, the Evansville Democratic who defeated Handley in the Senate race by 242,000 votes] *doesn't think he won the election himself. He just happened to be at the right place at the right time like I was in 1934. He is a hard worker & I hope will make a good Senator. It looks like Jenner may be on his way out tho he is the smartest politician of them all.*

Where the Republicans won they had disassociated themselves with Ike & Dick.

I just wanted you to know I was thinking about you in this hour of triumph. I hope Sam [Rayburn] *& Lyndon* [Johnson] *those old "radicals" can keep the mavericks in line.*[20]

Justice and Mrs. Minton took a trip around the world in early 1959. This tour, which lasted two months, began on January 12 when the couple took a Pan-American jetliner from New York to Paris. The trip included a stop at Karachi, Pakistan, for a visit with their son Sherman, who at the time was teaching and doing field studies on snake and scorpion venoms at the Jinnah Postgraduate Medical Center in Karachi. The Mintons, always strong family people, were savoring the time they had to see their son, his wife, and their grandchildren.

As a boy growing up in New Albany, young Sherman had a keen interest in natural history, with an emphasis on reptiles. His parents had bought him books on the subject, and his father took him to the great fossil beds at the Falls of the Ohio and to the hills near New Albany, where rattlesnakes could still be found about 1930.

Young Sherman's continuing career was a source of interest—and sometimes incredulous amusement—to his father. Still, the parents had been surprised at his dedication to poisonous snakes. The senior Minton, according to Sherman, had visions of him as a carnival performer or, at best, an impoverished biology teacher. About the time the son graduated from high school, the Mintons' encouragement of their son's interests was sorely tested. Although he had been forbidden to keep poisonous snakes, that summer he and a friend kept two copperheads and a small rattlesnake in a cage hidden in woods just outside New Albany. A copperhead bit his friend, and panic ensued since copperhead bites were considered quite serious. A neighbor told the friend's parents their son would be dead before the next day. Fortunately, serum was located and rushed from Louisville, and Sherman's friend made a quick and uneventful recovery.

The younger Minton was sure his career as a herpetologist was over. Instead, his parents told him that if he was going to have such a great interest in these creatures he had better learn how to work with them safely. As a result, Sherman had concentrated his studies on snake venoms since the fifties, and his parents were able to observe him in action during their visit to Pakistan.

The Mintons finished their global trip and returned to America, and on May 15 he wrote to his friend Truman:

> I attended a dinner in Louisville last week at which Robert Murphy of the State Department was presented a medal by Bellarmine College. As usual a number of congratulatory telegrams were read. The first one was from the President. It received the usual courteous applause. As the next one was read the first words were INDEPENDENCE MO and the large dinner crowd burst into good-natured laughter & uproarious applause with a spontaneity that manifested only affection and good will to the sender Harry

*Truman. Boy if you could only recall ten or twelve years you would sweep
the country. The people love you because they think you are a straight
shooter & know what you are talking about.*

*It sure was a delight to see you in Washington. I often think of a White
House reception when you were President and as I came through the line
you stood with all that gallery at your back and you said to me Go around
behind these bushes and sit down & wait until this thing is over & you &
Lew Schwellenbach & I will have a visit. It doesn't look like I will ever
have a chance to sit down & visit with you like we use to do. The public
won't let you!*

*Gertrude & I were concerned when we read in the paper that Mrs.
Truman was in the hospital. I hope she is out by this time & good as new.
Give her our love.*[21]

Truman replied on May 29:

*I have been trying for the last four or five days to get off a handwritten
letter to you in reply to yours of the 18th, but I just have not been able to do
it.*

*My birthday celebration [he turned seventy-five on May 8] started
in April and still seems to be going on, and the letters that accumulated
here because of that occasion and those that keep coming in about Mrs.
Truman are almost more than I can handle.*

*Just as soon as I get my ducks in a row and Mrs. Truman returns from
the hospital, you will hear from me along the lines you and I usually use in
correspondence.*[22]

Minton was hospitalized in October 1959 with a blood clot near the
heart. When he was released, he wrote to Truman on November 9 and his
handwriting evidenced the seriousness of his illness—it was a barely legible
scrawl:

*I am just home from the hospital & can't write much but the first thing I
wanted to do was to write to you & to tell you how much your calls,
flowers & letters to Gertrude meant to me as I lay there in the hospital with
about as close call as I ever had. To know of these things was wonderfully*

*comforting but the thing I cherish most is the friendship that prompted them.
Word from you even thrilled the doctors, nurses & hospital attendants.*

*What did you think of the elections Tuesday, especially in Indiana &
Ky? Good bye "Happy"!* [A. B. "Happy" Chandler of Kentucky][23]

Truman replied on November 16, 1959:

*I have never received a letter that pleased me more than yours of the 9th.
The report that you are back home in New Albany, Indiana, made me as
happy as I could be. When you were in the hospital I kept in touch with
Mrs. Minton and I don't think I ever worried about anything more than
your condition at the time I talked to her. I hope you will take care of
yourself as I have said time and again that we need men like you around.
Please tell Mrs. Minton to put handcuffs on you if necessary to keep you
down.*[24]

On March 28, 1960, in the same shaky handwriting, Minton wrote to
Truman:

*It sure warmed my heart to hear your voice the other day. If it had not been
such an awful day I would have gotten a cab & run over to see you. But I
get around so badly I was afraid of slipping and falling. Since I was sick I
have lost a great deal of the use of my legs. And I have my sleeping all
turned around & have to take sleeping pills they make me a bit woozy &
half intoxicated. If I can work it in agreeable with your time I am going to
drive out to see you this spring.*

*Some Democrat friends were in the other night & talked about how
much they enjoyed the rebroadcast of your Louisville speech. I missed it
damn it!*

*Kennedy looks awfully strong from where I sit for the nomination. But
Harry I am afraid the Ku Kluxers will take him in the election. The
anti-Catholic sentiment has diminished some but it is still here. I find it in
my contacts with the old OPAs around here. You know "Chip" Morrison's
defeat for governor of La was the hillbilly Kluxer vote. Sam Lubell the
pollster found a lot of it in the South on his recent poll. When Kennedy
filed for the Indiana primary the Baptist & others picketed him. Why nomi-*

nate a man who has two strikes on him to go with. Symington [Stuart from Missouri, another Democrat who pursued the Democratic presidential nomination in 1960] doesn't generate any enthusiasm—sorta like Cox or Davis in the days of other compromises. Lyndon Johnson has great ability but he has the curse of the South upon him.

Speaking of the South you are dead right about what you said about the Negro sit down strikes. Their action is unlawful. It is alright to picket & to demonstrate so long as they don't trespass or violate the law & the right of others. They claim to be against lawlessness & they practice it themselves.

I am sorry you could not accommodate my old friend Professor Miles [E. J. Miles, of Colorado College, had asked Truman to speak there]. He comes from a good old Democratic family in this part of the state.[25]

Truman responded on April 9:

Dear Shay:
Here I am two weeks late telling you how much I appreciated your letter of March 28th. I had expected to call on you—but Shay, the Devil has a hand in most things. He was represented—not by their consent—by the people around Louisville who were sure the world and the Democrats would be ruined unless I could talk to them. You know very well that I'm only a retired farmer who was lucky as hell in a political career which was forced on him. I'm neither a prophet, and thank God, nor a pollster. These pollsters are still on the make.

Look at Wisconsin. Kennedy was supposed to clobber [Hubert H.] Humphrey. With 100,000 Republican crossovers he didn't make the showings that the old man and his money thought he would. I like the boy—but he is still a boy. In 1944 Franklin Roosevelt had me to pay him a visit for lunch in back yard (which in the beginning was the front yard) of the White House. We are under the magnolia trees set out by Andrew Jackson. He told me he wanted me to go around the U.S. from New Orleans to Los Angeles to Seattle to Boston on the train. I told him I'd made plane reservations for the trip anticipating what he would tell me. Then he scared the hell out of me by saying "We can't both take chances."

Well I went to New Orleans, got on a Southern Pacific train with a special car for me and one for the press. We stopped a dozen time [sic] *before we arrived at L.A. The paper boys bet that John Garner wouldn't come to the station at Uvalde [Texas, Garner's hometown]—but he did—and we struck a blow for "liberty."*

In L.A. I saw all the top picture makers and collected $80,000.00 for the campaign, gave it to George Allen [Democratic National Commit-tee Secretary] and made him give me a receipt for the National Commit-tee. Must have obtained twice that on the way around, but I won't handle political money just made the unreliable Mr. Allen sign receipts for it and I made speeches.

Finally arrived in Boston after being called a Klu Kluxer in Chicago by Bertie [Colonel Robert R. "Bertie" McCormick of The Chicago Tri-bune] and an organization stooge everywhere else. In Boston at the Ritz who should be in my suite but old man Kennedy, the boy's father. He began cussing Roosevelt and called him a murderer because his boy was killed in Germany. I stood up and told him if he would repeat that state-ment I'd throw him out the window. Bob Hannegan [chairman of the Democratic National Committee] came in then and kept me from doing it. I haven't seen the old bastard since. Roosevelt made him and made him rich. Of course the boy's not to blame for the old man's shitass attitude—but I can't forget it. We've got to have a man for the Democratic candidate who not only can be elected but who can be President when he is elected. Two Coolidges in two generations are enough! History only repeats: Van Buren, Franklin Pierce, Jim Buchanan after Jackson, Grant, Hayes & Chester Arthur after Lincoln, Ben Harrison and McKinley after Cleve-land and me & Ike after Franklin.

Keep a stiff upper lip. We need men like you.[26]

Minton wrote to Truman on May 7:

Here it is Derby Day and I am sitting at home with the race track only a few miles away. I have never been since we went with Joe Guffey & Jack Garner & I have never wanted to. Once you have seen the Derby you have had it. You don't want to do that any more.

I was in Washington ten days ago & was tempted to stay over for the Democratic Pow Wow on April 30th. Vance Hartke invited me but I couldn't. I am sorry I missed seeing you as I was when you were in Louisville.

The weather was so bad that day I was afraid to venture out. My loss was the Kentuckians gain!

Yes I know you are just a "dumb" farm boy who was lucky in politics! Thank God for such luck! I had lunch in Washington and sat beside Daisy Harriman. She told me she asked Churchill if he thought you were a great President & if you would go down in history as a great American President. Churchill responded—"Truman will go down in history not as a great American President but one of the greatest!" "Them's" my sentiments & on the highest authority. In those days we had leadership in the White House & not a chocolate soldier.

Kennedy's showing in Indiana continues to emphasize the bigot vote in the country & W. Va. will really show it I am afraid. The crackpot candidates on the Democratic ticket got over 80,000 votes. That is only a sample of the Ku Klux vote in this state. Kennedy's father scared the hell out of me in December 1939 when Lew Schwellenbach & I had lunch with him in Jimmy Byrne's office. He was then Ambassador to England & he said England was through—Hitler would win & we could do business with Hitler etc. How wrong can a man get? His influence over the boy would be considerable. Senator K. is not so great that he can go into the race with his handicaps & win. You can't spot Nixon that anti-Catholic vote. So why nominate K? If not K—who? I was disturbed while I was in Washington to hear the Chief Justice who doesn't like Nixon say he felt he would be elected whoever the Democrats nominate. I know you don't like him but I am still for Stevenson.

If I could catch you home I might run out to see you. Best regards![27]

His avid interest in politics was not limited to the national scene; Minton was equally interested in and concerned with politics on the state and local level. He attended the Democratic State Convention in the Coliseum in Indianapolis on June 21, after which Truman wrote to him on June 24:

As I came through Indianapolis on June 22 I obtained a newspaper with a picture in it showing you talking to former Governor Schricker. I just had to tell you that I was highly pleased to know that you are still a "working" Democrat.[28]

Matthew Empson Welsh from Vincennes was nominated at this convention as the Democratic candidate for governor. He had been United States attorney for the Southern District of Indiana from 1950 to 1951; representative from Knox County in the Indiana General Assembly 1941 to 1943; senator from Knox and Daviess counties from 1955 to 1959; and Democratic floor leader of the Indiana Senate in 1957 and 1959.

Minton wanted to help elect Welsh as governor. On August 18, 1960, he wrote:

> My dear Matt:
> You are coming to this city [New Albany] soon. Do not fail to call on the Mayor. He has been elected four times and is a power here. He & the [Floyd County Democratic party] Chairman Bornwasser are not friends so he will try to keep you away from the Mayor. Both are good Democrats but political enemies. The Mayor thinks you are "high hat" so put him right by giving him a call.[29]

Welsh sent a congratulatory telegram to Minton on the occasion of his seventieth birthday on October 20, 1960, to which Minton responded on October 28:

> Thanks for your good telegram. It was good of you to remember me in the midst of your hot campaign. It looks like a victory to me—especially for you. My "scouts" all give you good reports. Again my thanks & I hope to be at your inauguration. Good luck.[30]

Welsh defeated his Republican opponent, Crawford F. Parker, on November 8 by the narrow margin of 23,177 votes out of more than 2,122,000 cast. He gave Minton the opportunity to attend his inauguration despite the fact that Nixon carried Indiana over Kennedy by a margin of almost 223,000 votes in the presidential race. (Kennedy carried only nine of the ninety-two counties in Indiana in 1960.) Governor Welsh took office on January 9, 1961.

The campaign had been an agonizing one for Minton and Truman, both of whom seemed to distrust Kennedy's controversial father, his Catholicism,

and his silver-spoon upbringing. On August 16, 1960, Minton wrote to
Truman after Kennedy had been nominated:

> I am sorry you were unable to make the Convention. I hope your sister is
> doing well. As a Democrat I of course accept the ticket. The thing that
> encourages me to believe it will be a winner is that the Republicans don't
> like it. Kennedy has made the Primary system look good. But a moment's
> reflection will show that the Primary is cut out for men like Kennedy who
> have wealth of their own to pay for putting an organization in the field &
> paying the campaign bills. One thing cannot be denied he has an effective
> organization & has conducted a vigorous campaign. If he can organize for
> the election as well he should overcome the spot handicap of his religion, I
> look for K to do much better than Al Smith who was crude & his family
> showed up poorly. Then too he had prohibition going against him. Never-
> theless as far as Indiana is concerned I am fearful because it is lousy with
> Ku Kluxers. I remember that in this campaign that Lov Daly & some other
> crackpot got 85,000 votes in the Primary.
>
> In my opinion that is an anti-Kennedy vote that is anti enough to go to
> the polls. How many of the Humphrey votes in W. Va. & Wis. were
> anti-Catholic & will remain so. On the other hand my barber says don't
> worry—the people are tired of this administration & want a change!!
>
> One thing the powers that be did not do & for which I hold them re-
> sponsible is that they didn't have you down for a speech to the convention
> from the start & not as an after thought. That I didn't like & I heard others
> say the same thing. I wish you had been there to give them a few solid
> punches.
>
> I am still hoping to see you in Independence before the year is out.
>
> With all good wishes & the hope that you will be on the firing line this
> campaign.[31]

Truman replied on August 30:

> You'll never know how very much I appreciated you letter of Aug. 16th.
> We are in a hell of a fix. Why, because Old Man Kennedy was & is the
> possessor of 200 million dollars made by selling short the country in 1930–
> 31 & 32 and using his position as Ambassador to Great Britain to make a

deal with the Scotch Whiskey boys to take a cut on every case sent to U.S.A. Now we have a situation as a result of Franklin Roosevelt's more than political smartness in Kennedy's son having been nominated for the greatest office in the history of the world.

What can we do? You and I will have to support the lesser of the two evils. Nixon is outside the pale. He said that the Democrats from 1934 to 1952 were the traitors of the age! Well if I'm a traitor and if General Marshall is one as the no good Senator Jenner stated at Milwaukee in 1952, with Ike on the platform, what are you & I to do? Well we'll support the Democrats as we have always done. I'm not so sure it won't be in vain. And then where do we go—God only knows.

I shall be in Marion, Indiana, on Sept. 5th for a labor day speech, in Abingdon, Virginia some time after that and then in Iowa—maybe—for a farm speech. I'm only supporting the Party and that's all I can do.[32]

Minton wrote to Truman on September 5:

I think I told you I am a pathological Democrat & when the baby is named he is my baby. Nixon is impossible for you & me. I would have been happier with another candidate. In his [Kennedy's] public speeches on TV he just doesn't come across. He appears immature but I hope he impresses other people more than he does me. I don't worry too much about old Joe K. I do think the boy is free from that influence in his public life.

Joe Alsop surprises me. He seems to be cool on Nixon to say the least. The polls he has been taking are all favorable to K.

We have a good ticket in Indiana but I am afraid they are making a mistake by divorcing the State ticket from the National. We did that in 1928 & got the hell beat out of us. There is no place for division in a campaign. You must have unity. K will never carry Indiana anyway. There are too many Klu Kluxers here. The Baptists are going to town on the religious issue. By the way you are a Baptist aren't you? Why don't you come out with a statement giving them hell. I sure would if I were a Baptist! I am afraid of the religious issue. It is being used & stirred skillfully by the opposition. Maybe if K meets it head on he might stop its catastrophic effect.

I am sorry I didn't get to Marion to see you today. It was very hot here

& none of my friends were going & it was impossible for me to drive up. I hope you got a good crowd & that Alex Campbell took good care of you.

Thanks a million for that picture you sent to me. I sure appreciate it. What a difference there is in your countenance & mine! My sins are catching up with me.[33]

On October 13 Minton sent another letter to Truman:

Thanks a million for the beautiful book, "Mr. Citizen." I almost read it in one sitting I was so interested. It reads just like talking to you!

In the "Great Debate" I heard them try to draw you in for your forthright speech but it backfired. The folks like your straight talk. Speaking of the "debate" I have the feeling Kennedy is doing Okay with Nixon. The religious thing is not as bad as it was but it still cuts deep. . . .[34]

On October 20 more than one hundred people gathered at the New Albany Country Club to honor Minton and join in celebrating his seventieth birthday. Truman sent a congratulatory telegram in which he called Minton "a great senator, a great judge and a great justice" and added that the country "certainly needs men of his caliber."[35] John Simpson Hastings, Chief Judge of the Seventh Circuit Court of Appeals in Chicago, told the audience that it was the first day in history his court had been adjourned without a legal explanation, but that he wanted to be in New Albany to honor a great Hoosier and a great American. Cale J. Holder, judge of the U.S. District Court at Indianapolis, recalled in a speech at the party that the appointment of Minton to the Supreme Court came after the only time he could remember when Republicans throughout Indiana supported a Democrat for a federal appointment. The centerpiece for the dinner was a huge cake in the shape of the Supreme Court Building.[36]

In an interview with reporters prior to this birthday, Minton had been asked about the upcoming presidential election. He modestly restrained himself with the suggestion that perhaps as a retired, but still neutral justice, he should not express any opinions on politics but added "I sure as hell intend to vote for Kennedy."[37]

Minton wrote to Truman on October 23:

Thanks for your birthday telegram but most of all for your friendship over the years. The older I get the more appreciative I am of it. I wish you could have been at the party. My friends never gave up hoping that you would turn up at the last minute but I told them you were too absorbed in the campaign. Some one got hold of your schedule & found out you were to be in Sykesville [Sikeston] Mo. just over the line but they didn't know where your next stop was!!

The campaign seems to be going or trending our way. The commentators all seem to feel the drift is Democratic. I did see one of your friend Gallup's polls that 8 percent more Republicans would go to the polls than Democrats. If that is true & the South is not too heavy in the sample it would look bad. We are still up to our ass in Ku Kluxers in Indiana. This is the most reactionary state in the Union. Kefauver [Estes] was here the other day but nothing helps in Indiana except on the local & state ticket.

I wish you could drop me a short note & let me know what you think. Sam Rayburn will be in Jeffersonville Nov. 2. I hope to see him. I wish I could have been with you and Sam on your visit with John Garner. There was an awfully good picture of you all in the Courier-Journal. Jack looked like an old "prospector" from the desert land.

I have toddled up to my old school at Bloomington for a couple of football games but it is some effort. My brother has been here from Texas. He is not too confident in Texas. He is a county level politician more interested in keeping his job as County Commissioner than anything else.

If K is defeated his Cuban "policy" will have a big part. Who let him get away with that?[38]

Kennedy won despite his Cuban "policy." In a letter to Truman, dated January 16, 1961, Minton observed about Kennedy that "I think his appointments have been very good with the exception of his brother [Robert F., nominee for Attorney General] & I hope he will prove a better lawyer than I think he is."[39]

Chief Justice Warren administered the oath of office to President Kennedy at 12:51 P.M. on Friday, January 20, 1961, on the East Portico of the Capitol. More than six inches of snow had blanketed Washington the night before and the temperature at the time of the swearing-in was twenty degrees with punishing winds. Despite the snow and frigid temperatures, the vigorous young President, hatless and coatless, spoke the memorable words: "And so, my fellow Americans, ask not what your country can do for you—ask what you can do for your country."[40] Truman, a prominent guest at the inauguration, wrote to Minton on January 29, 1961:

> I had a great time in Washington on the inauguration program. The new President was as courteous as anyone could expect. Wish most sincerely that you could have been present. I had a great time. The President was most kind to me. I had a chance to go to the White House which I hadn't had for eight years.[41]

On April 10 Minton wrote to Truman:

> I am sorry I did not get to your party in Washington. I just got the letter from Charlie Clark the day I got back from Florida where I spent February and the first week in March. I rather hoped you might stay over for the Gridiron Dinner & I would get to see you there. It is good to know that you are welcome at the White House again. When I was in Washington everyone had a good word for Kennedy, except Charlie Halleck [longtime Republican Congressman from Rensselaer, Indiana] & Ev Dirksen [longtime Republican Senator from Illinois]. As for them there just wasn't any honeymoon. He can't please those bastards no matter what he did.
>
> It is a most dangerous time & I don't go to bed sure I won't be awakened by an atomic explosion.
>
> I heard a good joke while in Florida. A negro was arraigned in court for rape. The judge explained to him that he could plead guilty, not guilty & not guilty because of insanity. The boy replied, "That's it jedge! I pleads not guilty because of insanity—I'se crazy about that stuff." Reckon the NAACP would disapprove that joke? Maybe the former President will disagree too! If he does he has sure changed!
>
> This administration seems stronger to me. I don't know a soul connected with it but Lyndon Johnson. In any event it is better than Nixon. I see where Nixon is going to start after Kennedy come May 1st or is it sooner? The Democrats should turn loose on little Richard with both bar-

rels. How about you taking after him. You would handle him the way I would like him to be handled.

I hope you can read this scribbling. With all good wishes to you & Mrs. Truman in which Gertrude joins.[42]

Minton himself acknowledged that the crude racial joke would offend the NAACP; that both Truman and Minton would have found it amusing offends almost everyone today. However, this instance reflects the biases of the time of which they themselves complained but were nonetheless subject to also.

Minton slipped and fell near his home on July 29, 1961, while taking an evening stroll. A small bone in his left ankle was broken. He was admitted to St. Edward's Hospital in New Albany, where on admittance his overall condition was described as excellent. He sent a note to Truman on August 11: "I am still laid up in the hospital. While I had only a simple fracture, I had two bad legs to start with. I can't put my weight on either one. They buckle."

While still on the mend, on the night of August 17 as he was sitting on the hospital porch, Minton suffered a cerebral hemorrhage and immediately was listed in "very grave condition."[43] A month later, on September 15, he was released from the hospital.

Minton wrote to Truman on September 23 and described the ordeal:

A week ago today they brought me home. I had a broken leg & then I had a stroke while I was there. I would be paralyzed if it were not for the fast action of the doctors who gave me a couple of spinal punctures. I have a nurse with me helping me to learn to walk with the aid of polio crutches. You see how poorly I write. I will have my wife keep you posted. Thank you so much for your many inquiries.[44]

September 28, 1961:

Dear Shay:

I am glad you are at home. A broken leg and a stroke is just too much.

Tell 'em all to go to hell and get well in spite of them. When I was living in the great White Jail at 1600 Pennsylvania Ave., my doctor told me I didn't have a Chinaman's chance to come out of that jail alive. Well, I fooled 'em, and here I am telling you to do the same thing for your own welfare and benefit.

You talk to me about how you write. I can read it and so what the hell's the difference. You and I have been through the mill together.

You remember, in Mexico City, when Ambassador [Josephus] Daniels had fiz water and plain water for lunch? You and I went back to the Reforma Hotel and remedied the situation!

Maybe it was dinner, any way you and I remedied it.

Then we had been to Panama, Costa Rica, San Salvador, Nicaragua, Guatemala before our visit to Mexico. That trip was made in DC3s and it was a good one.

Now I hope we can take another one like it![45]

On November 3 Minton responded:

Just a note to tell you how much I enjoyed your remarks at the various meetings in Washington and especially that dig you gave the pompous Eisenhower. It must have been a most satisfying experience to have dinner with the President & your old friends & to also have dinner with Tom Clark & my old colleagues on the Court. Tom invited me but of course I could not go. I am afraid I shall never get back to Washington. I am still unable to bathe & dress myself. What a fix to be in! I would like [to] know what you think about Berlin & whether we will get into war. If we do we are all cooked. You & I haven't too many years to go but think of our grandchildren & the world full of younger people.[46]

November 6, 1961

Dear Shay:
You'll never know how much I appreciated your note of the 3rd. I wish you and I could get together and rehash a few things. The damned commies haven't changed one little bit.

Berlin is as it was when the air lift made them back up. They understand when there are more divisions on your side than on theirs.

I think I told you about what happened at Potsdam when Winston Churchill & I were trying to obtain a free government for Poland. Old

Stalin had agreed with me that they should have free elections and so had the British Prime Minister. Churchill then made a remark that the Pope would not be pleased if Poland happened to be mistreated. Stalin put his elbow on the table, pulled his big mustache and said "Mr. Prime Minister, how many divisions has the Pope?"

But, Shay, I got off the subject. We could not have had a more cordial reception at the White House. Had dinner with a lot of our friends, the President and the First Lady and stayed all night. I slept in Lincoln's bed for the first time although I was a resident for almost 8 years!

I'll say to you I didn't do what my mother did. You know she died unreconstructed. When I sent for her to visit me when I moved into the "great white jail" in May 1945 she was 92 years old. My brother told her that she would have to sleep in Lincoln's bed as it was the only extra one in the White House. The good old lady told my brother to tell me that she'd sleep on the floor before she would sleep in Lincoln's bed! And she would have.

After that visit I went back to the Mayflower and answered some questions for the Newspaper Women and then went back to the White House to a Security Council meeting and then to the Press Club where I had a riotous meeting.

The next day I had luncheon with the High Court, of which you are a member, and Hugo Black brought up my comment on the steel case decision [Youngstown Sheet & Tube Company v. Sawyer, 343 U.S. 579; 96 L.Ed. 1153; 72 Sup. Ct. 863 (1952)] in which I had said it was in line with the Dred Scott decision, only worse. What a laugh they got out [of] that. And I had to tell 'em the round barn story and what drove the hired man crazy and they told me about your decision [Bell v. United States, 349 U.S. 81 (1955), with Minton dissenting] that it is cheaper to transport whores across state lines by the dozen than singly! Wish you could have been there. Get well. The Country needs you![47]

On December 15 Minton wrote to Truman:

It did my heart good to receive your letter & then to see "Mohammed go to the mountain"—that is to see Ike go to visit the Truman Library. He had a hang dog look on his face.

I was saddened by the death of dear old Sam Rayburn. It was good that you could go to the funeral. They don't make 'em like you and Sam any more.

When I look back on our service together I recall the cherished days of my life. You are still in the fight but I am a casualty. I hope you are healthy & happy & live to be 100.[48]

Truman replied on December 28:

I was at Sam Rayburn's funeral and I sat there and thought about the many incidences which you and I had gone through while we were both in the Senate. The main difficulty with living too long, I have found, is to weep over the deaths of your good friends.[49]

Almost a year later, on November 2, 1962, Minton wrote to Truman:

You were in Indiana & I didn't get to see you. I was unable to make the trip. I am sure you had a warm reception in this terrible Republican state & you took care of them with a good old Truman style Democratic speech. Kennedy pulled out all the stops on the poor old steel companies. [On April 10, 1962, United States Steel, followed by other major steel companies, announced price increases of six dollars a ton; Kennedy was enraged; he attacked the steel companies and forced the companies to roll back their prices; and on April 26, 1962, United States Steel and three other companies were indicted on price-fixing charges in violation of anti-trust laws.] *The belated criticism of the Republicans was flat & ridiculous. I think of those battles you had with them one of which you lost in our court. I still think Vinson's dissent in which Reed & I concurred stated the law correctly. I hope they will give you the customary birthday party in Washington. I sure enjoyed the one I attended.*

Kennedy's popularity holds up remarkably high & I believe we will do alright in next November tho the Republicans are working hard. I hope we can beat Capehart but I am afraid we don't have the candidate. Wilson Wyatt will be nominated in Ky but Happy [Chandler] will knife him. He is still a power in Ky a damned hill billy state.[50]

Truman himself was hospitalized in January 1963. On January 31 he wrote to "Shay and Mrs. Minton" thanking them for the "beautiful red roses you sent to me while I was in the hospital." He added a handwritten note at the end of the letter: "When I'm around again we'll pursue our 'personal and confidential correspondence'!"[51]

On February 17, 1963, Minton wrote to Truman:

I was delighted to get your letter and to learn that you are convalescing fine. I was distressed when I heard you were in the hospital altho I knew you were a tough customer! In my condition of semi-invalidism I am always conscious that I get feebler every month. I am now confined to my house almost entirely. I am unable to sleep. I am up all night and try to sleep in the day time. I am writing this at 2:30 A.M.

I am sorry I didn't get to talk to you when you were speaking in the campaign but by the time I got you located you were gone. I sure hated to see Wyatt [Wilson, of Kentucky] defeated. Of course the Democrats in Kentucky are split all to hell and Happy Chandler and his people voted for Morton [Thurston B., Republican, elected to the Senate from Kentucky in 1962]. What should the Democrats do about Chandler? He will surely win the nomination for Governor. Should the other faction vote for the Republican. I dislike Happy so but I dislike Rep. more! What would you do? We certainly put Capehart away for keeps. I knew we had a good young campaigning candidate [Birch E. Bayh, Jr., Democrat senator from Indiana from 1962 to 1980] but I didn't think he could make it but he did. For the first time since McNutt we have a Democrat Governor and two Democrat Senators. But we have a tax problem and you can't tell where the ball will bounce in Indiana. Mr. Kennedy has a tax problem too. I don't think he will get a satisfactory tax bill. He knocked hell out of Congress when he threw that big deficit at them and then said now we will make it up with a nice big tax cut! Is that possible? They talk about balancing the economy and the budget will take care of itself. Probably so but we are not getting very far balancing the economy. It is a real tough nut!

And so is Cuba! Too bad we could not have gone in there April 17, 1961 at the Bay of Pigs. I don't see how the President let the refugee army go in there and fail! What was the alternative. I am sure you would have thought that one through.

Take care of yourself. There are damned few of us left![52]

Truman replied on March 13:

You don't know how much I appreciate your letter of the 17th. The doctor did his best on me but still it wasn't very pleasant. I am getting along all right and hope to be able to be around in the usual manner before many days go by.

Of course, you and I both hated to see Wilson Wyatt defeated in Kentucky but if you and I had had a conference we would have known what was to take place.

It looks now as if Chandler expects to run for Governor. I will never forget Happy Chandler in the Senate. Barkley was the reason for his arrival there and he never could do anything mean enough to show he disapproved of the man who made him. I don't like people like that. I am sending you copies of the two articles which I have prepared for distribution. The one on Cuba and the other one on DeGaulle. I don't know what you will think of them but I can't stand their counterfeit publicity men. . . .

. . . Tell me what you think of the articles and don't mince words.[53]

Minton responded to Truman on April 5:

I was glad to get your letter and to know you are up and at 'em again. . . . The GOP has, with the aid of the press, driven Kennedy from the heights of success in Oct. in Cuba to the depths to where Cuba is now referred to as a mess. I think I approve of his policy toward Cuba since the Bay of Pigs which was the root of all our trouble. Why he would let those Cubans invade Cuba without any consideration of what was to be done if the invasion ran into deep trouble as they did. I suppose you deliberately refrained from saying what you would do about Cuba. All your remarks dealt with the past. I can't imagine you letting those Cubans invade with no provision for failure of the landing force.

The President is losing his popularity. The Gallup Poll shows a loss of 10 percent since January. If he keeps skidding by 1964, he will be scooping the bottom. I see where you are a grandfather again. Congratulations. My grandchildren (8) are the joy of my life. But when they have visited you a week or two you wish they would go home and when they go, they are hardly out of sight until you wish them back.

I give up on Happy Chandler. But it looks like he will win notwithstanding the party has a good young candidate backed by what I think is a good State administration.[54]

Truman replied to Minton on April 12:

I had quite a time with DeGaulle when I was President of the United States and he was the first President of France. I think I know pretty well what his viewpoint is, a laudable one, because he is trying to restore France to the point it was when Louis XIV was the head of the most powerful nation in Europe. I don't think he is able to do what he has in view but, whether you like him or not, you have to give him credit for the effort.[55]

On July 29, 1963, Minton wrote to Truman:

A few days ago I saw your biography on TV. Too sketchy for a great career such as yours, but it was pretty good. Mike Wallace is not noted for his objectivity. You have a great loyal public following.

I hope you will give the test ban treaty your hearty endorsement. The argument that no good can come out of the Russians isn't quite true. The treaty is all to the contrary and came rather suddenly.

Khrushchev may have something up his sleeve that we don't know about and this treaty would give him an advantage or he may be getting into position opposite China as Harriman pointed out. I can't see where the treaty will do much but it is a step away from war as the President says. [On July 15, 1963, the United States and the Soviet Union opened talks in Moscow on a nuclear test ban treaty. They reached a tentative accord five days later.]

I get a little fed up with Rockefeller [Nelson, who divorced his wife to marry a divorcée]. *He deliberately flaunted the moral standard of the nation with an arrogance typical of a Rockefeller who can do no wrong. His old grandfather had a public-be-damned attitude.*

As of today Kennedy could not carry a single Southern state altho he is dead right on the Negro question. It is time someone had a show down with the South.[56]

Truman replied to Minton on August 8:

That television biography you saw is not more than one-third true. I am getting together a series of broadcasts which will cover the history of the Presidency from the beginning of my administration to now and when I get that done, I'll invite you to come and sit with me while we criticize it— either in Louisville or St. Louis, whichever is more convenient to you. It is going to be a long time before I get it done. They will not be scheduled for release until next winter. I understand the question which has cost Kennedy a lot of votes down South but I will say this for him—he stood up for what he believed. What you had to say about Rockefeller is one hundred per cent correct. Please keep in mind that I am always glad to hear from you and your letters get priority on my desk, so write anytime you feel like it.[57]

Minton, now an invalid, received honors due a distinguished son of Indiana. On December 6, 1963, Governor Matthew E. Welsh dedicated the bridge over the Ohio River linking New Albany and Louisville on Interstate 64 as the "Sherman Minton Bridge." Welsh spoke briefly as he uncovered the stainless steel marker: "Shay, it is a personal pleasure to have you and Mrs. Minton here at a time when we can name this magnificent structure here in your home town in your honor. This is the wish of the people not only of your town and your county, but of the people of Indiana. I don't mean to be sentimental, but you are one of us."[58] Standing between Gertrude and New Albany Mayor C. Pralle Erni, Minton said that he was "grateful for this distinguished honor. It is one I'll always cherish."[59]

Indiana University and its School of Law also bestowed honors on Minton. On June 12, 1950, after he was elevated to the Supreme Court, Indiana University conferred upon him an honorary law degree. In 1963 he was one of the first recipients of a Zora G. Clevenger Award, an honor presented annually to living I-Men who, as graduates, have made significant contributions to Indiana University athletics and best perpetuate the ideals personified by Clevenger as a student, athlete, coach and administrator. Minton's health prevented him from making the trip from New Albany to Bloomington to receive the award; so Zora Clevenger himself, the retired athletic director at Indiana made the trip to New Albany and presented the award to Minton at his home. After his retirement from the Supreme Court, Minton was named a Professorial Lecturer in law on December 17, 1958, at the IU School of Law. (After his death, the Indiana University Board of Trustees on March 24, 1973, designated the moot courtroom in the Indiana University School Law as the Minton Moot Courtroom. On September 13, 1985, he was inducted posthumously as a charter member into the Academy of Law Alumni Fellows.)

Truman celebrated his eightieth birthday on May 8, 1964, and Minton sent congratulations to him on the occasion. On May 22, 1964, Truman expressed his thanks:

> I didn't receive a greeting, and there were hundreds of them, that I appreciated more than I did the one you sent me on my eightieth birthday. Your letter helped to make May 8th one of the happiest days of my life. I hope everything is going well with you and I am sure it is.[60]

Despite Truman's hopes, everything was not going well with Minton. Plagued by circulatory disorders, he still could not walk without the aid of a walker and a companion. Mrs. Minton gave him constant care. Most days he sat in a big chair in the living room of his home alone with his memories.

About his only diversion and enjoyment now was a daily outing with his wife, driving for an hour or so in the late afternoon. In the spring of 1964, son John took his mother's place on one of these drives. John recalled that his father knew all the roads in Floyd County—some of which were not even paved. Minton "enjoyed looking at the countryside and sometimes reflecting on the changes that he had seen in his lifetime." This fine memory, according to John, "extended to people and probably accounted for much of his success as a politician."

A letter that Minton wrote to a young female admirer on April 23, 1962, demonstrated his pathetic condition and his despair because of it. She had asked for a picture of him. He responded with an almost illegible handwritten note:

Dear Patricia:

I am sorry I have no more pictures. Since my stroke I am a semi-invalid and I am unable to write. Please forgive my long delay in answering your letter.

May God bless & keep you.

Sincerely, Sherman Minton[61]

On the tenth anniversary of the Supreme Court decision in *Brown v. Board of Education*, [62] Minton told reporters: "It was an inevitable decision. It was coming for quite a time."[63]

Minton, then seventy-three years old, added that he missed the deliberations on the high court but said that he rarely read the opinions of the Supreme Court because "I have trouble remembering what I read."[64]

LAST ILLNESS AND REFLECTIONS

RETIRED JUSTICE SHERMAN MINTON, NOW SEVENTY-FOUR, WAS ADMITTED TO FLOYD County Memorial Hospital in New Albany at 9:50 A.M. on Friday, April 2, 1965, after suffering severe intestinal bleeding at his home.

One physician listed him in fair condition upon admission. However, his personal physician, Harry E. Voyles, said that "when a man his age is taken to the hospital, we always worry."

That night his condition was changed to critical and it steadily deteriorated in the following week.

He died in his sleep at 2:33 A.M. on Friday, April 9, with Gertrude by his side. The death record stated the primary cause of death as "Liver failure due to multiple thrombo [sic] and hemorrhage from colon due to diverticula."[1] Undoubtedly the anemia which he had battled for years weakened his body and contributed to his death.

On the day of his death, Governor Roger D. Branigin ordered state flags flown at half-staff[2] and issued a handwritten tribute:

Sherman Minton was a great Hoosier. His bust in the State Capitol and his portrait in the Indiana University School of Law bear witness to his eminence in the law and his place in the hearts of our people.

Born with uncommon energy and courage, high ambition and a delightful wit, he made his way through IU and Yale and went on to become the first Hoosier to be appointed justice of the Supreme Court of the United States.

As our first public counselor and later as our senator and judge of the United States Court of Appeals, he had a distinguished record of public service.

*In tribute to his memory, the Capitol flag will remain at half-staff through
Monday. This is our farewell to one of our favorite Hoosiers, Shay Minton.*[3]

Gertrude Minton had been a devout Catholic all of her life, and the
children had been reared in the church. But Minton, to the concern and
even dismay of his wife, did not belong to any church until late in life.
There is evidence that this lack of religious faith stemmed from the early,
tragic death of his mother. Allegedly he had cried out at that time, "Why
did God take my mother?"[4]

But in 1961 Minton had converted to Catholicism. Father Paul Sweeny,
assistant pastor of Holy Trinity Catholic Church in New Albany, instructed
him and prepared him for confirmation. Funeral services for Minton were
held at 9:00 A.M. on Monday, April 12, at Holy Trinity.

Among the dignitaries who attended were Chief Justice Earl Warren,
Associate Justice Hugo L. and Mrs. Black; Associate Justice Tom C. Clark,
retired Justice Stanley F. Reed, Governor Roger D. Branigin, John S.
Hastings, chief judge of the Seventh Circuit Court of Appeals, Judge J. Earl
Major from the Seventh Circuit; and former governor of Kentucky,
A. B. "Happy" Chandler.

Pallbearers were Judge Paul J. Tegart of the Floyd Circuit Court; Judge
Henry N. Leist of the New Albany City Court, and New Albany attorneys
John A. Cody, Jr., Robert R. Kelso, Chester V. Lorch, and G. Kenneth Hay.

The requiem mass was celebrated in Holy Trinity by Father Bernard
Gerdon, pastor. Prior to the funeral oration, Father Richard Lawler, assistant pastor read from First Thessalonians: "And the dead in Christ will rise
first; then we who are alive, who are left, shall be caught up together with
them in the clouds to meet the Lord in the air; and so we shall always be
with the Lord."

The funeral oration was given by the Reverend Robert Minton, a cousin
who was pastor of Holy Family Catholic Church in Richmond, Indiana.
Burial was in the cemetery of Holy Trinity Catholic Church on Green Valley Road in New Albany.

Son John recalled that his feelings of grief peaked when the funeral pro-
cession passed the firehouse on State Street and he saw the firemen standing at attention. He thought about the many, many times he and his dad
had driven past the firehouse, and that this would be the last time. Son

Sherman recalled the way the people of New Albany turned out at the funeral home and on the streets. His dad had had many friends in all walks of life.

Truman sent a telegram to Mrs. Minton on the date of his old friend's death:

THE PASSING OF JUSTICE MINTON SADDENS ME AS IT STIRS DEEP MEMORIES OF A LONG AND MEANINGFUL FRIENDSHIP. HIS CONTRIBUTION IN THE U.S. SENATE AND ON THE BENCH OF THE SUPREME COURT LEAVE AN ENDURING MEMORIAL TO HIS SERVICES TO THE NATION. MRS. TRUMAN JOINS ME IN SENDING YOU OUR DEEPEST SYMPATHY.[5]

On the day of Minton's death, Indianapolis attorney Kurt F. Pantzer, a longtime friend, wrote to Mrs. Minton: "Word has arrived that my career-long friend, your husband, Shay Minton, has lost his last battle. It must indeed have been bitter to such a fighter to lose that battle to ill health rather than to one of the many more mighty adversaries whom he overcame during his lifetime."[6]

Minton's younger brother, Rosco, was a commissioner of Tarrant County, Texas. Older brother Herbert still lived in Fort Worth. Because of these close ties, on April 29, the Texas House of Representatives, with the Senate concurring on May, 5, 1965, unanimously adopted a resolution recognizing the great loss to Texas and the nation by the death of Sherman Minton. The House and Senate of Texas adjourned on April 29, 1965, "in memory of the Honorable Sherman Minton."

On June 7, Chief Justice Warren made these remarks "IN MEMORIAM JUSTICE MINTON":

Before rising for the Term, the Court records with sadness the passing of Retired Justice Sherman Minton. He is the third of our Retired Justices to have gone to his reward during this 1964 Term of Court. The deaths of Mr. Justice Burton and Mr. Justice Frankfurter have already been recorded in our proceedings. Justice Minton died peacefully at his home [sic] in New Albany, Indiana, at the age of seventy-four on April 9, 1965, after a long debilitating illness that had caused his retirement from the Court on October 15, 1956. Prior to that date, he had devoted most of his adult life to the service of his native State and Nation. As a gallant combat officer in World War I, as public counselor for the Public Service Commission of Indiana, as United States Senator from the State, as Presidential Assistant, as Judge of the United States Court of Appeals for the Seventh Circuit, and for seven years before his retirement as an Associate Justice of this Court, he made important contributions in each of the offices he held to the history of our time. For this devoted public service, he will be long remembered. Those of us who had the privilege of serving with him on the Supreme Court mourn his loss as we would a brother.[7]

In keeping with a long tradition, the Supreme Court held proceedings in memory of Justice Minton on Monday, May 2. At 11:00 A.M., a meeting of the Bar of the Supreme Court was held in his memory. Leon H. Wallace, dean of the Indiana University School of Law, was selected as chairman of the Resolutions Committee, which adopted resolutions highlighting the life of the late justice. The resolutions were read in open Court by the solicitor general and copies were presented to Mrs. Minton and his children. Attorney General Nicholas B. Katzenbach addressed the court and spoke highly of Minton. The proceedings concluded with warm words of praise from Warren: "We enjoyed Justice Minton as a colleague; we cherished him as a friend; and we admired him as a dedicated public servant."[8]

Minton's former law clerks, Marshall E. Hanley of Muncie and Alan T. Nolan of Indianapolis, shared some personal recollections of the Justice. Charles E. Kelso of New Albany, another former law clerk and a professor at the IU School of Law in Indianapolis, was also present.[9]

After her husband's death, Gertrude Gurtz Minton sold the family home in New Albany and lived with her daughter, Mary-Anne, in Potomac, Maryland. She died there on June 4, 1982, at the age of eighty-nine. She is buried beside her husband.

Sherman Minton died and was buried within a few miles of his birthplace in the hills of southern Indiana that he loved so much. He had come full circle, with intermediate stops in high positions in all three branches of our government and had experienced life in Indianapolis, Washington, D.C., and Chicago.

One may logically wonder what qualities of character and what charac-
teristics of personality impelled Sherman Minton of Floyd County, Indiana,
beyond the state. What properties caused him to defy the circumstances of
his birth and reach for such eminent heights of achievement?

When he lost his senatorial seat in 1940, veteran correspondents Joseph
Alsop and Turner Catledge, wrote: "He was one of those rare politicians
who really mean most of what they say about 'the common man.' Alto-
gether he commanded the respect of those with whom he worked, and his
qualities were rewarded when the administration leadership chose him out
as their leading lieutenant among the younger men."[10]

Max Lerner, another keen observer of the era, wrote: "Broad-shouldered,
square-jawed, he [Minton] looked in his Senate days like a handsome prize
fighter. . . . It was quite apparent that he was one of the ablest of the freshman Senators, and others of the 1934 crop, like Senator Truman of Missouri, who sat next to him, were impressed by his legal knowledge and his
fluent and militant manner in debate. He became assistant Democratic Whip,
and got to be known as one of the toughest New Deal militants, a sort of
FDR-Dead End kid, whose sharp wit and flaying words even the strong men
of the opposition were not anxious to provoke."[11]

Perhaps former Senator Claude Pepper said it best in a letter which he
wrote to Gordon R. Owen on August 25, 1961: "Senator Minton, as Carlyle
said about Mirabeau 'had an eye that could see; and senses that could feel
the times we are in, and he had the capacity to arouse others to see and feel
the challenge of such times.' There is no way to measure what he could
have done for America and freedom . . . if he had been permitted to remain
in the Senate."[12]

The favorite years of his life were his six years as a senator from Indiana
from 1935 to 1941. When asked at the age of seventy about the "most exciting period" of his life, Minton told the press that it was the New Deal era.
"We were in a revolution," he said, "and I was close to the throne."[13]

Certainly Minton also possessed traits that were less praiseworthy.

As an active and loyal Democrat in Senate, he supported President
Roosevelt and the New Deal with sometimes overzealous partisanship. When
asked about this unwavering support, the guileless and disarming Minton
responded: "Sure, I'm a New Dealer. I'd be ashamed to be an Old Dealer."

Minton could also be pugnacious and pedantic. His critics sometimes said that the bellicosity with which he asserted the law was in inverse proportion to his knowledge of it.[14]

Judicial historians and legal scholars have not been kind with respect to Minton's work on the Supreme Court. One wrote that "his seven-year stint on the Court has been universally and justly regarded as a failure."[15] Another one found that "Minton was considered by most contemporary students of the Court as the poorest of Truman's unremarkable selections for the high tribune."[16]

In 1970 Albert P. Blaustein, a professor at Rutgers University School of Law, and Roy M. Mersky, professor and director of research at the University of Texas School of Law, invited sixty-five law school deans and professors of law, history and political science who dealt with constitutional law to evaluate the Supreme Court justices who served from its establishment in 1789 until just prior to the appointment of Chief Justice Burger in 1969. They were not given any criteria but were free to select their own criteria. They were asked to rate all the justices in a continuum from "A" to "E."

Eight justices were named as failures, including Minton, Vinson, Burton, and Byrnes. McReynolds and Whittaker were at the bottom of the list.

It is difficult to understand why Minton should be rated as a failure by these participants in the survey; the facts and a careful examination of his opinions do not fully bear out this harsh judgment.

He was not dishonest, corrupt, obtuse, or incompetent. He was not mean-spirited, bigoted, petty, or prejudiced. He did not shirk his responsibilities. In fact he resigned from the Court when he felt he could no longer carry his share of the load.[17] Moreover, Minton was intelligent; he had more formal education and training in the law than many of the other justices. He had practiced law for fifteen years and had been a judge for eight years on the second-highest court in the land before his appointment to the Supreme Court.

Some critics have said he wrote no opinions of lasting significance. This may be true; however, most, if not all of the court's opinions are of temporary significance.

It is quite evident, as has been amply shown in this work, that Minton was a strict constructionist. He construed legislation with extreme literalness. With an eye always on precedent, he decided cases by an impersonal interpretation of statutory and constitutional law. His strict constructivism explains why he voted differently as a justice from the way he probably would have voted as a senator. He was less influenced by his own predilections than were many, if not all, of his colleagues. Certainly this trait should be in his favor.

Minton was aware that most popular critics seemed to look for a strong "legislative judiciary" and provided his own answer to charges that his judgments were uninspired.

George D. Braden, associate professor of law at Yale University, wrote an article entitled "Mr. Justice Minton and the Truman Bloc" which was published in 26 *Indiana Law Journal* 153, Winter, 1951. The article criticized Minton and his colleagues for abandoning the great tradition of an independent and spirited judiciary. Braden submitted an advance copy of the article to Minton for comment. Minton commented by letter to the author on November 20, 1950:

> *I had somehow gotten this idea when I was a Senator that the Nine Old Men were engaged in a little very judicial legislation. I did not like it then, and I don't think I like it now.*
>
> *I get the impression from most of the commentators and law professors that they are interested in seeing their point of view prevail and that if it is not the law, that it ought to be, and that they pay scant attention to many cases decided by this Court that do not come within their objective to save the world quickly. I agree that the law grows, but I do not think it grows by leaps and bounds. There is also another bit of philosophy that keeps popping up in the law and goes as far back as Montesquieu and certainly as John Adams, and that is that this is a government of laws and not of men.*
>
> *I suppose all we can do is the best we can according to the lights we have. I hope you will help me keep my lamps trimmed and burning.*[18]

Before one can contribute to the growth of the law as a justice of the Supreme Court, that person must be nominated by an incumbent President and with the advice and consent of the Senate, appointed by the President. Perhaps, then, when weighing the performance of a particular justice on the high court, the judgment of the appointing authority should be considered. In other words: What did Truman think?

Unlike Eisenhower who privately called his appointment of Chief Justice Earl Warren "the biggest damfool mistake I ever made,"[19] Truman was pleased with his appointee. (Truman, however, was disappointed in one of his appointments to the Supreme Court—Justice Tom C. Clark—and described that appointment as "my biggest mistake."[20])

In 1961 Gordon R. Owen, an instructor and graduate student at Purdue University, was working on his doctoral dissertation: A biographical and rhetorical analysis of Minton. He wrote to Truman and asked for his viewpoint on Minton. On July 19, 1961, Truman sent his viewpoint to Mr. Owen:

> *In 1934 on November election day two new senators were elected—one in Indiana and one in Missouri. They were sworn in as senators on January 3, 1935, with eleven other new Democratic senators.*
>
> *Senator Minton and Senator Truman were given seats in the back row alongside of each other. They became lifelong friends. Both believed in President Franklin D. Roosevelt and what he stood for. Both had been elected on the Roosevelt platform and both stayed with that platform.*
>
> *Sherman Minton is among the greatest men Truman has been associated with in his forty years in public life. Senator Minton has a keen mind— one of the keenest—he has a true sense of honor and he acts on that basis, both publicly and privately.*
>
> *In the Senate, Minton and Truman were together on every big issue. In 1940 both were up for re-election. Both had hard struggles. Minton was defeated by a reactionary and Truman was, almost but not quite.*
>
> *Senator Minton, after that 1940 election, became a member of President Roosevelt's staff. Later he was appointed a member of the U.S. Court of Appeals in Chicago.*
>
> *When Truman became the President of the United States he appointed Sherman Minton to the Supreme Court, his top-notch appointment after the Chief Justice [Fred Moore Vinson].*
>
> *There never was a finer man nor an abler public servant than the Honorable Sherman Minton.*[21]

NOTES

CHAPTER ONE

1. *The Indianapolis Star*, October 13, 1949; *The Indianapolis Times*, October 13, 1949.
2. List of those accepting the invitation to Minton's swearing-in ceremony as associate justice of the Supreme Court. Truman papers, Official File, Truman Library.
3. *The Indianapolis Star*, October 13, 1949; *The Indianapolis Times*, October 13, 1949.
4. Supreme Court Journal, October 12, 1949. Kurt F. Pantzer papers, Indiana Division, Indiana State Library, Indianapolis.

CHAPTER TWO

1. Letter from Mary-Anne Minton Callanan to author, February 18, 1992.
2. Grandmother Minton, Savannah Cline Minton, married Peter Smith after the death of Grandfather Minton, Jonathan S. Minton. So she did not rear the children alone as Minton intimated. Letter from Mary-Anne Minton Callanan to author, dated February 18, 1992.
3. *The Louisville Times*. October 25, 1960.
4. Inscription on photograph, "Old Hill Farm." Mary-Anne Minton Callanan collection, Bethesda, Md.
5. Haffner, "A Hoosier Country Doctor." *Indiana Magazine of History* , June 1989, pp. 151–2.
6. Marriage Book, no. 11, page 499, Floyd County, New Albany.
7. Corcoran, *Sherman Minton: New Deal Senator,* doctoral dissertation in history, University of Kentucky, 1977, p. 16. A copy of this dissertation is in the Indiana Room, New Albany-Floyd County Public Library. Hereafter cited as "Corcoran, p. _____."
8. Corcoran, p. 16.
9. Owen, *The Public Speaking of Sherman Minton,* doctoral dissertation in speech, Purdue University, 1962, p. 36. A copy of this dissertation is in the Indiana Room, New Albany-Floyd County Public Library. Hereafter cited as "Owen, p. _____."
10. Among the Minton papers in the Indiana Room of the New Albany-Floyd County Public Library there is a file labeled "Minton Genealogy File." In this file there is a document by David H. Corcoran entitled "The Preconditions for Greatness: A Case Study of Sherman Minton," which appears to be the first draft of his dissertation, *Sherman Minton: New Deal Senator.*; This incident is related on p. 16 of "The Preconditions for Greatness: A Case Study of Sherman Minton." Hereafter this work will be cited as "Corcoran, 'Preconditions,' p. _____."

11. Corcoran, "Preconditions," p. 15.
12. Ibid, pp. 14–15.
13. Owen, p. 35, quoting the *Courier-Journal*, Louisville, Ky., September 14, 1950.
14. *The Louisville Times*, October 25, 1960: 1.
15. Owen, p. 37; *The New Albany Tribune*, September 18, 1950, and July 23, 1959; Minton in a note to Kurt F. Pantzer, Pantzer papers, Indiana Division, Indiana State Library, Indianapolis.
16. Copy of this script is in the Minton papers, Indiana Room, New Albany-Floyd County Public Library.
17. Corcoran, "Preconditions," p. 18.
18. Owen, p. 39, quoting a statement by Minton during a personal interview on June 12, 1961.
19. Owen, p. 39.
20. *Washington Post*, October 12, 1949; Louisville *Courier-Journal*, September 18, 1949.
21. *The Vista*, Vol. VI, published by the senior class of the New Albany High School, 1910.
22. Owen, p. 39.
23. Louisville *Courier-Journal*, September 18, 1950.
24. Heazlitt, "Minton Named Supreme Court Justice," *The Scroll of Phi Delta Theta*, November 1949. Hereafter cited as: "Heazlitt."
25. *The Indianapolis Star*, October 16, 1960.
26. Corcoran, "Preconditions," pp. 28–9.
27. Minton papers, New Albany High School collection, New Albany.
28. Corcoran, "Preconditions," p. 29.
29. *The Indianapolis News*, September 8, 1956.
30. Radio Station WLW, Cincinnati, Ohio, "Personalities in Your Government," October 21, 1952. A copy of this script is in the Minton papers, Indiana Room, New Albany-Floyd County Public Library.
31. Owen, p. 44.
32. Minton's student record, Indiana University, Office of the Registrar, Bloomington.
33. *Indiana Alumni Magazine*, Vol. XII, No. 3, November, 1949, p. 25.
34. "Retired U.S. Supreme Court Justice Dies," *Indiana Alumni Magazine*, May 1965, p. 21.
35. Louisville *Courier-Journal*, April 10, 1965.
36. Minton's student record, Indiana University, Office of the Registrar, Bloomington.
37. Ibid.
38. *Indiana Alumni Magazine*, Vol. XII, No. 3, November, 1949, p. 26.
39. "Retired U.S. Supreme Court Justice Dies," *Indiana Alumni Magazine*, May 1965, p. 21.

40. Louisville *Courier-Journal*, September 18, 1949.
41. "Sherman Minton's Greatest Sports Thrill," *Indiana Alumni Magazine*, December 1956, p. 18.
42. Ibid.
43. *Arbutus*, 1914 yearbook of Indiana University, p. 356.
44. Ibid.
45. "The Minton Story," *Indiana Alumni Magazine*, November 1956, p. 26.
46. Ibid.
47. *Arbutus*, 1914 yearbook of Indiana University, p. 358.
48. Heazlitt.
49. Pantzer, Kurt. F., "Sherman Minton, Son of Indiana," address at the presentation of Minton's portrait to the Seventh Circuit Court of Appeals in Chicago, June 15, 1951, p. 11. Hereafter cited as: "Pantzer, p. _____."
50. Atkinson, David Neal. *Mr. Justice Minton and the Supreme Court, 1949–1956*; doctoral dissertation in political science, University of Iowa, 1969, p. 56. Hereafter cited as "Atkinson, p. _____."
51. Elizabeth Anne Hull, *Sherman Minton and the Cold War Court*, doctoral dissertation in political science, New School for Social Research, 1977, p. 4. Hereafter cited as "Hull, p. _____."
52. Owen, pp. 45-46; Atkinson, p. 56.
53. Several versions of this incident are extant. See, for example, "Mickey McCarty Says," *The Indianapolis News*, September 10, 1956; Gordon Englehart, "His Friends Remember," Louisville *Courier-Journal*, April 10, 1965; and Wayne Guthrie, "Ringside in Hoosierland," *The Indianapolis News*, November 19, 1965. The author prefers the version contained in Radio Station WLW script, Cincinnati, Ohio, "Personalities in Your Government," October 21, 1952.
54. Rothe (ed.), *Current Biography . . . 1949*, pp. 429–31.
55. Owen, p. 46, based on a statement by Minton during a personal interview on June 12, 1961.
56. Hull, pp. 4–5.
57. Owen, p. 45; Station WHAS, Louisville, Ky.; special broadcast on October 12, 1949.
58. Atkinson, p. 57.
59. *The Indianapolis Star*, September 16, 1949.
60. *The Indianapolis News*, September 10, 1956.
61. A copy of this address in the Minton papers, Indiana Historical Society, Indianapolis; courtesy of New Albany attorney John A. Cody, Jr.
62. When the author requested Minton's complete military record during World War I from the National Personnel Records center, I was informed the records were destroyed in a fire on July 12, 1973. Secondary sources have been used for information about Minton's World War I service.
63. Louisville *Courier-Journal*, April 10, 1965.

64. Copy of Minton's service medical records from the Veterans Administration regional office in Indianapolis.

65. Minton papers, Mary-Anne Minton Callanan collection, Bethesda, Md.

66. Pantzer, p. 11.

67. Student record for Gertrude Gurtz, freshman at St. Mary-of-the-Woods College in Terre Haute, March 1912, Mary-Anne Minton Callanan collection, Bethesda, Md.

68. Author's interview with Mary-Anne Minton Callanan, March 30, 1988.

69. Louisville *Courier-Journal*, April 10, 1965.

70. Ibid.

71. Copy of Minton's service medical records from the Veterans Administration regional office in Indianapolis.

CHAPTER THREE

1. *New Albany Daily Ledger*, May 3, 5, and 8, 1920.

2. Owen, p. 51.

3. *In Memoriam Justice Minton*, May 2, 1966, 16 Law Ed. XLVI.

4. Letter to the author from John A. Cody, Jr., partner in the law firm of Cody and Cody (successor firm to Stotsenburg, Weathers and Minton), dated November 12, 1987. Hereafter cited as "Cody letter to the author."

5. Pantzer, p. 14.

6. Most of the information about Shutts & Bowen came to the author in a letter from Preston L. Prevatt, partner in the law firm of Shutts & Bowen, dated April 20, 1988, and a copy of a portion of the history of the firm enclosed therewith.

7. Cody letter to the author.

8. Radio Station WLW, Cincinnati, Ohio, "Personalities in Your Government," October 21, 1952.

9. Owen, p. 50.

10. Ibid.

11. Owen, p. 51.

12. Blake, *Paul V. McNutt*, pp. 7–8.

13. Ibid., p. 118.

14. *Yearbook of the State of Indiana*, 1933, Indiana State Library, Indianapolis.

15. *The Indianapolis Star*, February 22, 1934.

16. Ibid.

17. Corcoran, p.6.

18. Louisville *Courier-Journal*, April 10, 1965.

19. *The Indianapolis Star*, June 13, 1934.

20. Ibid.

21. Ibid.

22. Ibid.

23. Ibid.

24. Ibid.
25. *New Albany Tribune*, June 20, 1934.
26. Louisville *Courier-Journal*, August 23, 1934.
27. *Time*, September 17, 1956.
28. Blake, *Paul V. McNutt*, p. 150.
29. *New Albany Tribune*, November 7, 1934.
30. Meredith Nicholson papers, 1890-1947, Indiana Historical Society, Indianapolis.
31. Minton papers, Mary-Anne Minton Callanan collection, Bethesda, Md.
32. Truman, *Memoirs* , p. 155.
33. Corcoran, p. 12.
34. Ibid., p. 16.
35. Ibid.
36. *Congressional Record*, Vol. 79, Part 1, January 7, 1935, p. 129.
37. Ibid, Vol. 79, Part 2, March 18, 1935, p. 3807.
38. Corcoran, p. 18.
39. Ibid.
40. The account of the Senate fight is from Williams, *Huey Long*, pp. 831–2; Hull, p. 14.
41. Manchester, *The Glory and the Dream*, p. 114.
42. Ibid.
43. *Congressional Record*, Vol. 79, Part 8, June 12, 1935, p. 9116.
44. Ibid, Vol. 79, Part 13, August 24, 1935, p. 14546.
45. Ibid, Vol. 79, Part 13, August 26, 1935, p. 14747.
46. Manchester, *The Glory and the Dream*, p. 114.
47. *Traverse City* (Michigan) *Record Eagle*, June 26, 1991.
48. *New Albany Tribune*, September 11, 1935.
49. Manchester, *The Glory and the Dream*, p. 115.
50. *Congressional Record*, Vol. 79, Part 8, May 31–June 10, 1935, pp. 8439–47.
51. Frank, *Mr. Justice Black*, p. 75.
52. Ibid., pp. 77–8.
53. Owen, p. 72.
54. *United States v. William M. Butler, et al., Receivers of Hoosac Mills Corporation*, 297 U.S. 1 (1936).
55. *Schechter v. United States*, 295 U.S. 495 (1935).
56. Owen, p. 74.
57. *Congressional Record*, Vol. 80, Part 1, January 16, 1936, pp. 497–8.
58. Ibid.
59. Ibid.
60. Ibid.
61. Ibid.
62. Ibid, Vol. 80, Part 1, January 16, 1936, p. 499.

63. Ibid., p. 500.

CHAPTER FOUR

1. Woodburn papers, Lilly Library, Indiana University, Bloomington.
2. *Congressional Record*, Vol. 80, Part 1, February 4, 1936, p. 1436.
3. Ibid, Vol. 80, Part 3–5, March 3, 1936, pp. 3103–5.
4. Ibid, Vol. 80, Part 3–5, March 23, 1936, pp. 4154–6.
5. Ibid, Vol. 80, Part 3–5, March 23, 1936, p. 4154.
6. Ibid, Vol. 80, Part 3–5, March 23, 1936, p. 4155.
7. *Congressional Record*, 74th Congress, 2 Session, p. 3213.
8. Ibid, pp. 3216–19.
9. Ibid, pp. 5602–6.
10. Carmony, *Handbook on Indiana History*, pp. 54–69.
11. Campaign speech at Shelbyville, Ind., February 14, 1936, Minton papers, John A. Cody Jr. collection, New Albany.
12. Owen, pp. 167–8; *Lafayette Leader*, December 11, 1936, p. 1.
13. *New Albany Tribune*, January 12, 1937.
14. Ibid, January 19, 1937.
15. Rehnquist, *The Supreme Court*, p. 220.
16. Manchester, *The Glory and the Dream*, p. 151.
17. Alsop and Catledge, *The 168 Days*, p. 36.
18. Reid, p. 36.
19. Ibid.
20. *New Albany Tribune*, February 9, 1937.
21. Rehnquist, *The Supreme Court*, p. 220.
22. Owen, p. 119; *New York Times*, February 5–6, 1937.
23. Manchester, *The Glory and the Dream*, p. 137.
24. Ibid.
25. 298 U.S. 587 (1936).
26. *Adkins v. Children's Hospital*, 261 U.S. 525 (1923).
27. Minton, "A Larger Supreme Court," radio address, February 15, 1937, Minton papers, John A. Cody, Jr. collection, New Albany.
28. Manchester, *The Glory and the Dream*, p. 151.
29. *Congressional Record*, 75th Congress, 1 Session, pp. 1284–7, 1293–4.
30. Ibid, pp. 1717–21.
31. Ibid, pp. 1721–9.
32. Ibid, p. 2611; Index, p. 381.
33. Ibid, pp. 6791–3, 6798–6800, 6803–10, 6873–87, 6895–6922.
34. Rehnquist, *The Supreme Court*, p. 227.
35. Ibid., pp. 227–8.
36. Manchester, *The Glory and the Dream*, p. 152.
37. *West Coast Hotel Company v. Parrish*, 300 U.S. 379 (1937).

38. *The Indianapolis Star*, April 1, 1937.
39. *National Labor Relations Board v. Jones & Laughlin Steel Corporation*, 301 U.S. 1 (1937).
40. *Charles C. Steward Machine Co. v. Davis*, 301 U.S. 548 (1937).
41. Generally, on the fight in the Senate over the court-packing bill, see Alsop and Catledge, *The 168 Days*; Farley, *Jim Farley's Story*; and Alsop, *FDR 1882–1945*:
42. Pusey, "F.D.R. vs. the Supreme Court," p. 1257.
43. Corcoran, p. 387; *Congressional Record*, 75th Congress, 1 Session, pp. 6986–7.
44. Corcoran, pp. 148–9.
45. Rehnquist, *The Supreme Court*, p. 232.
46. Morgan, *FDR: A Biography*, p. 478.
47. Corcoran, p. 153.
48. Owen, p. 139.
49. Corcoran, pp. 151–2; *New Albany Tribune*, July 21, 1937.
50. Corcoran, pp. 163–4.
51. *Congressional Record*, 75th Congress, 1 Session, p. 3066.
52. Ibid, pp. 2476–95.
53. Corcoran, p. 170.
54. Ickes, *The Secret Diary*, pp. 182–3.
55. Swindler, *Court and Constitution*, p. 82.
56. Corcoran, p. 171.
57. Swindler, *Court and Constitution* , pp. 83–6.
58. Morgan, *FDR: A Biography*, p. 479.
59. Farley, *Jim Farley's Story*, p. 98.
60. Corcoran, p. 171.
61. *The Indianapolis Times*, August 14, 1937.
62. Corcoran, pp. 171–75; Swindler, *Court and Constitution*, pp. 82–6.
63. Swindler, *Court and Constitution*, pp. 82–6.
64. Corcoran, p. 175.
65. Farley, *Jim Farley's Story*, pp. 99–102; Swindler, *Court and Constitution*, p. 86.
66. Corcoran, pp. 182–3.
67. Corcoran, p. 184; *New Albany Tribune*, June 19, 1937.
68. Blake, *Paul V. McNutt*, p. 198; *New York Times*, August 26, 1937.

Chapter Five

1. Atkinson, p. 59, citing Felix Frankfurter to Minton, February 1, 1960, Frankfurter papers, Library of Congress.
2. Blake, *Paul V. McNutt*, p. 201.
3. Ibid.
4. Ibid., p. 202.
5. Ibid.
6. Ibid., pp. 202–3, citing Sidney Olson in *The Washington Post*, February 24, 1938.

7. Ibid., pp. 202–3.

8. Ibid., p. 201.

9. *Congressional Record*, Vol. 83, Part 5, April 28, 1938, pp. 5912–14.

10. *The Washington Post*, October 12, 1949, p. 1.

11. Corcoran, p. 201; *New Albany Tribune*, May 3, 1938.

12. *New Albany Tribune*, August 17, 1938.

13. Corcoran, pp. 205–6; Minton campaign speech, 1938, Minton papers, John A. Cody Jr. collection, New Albany.

14. Corcoran, p. 208; *New Albany Tribune*, December 22, 1938.

15. Corcoran, p. 243.

16. *Congressional Record*, 75th Congress, 1 Session, p. 6791.

17. Corcoran, p. 250.

18. "Colleagues Write about Senator Minton," copies of letters from U.S. senators to William A. Kunkel, Jr., publisher of the *Fort Wayne Journal-Gazette* (reprinted in *The Corydon Democrat*), Minton papers, Mary-Anne Minton Callanan collection, Bethesda, Md.

19. *The Indianapolis Star*, June 18, 1939.

20. *Congressional Record*, Vol. 84, Part 10, July 28, 1939, p. 10340.

21. Byrnes, *All in One Lifetime*, p. 111.

22. Morgan, *FDR: A Biography*, pp. 511–12.

23. Ibid., p. 513.

24. Ibid.

25. *The Indianapolis News*, September 23, 1939.

26. Roosevelt, Elliott (ed.), *Franklin D. Roosevelt, His Personal Letters*, p. 924.

27. Owen, p. 215; *The Indianapolis Star*, as quoted in the *New Albany Tribune*, May 27, 1940.

28. Ibid.

29. Atkinson, p. 62.

30. Owen, pp. 189–91.

31. Corcoran, pp. 317–20.

32. Owen, p. 207; *Congressional Record*, Vol. 86, Part 8, June 21, 1940, p. 8800.

33. Atkinson, p. 62.

34. *Congressional Record*, Appendix Vol. 86, Part 17, August 30, 1940.

35. *The Indianapolis News*, October 18, 1940.

36. Corcoran, p. 276; Owen, p. 179.

37. Morgan, *FDR: A Biography*, p. 524.

38. Ickes, *The Secret Diary*, p. 362.

39. Minton papers, Mary-Anne Minton Callanan collection, Bethesda, Md.

40. Ibid.

41. Barnhart (ed.), *American College Dictionary*.

42. Minton papers, Mary-Anne Minton Callanan collection, Bethesda, Md.

43. *The Indianapolis Star*, January 8, 1941.

44. Obituary, *The New York Times*, Saturday, April 10, 1965; Atkinson, p. 63; Hull, p. 28.
45. Truman papers, SV File, Truman Library.
46. Ibid.
47. Ibid.
48. Resolutions, Proceedings in the Supreme Court of the United States, *In Memoriam Justice Minton*, May 2, 1966, 16 Law Ed. 2d XLViii.
49. Alexander manuscripts, Manuscripts Department, Lilly Library, Indiana University, Bloomington.

Chapter Six

1. *The Indianapolis News*, October 7, 1941.
2. Hull, p. 41.
3. *Colgate-Palmolive-Peet Co. v. National Labor Relations Board*, 338 U.S. 355, 363 (1949).
4. *United States ex rel. Parker v. Carey*, 135 F.2d 205, 207 (7th Cir., 1943).
5. *United States v. Johnson*, 149 F.2d 31, 45 (7th Cir., 1945).
6. *Lutwak v. United States*, 344 U.S. 604, 619 (1953).
7. 302 U.S. 319, 324–5 (1937).
8. *In re George F. Nord Building Corporation*, 129 F.2d 173, 176 (7th Cir., 1942).
9. *United States v. One 1946 Plymouth Sedan Automobile*, 167 F.2d 3 (7th Cir., 1948).
10. *Carroll v. United States*, 267 U.S. 132 (1925).
11. *United States ex rel. Hack v. Clark*, 159 F.2d 552, 554 (7th Cir., 1947).
12. *United States v. Knauer*, 328 U.S. 654 (1946).
13. Hull, p. 58.
14. 16 *George Washington Law Review* 589, 592, June, 1948.
15. 173 F.2d 79 (7th Cir., 1949).
16. *The Indianapolis Star*, September 26, 1942.
17. Minton papers, Truman Library.
18. Ibid.
19. Ibid.
20. Ibid.
21. Ibid.
22. Ferrell (ed.), *Off the Record*, pp. 38–9.
23. Ibid., p. 61.
24. Minton papers, Mary-Anne Minton Callanan collection, Bethesda, Md.
25. Frank McNaughton papers, Truman Library.
26. Minton papers, Truman Library.
27. Ibid.
28. Ibid.
29 Manchester, *The Glory and the Dream*, p. 449.
30. Minton papers, Mary-Anne Minton Callanan collection, Bethesda, Md.

31. Ibid.
32. Ibid.
33. *The Indianapolis Star*, September 16, 1949.
34. Ibid.
35. *The Indianapolis Star*, September 17, 1949.
36. Minton papers, Truman Library.
37. Correspondence with Minton, Paul V. McNutt papers, Lilly Library, Indiana University, Bloomington.
38. *New Albany Tribune*, September 15, 1949.
39. Minton papers, Mary-Anne Minton Callanan collection, Bethesda, Md.
40. Hearing before the Senate Judiciary Committee on Minton's nomination to the Supreme Court, September 27, 1949; United States Government Printing Office, Washington, D.C.; 1949, p. 1.
41. Ibid., p. 20.
42. Ibid.
43. Ibid., pp. 20–1.
44. *The Indianapolis News*, September 27, 1949.
45. *The Indianapolis Star*, October 4, 1949.
46. Hull, p. 86.
47. *The Indianapolis Star*, October 5, 1949.
48. Ibid.
49. Hull, p. 84.
50. *The Indianapolis Star*, October 5, 1949.
51. Hearing, September 27, 1949, p. 19.
52. Kurt F. Pantzer papers, Indiana Division, Indiana State Library, Indianapolis.
53. Hull, p. 86.
54. Ibid.

CHAPTER SEVEN

1. Much of the material on the Supreme Court Building comes from a book published by the Foundation of the Federal Bar Association, *Equal Justice Under the Law: The Supreme Court in American Life*, Washington, D.C., 1965.
2. Ibid., p. 112.
3. Ibid.
4. Lerner, "The Supreme Court," *Holiday*, pp. 73, 122.
5. Remarks of Chief Justice Warren, *In Memoriam Justice Minton*, May 2, 1966, 16 Law Ed.2d Liii.
6. *Time*, September 17, 1956, p. 31; Hull, pp. 133–4.
7. Hull, p. 126.
8. Atkinson, pp. 101–2.
9. Ibid., p. 108.
10. Ibid., p. 133, Footnote 14.

11. Newman, *Hugo Black*, p. 399.
12. Atkinson, p. 102; Hull, p. 128.
13. Minton papers, Truman Library.
14. 338 U.S. 258 (1949).
15. *Commissioner of Internal Revenue v. Connelly* file, Minton papers, Truman Library.
16. 338 U.S. 537 (1950).
17. Minton papers, Truman Library.
18. 339 U.S. 56 (1950).
19. 339 U.S. 56, 63 (1950).
20. 339 U.S. 162 (1950).
21. 339 U.S. 162, 168 (1950).
22. 339 U.S. 162, 172 (1950).
23. *Eugene Dennis v. United States* file, Minton papers, Truman Library.
24. 338 U.S. 680 (1950).
25. 18 U.S.C. Sec. 1462.
26. 338 U.S. 680, 683 (1950).
27. 339 U.S. 827 (1950).
28. *Automatic Radio Manufacturing Company v. Hazeltime Research Inc.* file, Minton papers, Truman Library.
29. Minton papers, Mary-Anne Minton Callanan collection, Bethesda, Md.
30. Minton papers, Truman Library.
31. Ibid.
32. President's personal file, Truman papers, Truman Library.
33. 341 U.S. 329 (1951).
34. 341 U.S. 329, 337 (1951).
35. 342 U.S. 485 (1952).
36. 342 U.S. 485, 492–3, (1952).
37. 342 U.S. 485, 493 (1952).
38. Ibid.
39. Minton papers, Truman Library.
40. Minton papers, Mary-Anne Minton Callanan collection, Bethesda, Md.
41. 343 U.S. 579 (1952).
42. 333 U.S. 138 (1948).
43. Truman, *Memoirs*, Vol II, p. 428.
44. Rehnquist, *The Supreme Court*, pp. 94–5.
45. Minton papers, PSF-Personal, Truman Library.
46. Minton papers, Mary-Anne Minton Callanan collection, Bethesda, Md.
47. Minton papers, PSF-Personal, Truman Library.
48. Minton papers, Mary-Anne Minton Callanan collection, Bethesda, Md.
49. 344 U.S. 604 (1953).
50. 344 U.S. 604, 619–20 (1953).

51. 346 U.S. 249 (1953).

52. *Barrows v. Jackson* file, Minton papers, Truman Library.

53. Ibid.

54. Minton papers, Truman Library.

55. Minton papers, Mary-Anne Minton Callanan collection, Bethesda, Md.

56. Minton papers, Truman Library.

57. Minton papers, Mary-Anne Minton Callanan collection, Bethesda, Md.

58. Minton papers, Truman Library.

59. 347 U.S. 483 (1954).

60. 163 U.S. 537 (1896).

61. Ibid.

62. Kluger, *Simple Justice*, p. 587.

63. *In Memoriam Justice Minton* , May 2, 1966, 16 Law Ed.2d XLVii.

64. Kluger, *Simple Justice*, p.612.

65. Ibid., p. 613.

66. Atkinson, p. 229.

67. Minton papers, Truman Library.

68. 16 Law Ed. 2d Liii.

69. Kluger, *Simple Justice*, p. 682.

70. *Brown v. Board of Education*, 347 U.S. 483, 495 (1954).

71. Minton papers, Mary-Anne Minton Callanan collection, Bethesda, Md.

72. 347 U.S. 672 (1954).

73. Ibid., p. 682.

74. Ibid., p. 685.

75. Clark, "Sherman Minton," *Indiana Law Journal*, pp. 1–3.

76. 347 U.S. 227 (1954).

77. *Remmer v. United States* file, Minton papers, Truman Library.

78. 345 U.S. 461 (1953).

79. Civil rights cases, 109 U.S. 3 (1883).

80. *Terry v. Adams*, 345 U.S. 461, 484–5, 493–4 (1953) (dissenting opinion).

81. *Sullivan v. United States*, 348 U.S. 170 (1954).

82. *McAllister v. United States*, 348 U.S. 19 (1954).

83. *United States v. Liverpool & London & Globe Insurance Company*, 348 U.S. 215 (1955).

84. *United States v. Acri*, 348 U.S. 211 (1955).

85. *United States v. Scovil*, 348 U.S. 218 (1955).

86. *Lewis v. United States*, 348 U.S. 419 (1955).

87. Ibid., pp. 422–3.

88. *Norwood v. Kirkpatrick*, 349 U.S. 29 (1955).

89. 347 U.S. 483 (1954).

90. Kluger, *Simple Justice*, p. 741.

91. 349 U.S. 294, 301 (1955).

92. Minton papers, Mary-Anne Minton Callanan collection, Bethesda, Md.
93. Minton papers, Truman Library.
94. Ibid.
95. 350 U.S. 55 (1955).
96. Internal Revenue Code of 1954, Sec. 1032.
97. 350 U.S. 155 (1956).
98. 350 U.S. 318 (1956).
99. 36 Stat. 298 (1910), 45 U.S.C. Sec 11 (1952).
100. 350 U.S. 318, 324–5 (1956).
101. 350 U.S. 377 (1956).
102. Ibid., pp. 381–2.
103. 350 U.S. 485 (1956).
104. *Armstrong v. Armstrong*, 350 U.S. 568 (1956).
105. 351 U.S. 79 (1956).
106. 351 U.S. 493 (1956).
107. 351 U.S. 502 (1956).
108. 351 U.S. 536 (1956).
109. Unpublished dissent of Justice Minton, *Cole v. Young*, Minton papers, Truman Library.
110. Minton papers, Truman Library.
111. Minton papers, Eisenhower Library.
112. Ibid.
113. *Time*, September 17, 1956, p. 31.

CHAPTER EIGHT

1. Letter from Truman to Minton, July 12, 1956, Mary-Anne Minton Callanan collection, Bethesda, Md.
2. Enclosure to letter from Minton to Truman, August 24, 1956, Minton papers, Truman Library.
3. Minton papers, Truman Library.
4. Minton papers, Mary-Anne Minton Callanan collection, Bethesda, Md.
5. *The Indianapolis Star*, October 7, 1956.
6. *The Indianapolis Times*, October 15, 1956.
7. 1 Law Ed.2d LXXViii, October 15, 1956.
8. 1 Law Ed.2d LXXViii-LXXiX, October 15, 1956.
9. Ibid.
10. Louisville *Courier-Journal*, December 27, 1956.
11. Minton papers, Truman Library.
12. Minton papers, Mary-Anne Minton Callanan collection, Bethesda, Md.
13. Ibid.
14. Minton papers, Truman Library.
15. Ibid.

16. Ibid.
17. Minton papers, Mary-Anne Minton Callanan collection, Bethesda, Md.
18. Minton papers, Truman Library.
19. Minton papers, Mary-Anne Minton Callanan collection, Bethesda, Md.
20. Minton papers, Truman Library.
21. Ibid.
22. Minton papers, Mary-Anne Minton Callanan collection, Bethesda, Md.
23. Minton papers, Truman Library.
24. Minton papers, Mary-Anne Minton Callanan collection, Bethesda, Md.
25. Minton papers, Truman Library.
26. Minton papers, Mary-Anne Minton Callanan collection, Bethesda, Md.
27. Minton papers, Truman Library.
28. Minton papers, Mary-Anne Minton Callanan collection, Bethesda, Md.
29. Minton papers, Matthew E. Welsh collection, Indianapolis, Indiana.
30. Ibid.
31. Minton papers, Truman Library.
32. Minton papers, Mary-Anne Minton Callanan collection, Bethesda, Md.
33. Minton papers, Truman Library.
34. Ibid.
35. *The Indianapolis Star*, October 21, 1960.
36. Ibid.
37. *The Indianapolis Star*, October 16, 1960.
38. Minton papers, Truman Library.
39. Ibid.
40. Daniel (ed.), *Chronicle of the 20th Century*, p. 860.
41. Minton papers, Mary-Anne Minton Callanan collection, Bethesda, Md.
42. Minton papers, Truman Library.
43. *The Indianapolis Times*, August 18, 1961, p. 1, col. 8.
44. Minton papers, Truman Library.
45. Minton papers, Mary-Anne Minton Callanan collection, Bethesda, Md.
46. Minton papers, Truman Library.
47. Minton papers, Mary-Anne Minton Callanan collection, Bethesda, Md.
48. Minton papers, Truman Library.
49. Minton papers, Mary-Anne Minton Callanan collection, Bethesda, Md.
50. Minton papers, Truman Library.
51. Minton papers, Mary-Anne Minton Callanan collection, Bethesda, Maryland
52. Minton papers, Truman Library.
53. Minton papers, Mary-Anne Minton Callanan collection, Bethesda, Md.
54. Minton papers, Truman Library.
55. Minton papers, Mary-Anne Minton Callanan collection, Bethesda, Md.
56. Minton papers, Truman Library.
57. Ibid.

58. *New Albany Tribune*, December 6, 1963.
59. Ibid.
60. Minton papers, Mary-Anne Minton Callanan collection, Bethesda, Md.
61. Ibid.
62. 347 U.S. 483 (1954).
63. *The Indianapolis Star*, May 18, 1964.
64. Ibid.

Chapter Nine

1. Official record of Minton's death, Book no. CH-45, p. 258, Health Department, New Albany, Indiana.
2. *The Indianapolis News*, April 9, 1965.
3. Ibid.
4. Corcoran, "Preconditions," p. 13.
5. Minton papers, Truman Library.
6. Kurt F. Pantzer papers, Box 15, Indiana Division, Indiana State Library, Indianapolis.
7. 14 Law Ed.2d XL, June 7, 1965.
8. *In Memoriam Justice Minton*, 16 Law Ed.2d XLV–Liii.
9. Minton papers, Indiana Room, New Albany-Floyd County Public Library.
10. Alsop and Catledge, *The 168 Days*, p. 300.
11. Lerner, "The Supreme Court," *Holiday*, pp. 73, 122.
12. Owen, p. 218.
13. Dillard, *Dictionary of American Biography*, p. 542.
14. Swindler, *Court and Constitution*, p. 171.
15. Abraham, *Justices and Presidents*, p. 246.
16. Swindler, *Court and Constitution*, p. 171.
17. Louisville *Courier-Journal*, April 10, 1965.
18. Letter to George Dorsey Braden, correspondence between Braden and Minton (1936–1956), Minton papers, Truman Library, MHDC no. 515.
19. Manchester, *The Glory and the Dream*, p. 737.
20. Miller, *Plain Speaking*, an oral biography of Harry S. Truman p. 242.
21. Minton papers, Truman Library, PPNF.

240

BIBLIOGRAPHY

MANUSCRIPTS

Hull, Elizabeth Anne. "Sherman Minton and the Cold War Court," 1977. New School for Social Research, New York.

Owen, Gordon R. "The Public Speaking of Sherman Minton," 1962. Purdue University, Lafayette, Ind.

Atkinson, David Neal. "Mr. Justice Minton and the Supreme Court, 1949–1956," 1969. University of Iowa, Iowa City.

Corcoran, David H. "Sherman Minton: New Deal Senator," 1977. University of Kentucky, Lexington.

GOVERNMENT PUBLICATIONS

Yearbook of the State of Indiana, 1933, 1934, and 1935. Indiana State Library, Indianapolis, Indiana.

Resolution for Justice Sherman Minton Presented at Meeting of Federal Judges, Seventh Circuit. Chicago: May 12, 1965. Truman Library, Independence, Mo.

Congressional Record. 74th Cong. 1st sess. 1935, through 76th Cong. 2d sess. 1940, Vols. 79–86. Washington, D.C.

United States Reports of the Supreme Court, Vols. 338–52. United States Printing Office, Washington, D.C.

Hearing Before the Committee on the Judiciary on the Nomination of Sherman Minton of Indiana to be Associate Justice of the Supreme Court of the United States. United States Senate, 81st Cong. 1st sess. September 27, 1949. United States Printing Office, Washington, D.C.

In Memoriam Justice Minton. 14 Law Ed. 2d XL. June 7, 1965. United States Printing Office, Washington, D.C.

In Memoriam Justice Minton. 16 Law Ed. 2d XLV–Liii. May 2, 1966. United States Printing Office, Washington, D.C.

Federal Reporter. 2d ser., vols. 119–75. West Publishing Company, Eagan, Minn.

DOCUMENTS AND LETTERS

Black, Hugo L. Letter to Sherman Minton, September 19, 1945. From the personal collection of Mary-Anne Minton Callanan, Bethesda, Md.

Minton, Sherman. Letters to and from Harry S. Truman and others. From the personal collection of Mary-Anne Minton Callanan, Bethesda, Md.

Pantzer, Kurt F. Letters to and from Sherman Minton. Collection of the Indiana Division, Indiana State Library, Indianapolis.

Truman, Harry S. Letters to and from Sherman Minton and others. The Truman Library, Independence, Mo.

NEWSPAPERS AND PERIODICALS

Courier-Journal, Louisville, Ky.

Indiana Alumni Magazine

The Indianapolis Star

The Indianapolis News

Lafayette Leader, Lafayette, Ind.

The Tribune, New Albany, Ind.

Record-Eagle, Traverse City, Mich.

The Washington Post

JOURNAL ARTICLES

Atkinson, David N. "Justice Sherman Minton and the Balance of Liberty." *Indiana Law Journal* 50 (Fall, 1974): 34.

Bamberger, Fred P. "Sherman Minton, 1890–1965." *American Bar Association Journal* 51 (1965): 663.

Blaustein, Albert P. and Roy M. Mersky. "Rating Supreme Court Justices." *American Bar Association Journal* 58 (November 1972): 1183.

Braden, George D. "Mr. Justice Minton and the Truman Bloc." *Indiana Law Journal* 26 (1951): 153.

Clark, Tom C. "Sherman Minton." *Indiana Law Journal*. Vol. 41, No. 1 (Fall 1965).

Dillard, Irving. "Truman Reshapes the Supreme Court." *Atlantic Monthly* (December 1949): 30.

Frank, John P. "The United States Supreme Court: 1949–50." *University of Chicago Law Review* 18 (Autumn 1950): 1.

Frankfurter, Felix. "Mr. Justice Roberts." *University of Pennsylvania Law Review* 104 (December 1955): 311.

Haffner, Gerald O. "A Hoosier Country Doctor." *Indiana Magazine of History*, Vol. 85, No. 2 (June 1989): 151–2.

Heazlitt, Walter S., "Minton Named Supreme Court Justice," *The Scroll of Phi Delta Theta* (November 1949).

Lerner, Max. "The Supreme Court." *Holiday*, Vol. 7 No. 2 (February 1950).

Pusey, Merlo J. "FDR vs. the Supreme Court." *The American Heritage New Illustrated History of the United States*, Vol. 14, "The Roosevelt Era." New York: Dell, 1963.

Wallace, Harry L. "Mr. Justice Minton—Hoosier Justice on the Supreme Court." 34 Indiana Law Journal (Part I, Winter 1959): 145, and (Part II, Spring 1960): 378.

BOOKS

Abraham, Henry J. *Justices and Presidents: A Political History of Appointments to the Supreme Court*. 2d ed. New York: Oxford University Press. 1985.

Allen, Frederick Lewis. *Since Yesterday, The Nineteen Thirties in America*. New York: Harper and Brothers, 1939.

Allen, Robert S., and William V. Shannon. *The Truman Merry-Go-Round*. New York: Vanguard Press, 1950.

Alsop, Joseph, and Turner Catledge. *The 168 Days*. New York: Doubleday, Doran and Company, Inc., 1938.

Alsop, Joseph. *FDR 1882–1945: A Centenary Remembrance*. Thorndike Press, 1982.

Barnhart, Clarence L. (ed.). *The American College Dictionary*, New York: Random House, 1947–48.

Blake, Israel George. *Paul V. McNutt, Portait of a Hoosier Statesman*. Indianapolis: Central Publishing Co., 1966.

Burns, James MacGregor. *Roosevelt, The Lion and the Fox*. New York: Harcourt Brace and Company, 1956.

_____. *Roosevelt: The Soldier of Freedom*. New York: Harcourt Brace Jovanovich, Inc., 1970.

Byrnes, James F. *All in One Lifetime*. New York: Harper and Bros., 1958.

Cushman, Robert Eugene. *Leading Constitutional Decisions*. 10th ed. New York: Appleton-Century-Crofts, Inc., 1955.

Daniel, Clifton, Editor-in-Chief. *Chronicle of the 20th Century*. Mount Kisco, New York: Chronicle Publications, Inc., 1987.

Daniels, Jonathan Worth. *The Man of Independence*. Philadelphia: J.B. Lippincott Company, 1950.

Dillard, Irving. *Dictionary of American Biography*. Supplement Seven, 1961–65. John A. Garraty, ed., New York: Scribner's, 1981.

Equal Justice Under Law: The Supreme Court in American Life. Washington, D.C.: Foundation of the Federal Bar Association, 1965.

Farley, James A. *Jim Farley's Story: The Roosevelt Years*. New York: McGraw-Hill Book Co., Inc., 1948.

Ferrell, Robert H., ed. *Off the Record: The Private Papers of Harry S Truman*. New York: Harper and Row, 1980.

_____. *Truman: A Centenary Remembrance*. New York: The Viking Press, 1984.

Frank, John P. *Mr. Justice Black: The Man and His Opinions*. New York: Vanguard Press, 1950.

Gunther, John. *Roosevelt in Retrospect: A Profile in History*. New York: Harper and Brothers, 1950.

Ickes, Harold L. *The Secret Diary of Harold L. Ickes*. Vols. 1–3. New York: Simon and Schuster, Inc., 1953.

Kirkendall, Richard. "Sherman Minton." *The Justices of the United States Supreme Court 1789–1969: Their Lives and Major Opinions*. Vol. 4. Edited by Leon Friedman and Frank L. Israel. New York: Chelsea House, 1969.

Kluger, Richard. *Simple Justice: The History of Brown v. Board of Education and Black America's Struggle for Equality*. New York: Alfred A. Knopf, 1975.

Manchester, William. *The Glory and the Dream: A Narrative History of America, 1932–1972*. New York and Toronto: Bantam Books, 1973.

Miller, Merle. *Plain Speaking: An Oral Biography of Harry S Truman*. New York: Berkley Books, 1973.

Morgan, Ted. *FDR: A Biography*. New York: Simon and Schuster, 1985.

Newman, Roger K. *Hugo Black*. Pantheon Books, 1994.

Rehnquist, William H. *The Supreme Court: How It Was, How It Is*. New York: William Morrow and Company, Inc., 1987.

Reid Robert L. (ed.). *Back Home Again: Indiana in the Farm Security Administration Photographs, 1935–1943*. Bloomington: Indiana University Press, 1987.

Rodell, Fred. *Nine Men: A Political History of the Supreme Court from 1790 to 1955*. New York: Random House, Inc., 1955.

Roosevelt, Elliott, ed. *Franklin D. Roosevelt: His Personal Letters*. New York: Harper and Brothers, 1949.

Roosevelt, Elliott and James Brough. *A Rendezvous with Destiny, The Roosevelts of the White House*. New York: G.P. Putnam's Sons, 1975.

Rothe, Anna (ed.). *Current Biography, Who's Who and Why, 1949*. New York: H. W. Wilson Co., 1950.

Schlesinger, Arthur M. Jr. *The Age of Roosevelt: The Politics of Upheaval*. Vol. 2. Boston: Houghton-Mifflin Company, 1959–60.

_____. *The Coming of the New Deal*. Vol. 3. Boston: Houghton-Mifflin Company, 1959–60.

Steinberg, Alfred. *The Man from Missouri: The Life and Times of Harry S Truman*. New York: G.P. Putnam's Sons, 1962.

Swindler, William Finley. *Court and Constitution in the Twentieth Century: The New Legality 1932–1968*. Indianapolis: The Bobbs-Merrill Company, Inc., 1970.

Truman, Harry S. *Memoirs of Harry S Truman: Years of Decision*. Vol. 1. Garden City, N.Y.: Doubleday and Company, Inc., 1955.

Welsh, Matthew E. *View from the State House: Recollections and Reflections, 1961–1965*. Indianapolis: Indiana Historical Bureau, 1981.

Williams, Charlotte. *Hugo L. Black: A Study in the Judicial Process*. Baltimore: The Johns Hopkins Press, 1950.

Williams, Thomas Harry. *Huey Long*. New York: Alfred A. Knopf, 1969.

INDEX

Note: An asterisk (*) after a number indicates that a photo appears on that page.

Copeland, Royal S., 67, 83
Court reform ("court packing") plan, 68, 69–70, 71–7
    defeat, 79–80
Craig, George H., 188
Crowe, Eugene B., 32
Cuba and the Bay of Pigs invasion, 211, 212
Cummings, Homer S., 67, 68

Davis, John W., 59
Denton, Winfried K., 131
Dewey, Thomas E., 100, 128
Dickinson, Lester J., 62
Dietrich, William H., 79
Dixon, Edgar H., 193
Donahey, A. Victor, 41
Donnell, Forrest C., 53, 132
Douglas, William O., 138, 160, 180*, 181*, 187
Duchess County Association of New York, 43
Duffy, F. Ryan, 42
Dulles, John Foster, 125, 126
DuPont, Pierre S., 59

Early, Stephen T., 1
Eby, A. Dale, 186
Economic royalists, 59
Eisenhower, Dwight D., 137, 154, 161, 169, 174, 185
Ely, Joseph B., 59
Emergency Relief Appropriation Act, 49
Engleman, Harry K., 10
Erni, C. Pralle, 214
Ethridge, Mark F., 141
Evans, Evan A., 110

Fair Labor Standards Act, 115
Farley, James, 48, 78, 89
Farm Credit Act, 91
Farm Mortgage Moratorium Act, 49
Federal Employers' Liability Act, 115, 171

Federal Power Commission, 163
Feinburg Law, 147–148
Ferguson, Homer, 132
Fifteenth Infantry Company, Eighty-fourth Div., 25
Floyd, John, 7
Frank, Sir Oliver, 184
Frankfurter, Felix, 22, 53, 63, 87, 138, 139, 154, 160, 180*, 181*, 187, 219
Frazier, John O., 175*
Frazier, Lynn J., 48
Frazier v. United States, 144

Gannett, Frank E., 90
Garner, John Nance, 41, 44, 67, 77, 78, 89, 96
George, Walter F., 72, 90
Gerdon, Father Bernard, 218
Gerry, Peter G., 41
Gibson, Ernest W., 48
Gilbert, Cass, 135
Gillette, Guy M., 91
Glass, Carter, 67
Glenn, General, 24
Goodrich, James P., 63
Gray, Raymond W., 185
Greenlee, Pleas E., 4, 33, 34, 36–7, 38, 41, 64–5, 84
Guffey Coal Conservation Act, 43, 49, 70
Guffy, Joseph F., 41

Hanley, Marshall E., 185, 220
Harlan, John M., 138, 172, 181*, 187
Harrison, Pat, 67, 79
Hastings, John S., 204, 218
Hatch Act, 101
Hatch, Carl A., 41, 42, 101, 126
Hay, G. Kenneth, 218
Heazlitt, Walter S., 13, 15, 54*, 55*
Hedden, D. Kirke, 23
Hemenway, James A., 41
Hill, Lister, 105
Holder, Cale J., 204